STRATEGIC SPATIAL PROJECTS

How can spatial planning and design better contribute to fundamental changes and transformations of the spatial organisation of society that are at once qualitative, sustainable and socially inclusive?

Western society is facing major developments, challenges and opportunities. Governments are being urged to adopt a more proactive style in order to enhance the vitality and resilience of their cities and regions. The challenges they are faced with cannot be tackled adequately with purely market-based solutions or traditional land-use planning. This book starts from the position that spatial planning urgently needs to adopt a more strategic approach, combining the aim of socio-spatial transformation with a concern for action and implementation. Through a number of theoretical contributions and empirical case studies, it explores strategic spatial projects as a catalyst for socio-spatial change.

Theoretically and empirically, the book analyses three interrelated challenges for strategic spatial planning and the potential of strategic spatial projects to address these. How to make planning through projects socially innovative, how to mobilise design in strategic projects to communicate and bring about improved spatial quality and how to operationalise sustainability for strategic spatial projects and work through the land-use conflicts often associated with them.

Unique in its focus on the transformative potential and action-orientation of strategic projects, this book explores the potential role of design in communicating about and pursuing spatial quality in strategic projects. The book is for academics, students and practitioners in spatial planning and design, community development, human geography, public administration and policy studies and urban sociology.

Stijn Oosterlynck is Lecturer in Urban Sociology at the University of Antwerp and Post-doctoral Research Fellow of the Fund for Scientific Research – Flanders in the Department of Architecture, Urbanism and Spatial Planning and the Institute of Social and Economic Geography at K.U.Leuven, Belgium.

Jef Van den Broeck is Honorary Professor in the Department of Architecture, Urbanism and Spatial Planning at K.U.Leuven, Belgium.

Louis Albrechts is Emeritus Professor of Planning in the Department of Architecture, Urbanism and Spatial Planning at K.U.Leuven, Belgium.

Frank Moulaert is Professor of Spatial Planning in the Department of Architecture, Urbanism and Spatial Planning at K.U.Leuven, Belgium.

Ann Verhetsel is Professor of Economic Geography and Regional Economics in the Faculty of Applied Economics of the University of Antwerp, Belgium.

THE RTPI Library Series

Editors: Robert Upton, Infrastructure Planning Commission in England, and Patsy Healey, University of Newcastle, UK

Published by Routledge in conjunction with the Royal Town Planning Institute, this series of leading-edge texts looks at all aspects of spatial planning theory and practice from a comparative and international perspective.

Planning and Transformation
Learning from the Post-Apartheid Experience
Philip Harrison, Alison Todes and Vanessa Watson

Conceptions of Space and Place in Strategic Spatial Planning
Edited by Simin Davoudi and Ian Strange

Regional Planning for Open Space
Edited by Terry van Dijk and Arnold van der Valk

Crossing Borders
International Exchange and Planning Practices
Edited by Patsy Healey and Robert Upton

Effective Practice in Spatial Planning
Janice Morphet

Transport Matters
Angela Hull

Cohesion, Coherence, Co-operation
European Spatial Planning Coming of Age?
Andreas Faludi

Strategic Spatial Projects
Catalysts for Change
Edited by Stijn Oosterlynck, Jef Van den Broeck, Louis Albrechts, Frank Moulaert and Ann Verhetsel

Implementing Sustainability
The New Zealand Experience
Caroline L Miller

STRATEGIC SPATIAL PROJECTS

CATALYSTS FOR CHANGE

EDITED BY

STIJN OOSTERLYNCK, JEF VAN DEN BROECK,
LOUIS ALBRECHTS, FRANK MOULAERT
AND ANN VERHETSEL

Routledge
Taylor & Francis Group

LONDON AND NEW YORK

First published 2011
by Routledge
2 Park Square, Milton Park, Abingdon, Oxon, OX14 4RN

Simultaneously published in the USA and Canada
by Routledge
270 Madison Avenue, New York, NY 10016

Routledge is an imprint of the Taylor & Francis Group, an informa business

© 2011 selection and editorial material, Stijn Oosterlynck, Jef Van den Broeck,
Louis Albrechts, Frank Moulaert & Ann Verhetsel; individual chapters, the
contributors

The right of Stijn Oosterlynck, Jef Van den Broeck, Louis Albrechts, Frank
Moulaert & Ann Verhetsel to be identified as authors of the editorial material,
and of the authors for their individual chapters, has been asserted by them in
accordance with sections 77 and 78 of the Copyright, Designs and Patents Act
1988.

Typeset in Akzidenz Grotesk by Prepress Projects Ltd, UK
Printed and bound in Great Britain by TJ International Ltd, Padstow, Cornwall

British Library Cataloguing in Publication Data
A catalogue record for this book is available from the British Library

Library of Congress Cataloging-in-Publication Data
Strategic spatial projects catalysts for change/edited by Stijn Oosterlynck . . .
[et al.].
p. cm. – (The RTPI library series)
Includes bibliographical references and index.
1. City planning. 2. Strategic planning. 3. Sustainable development. I.
Oosterlynck, Stijn.
HT165.5.S77 2011
711'.4–dc22
2010019236

ISBN13: 978-0-415-56683-4 (hbk)
ISBN13: 978-0-415-56684-1 (pbk)
ISBN13: 978-0-203-83948-5 (ebk)

CONTENTS

FIGURES

TABLES

CONTRIBUTORS

Louis Albrechts is emeritus professor of planning in the Department of Architecture, Urbanism and Spatial Planning at K.U.Leuven, Belgium. His current research focuses on the practice and nature of strategic planning and on creativity and diversity in planning.

Tom Coppens is currently employed as an urban planner for the city of Antwerp. Between 2001 and 2009, he was a researcher in the Department of Architecture, Urbanism and Spatial Planning. His research topics are process management and conflict management in urban planning.

Marleen Goethals is a lecturer in the master course in Urbanism and Spatial Planning at Artesis Hogeschool Antwerp and a practising designer at various architecture firms. She is also a PhD researcher in the Department of Architecture, Urbanism and Spatial Planning at K.U.Leuven. Her research is concerned with spatial quality and research by design.

Jean Hillier is professor of town and country planning with the Global Urban Research Unit (GURU) in the School of Architecture, Planning and Landscape at Newcastle University, Newcastle upon Tyne, England. Research interests include planning theory and methodology for strategic practice in uncertainty, exploring concepts of resilience, and cities and planning systems as complex adaptive assemblages.

Trui Maes is an urban planner and research associate at the Centre for Sustainable Development at Ghent University, Belgium. She is a partner in the Flemish transition network of Sustainable Living and Building and an expert in Flanders' Ecopolis.

Frank Moulaert is professor of spatial planning in the Department of Architecture, Urbanism and Spatial Planning at K.U.Leuven, Belgium. His research focuses on social innovation and spatial development.

Stijn Oosterlynck is lecturer in urban sociology in the Department of Sociology at the University of Antwerp and post-doctoral research fellow of the Fund for Scientific Research – Flanders in the Department of Architecture, Urbanism and Spatial Planning and the Institute of Social and Economic Geography at K.U.Leuven, Belgium. His current research focuses on the sociology of urban development and policy, urban social movements and globalisation.

Constanza Parra is a post-doctoral researcher of the Maison Européenne des Sciences de l'Homme et de la Société (MESHS) and of the Centre Lillois d'Etudes et de Recherches Sociologiques et Economiques (CLERSE) at the University of Science and Technology in Lille, France. Her current research focuses on sustainable development, governance, protected areas and ecotourism.

Jan Schreurs is associate professor in the Department of Architecture, Urbanism and Planning at K.U.Leuven and professor at Sint-Lucas College of Art and Architecture in Brussels and Ghent. His current research focuses on urbanity and designerly research and on the role of spatial quality in sustainable development.

Bernardo Secchi is full professor of urbanism in the School of Architecture at the University IUAV in Venice. He is the director of the PhD Program in Urbanism at this university and Member of the Educational Board of the European Master in Urbanism.

Jef Van den Broeck is honorary professor at K.U.Leuven. He is a spatial planner/designer and was founder (1973) and general manager (1973–97) of Studiegroep OMGEVING. He was coordinator of the research project SP2SP (Spatial Planning to Strategic Projects). Both in his research and in his planning and design practice he deals with 'strategic spatial planning and design' at all spatial scales and policy levels (from local to supranational), in Europe as well as in developing countries. He is also involved in different organisations aiming at socio-spatial quality.

Pieter Van den Broeck is a doctoral researcher in the Department of Architecture, Urbanism and Spatial Planning at K.U.Leuven, Belgium and a senior planner at the independent urban design and planning firm OMGEVING. His current research interests are institutionalist planning theory, the analysis of planning systems and social innovation.

Barbara Van Dyck is a researcher in the Department of Architecture, Urbanism and Spatial Planning at K.U.Leuven and associated researcher at the Department of Transport and Regional Economics at the University of Antwerp, Belgium. Her research focuses on the political economy of spatial development, local development, urban wasteland and urban social movements.

Elke Vanempten is a doctoral researcher of the 'Prospective Research for Brussels' programme in the Department of Industrial Sciences and Technology at Erasmus University Colleges Brussels and the Department of Architecture, Urbanism and Spatial Planning at K.U.Leuven, Belgium. Her research focuses on integrated open space development in urban fringes, urban–rural relationships, and urban and landscape design and its relation with politics.

Ann Verhetsel is full professor of economic geography and regional economics in the Faculty of Applied Economics of the University of Antwerp, Belgium, where she teaches introductory and advanced courses in economic geography and social geography. Her research focuses on the intersection of economics, geography and spatial planning.

Han Verschure is emeritus professor of planning in the Department of Architecture, Urbanism and Spatial Planning at K.U.Leuven, Belgium. His research focuses on sustainable human settlements.

Paola Viganò is associate professor of urbanism at the University IUAV in Venice and currently guest professor in the Department of Architecture, Urbanism and Spatial Planning at K.U.Leuven, Belgium. She is a Member of the Board of the PhD Program in Urbanism in Venice and of the European Master in Urbanism Educational Board.

PREFACE

This book presents the results of four years of case study research and theoretical discussions on strategic spatial projects and planning. The cases have been examined within a large-scale Flemish research project called SP2SP (Spatial Planning to Strategic Projects), coordinated by Jef Van den Broeck and Louis Albrechts, and financed by IWT (Flemish Institute for Innovation, Science and Technology). The SP2SP research consortium consisted of the Department of Architecture, Urbanism and Spatial Planning (K.U.Leuven), the Centre for Sustainable Development (Ghent University), the Department of Transport and Spatial Economy (Antwerp University) and the two private consultancy, planning and design agencies IDEA Consult and OMGEVING. A group of stakeholders (regional and city planners, planning organisations, different public administrations, etc.) was guiding the research process (for instance by giving input on the research topics, questions and case studies, by giving feedback on the scientific results), thus helping to forge a strong link between academic research and planning, design and policy practice.

ACKNOWLEDGEMENTS

Many people have contributed in one way or another to the research process out of which this book results. Special thanks to Paul Schreurs from funding agency IWT, Tuna Taşan-Kok, who coordinated the SP2SP project during the first two years, Georgina Johnson-Cook for her editorial advice and patience, Robert Upton and Patsy Healey for their constructive advice as editors of the RTPI Library Series and the SP2SP user group of planning and design practitioners, who provided excellent feedback during the whole research process.

We would also like to acknowledge the contribution of the following people (in alphabetical order): Willem de Laat, Bruno De Meulder, Kaatje Molenberghs, Ruth Segers, Tania Vandenbroucke, Stefanie Vincke, Guy Vloebergh and Paul Wuillaume.

We gratefully acknowledge the following people and organisations who kindly granted us permission for the use of photographs and illustrations: Google Earth (Figures 3.1 and 7.1), Manuel de Solà-Morales and Dominique Macel (Figures 6.1, 6.2, 6.3, 6.4, 6.5 and 6.6), uapS (Figures 6.7, 6.8 and 6.9), Robbrecht, Daem, Van Hee and Technum (Figures 6.10 and 6.11), John Zeisel (Figure 6.12), Studiegroep OMGEVING (Figure 7.2, top), Econnection and Buck Consultants International (Figure 7.2, top), Departement Ruimtelijke Ordening, Woonbeleid en Onroerend Erfgoed, Afdeling Ruimtelijke Planning, Vlaanderen (Figure 7.2, bottom), OMGEVING and Idea Consult (Figure 7.3), Agence de Développement et d'Urbanisme de Lille Métropole/COPIT (Figure 7.4), Jacques Simon/JNC International (Figure 7.5) Yves Hubert for JNC International and Christian Louvet for Espace Naturel Lille Métropole (Figure 7.6) and Euro-Immostar (Figure 10.2).

CHAPTER 1

STRATEGIC SPATIAL PLANNING THROUGH STRATEGIC PROJECTS

STIJN OOSTERLYNCK, LOUIS ALBRECHTS AND JEF VAN DEN BROECK

FROM TRADITIONAL LAND-USE PLANNING TO STRATEGIC PLANNING

Our western society is facing major developments, challenges and opportunities that affect our cities and regions in manifold ways: globalisation, new technological developments, rising energy costs, the global financial crisis and the subsequent economic crisis, increasing diversity, the crisis of representative democracy, geographically uneven development, social polarisation, the ageing of the population, increasing environmental awareness at all spatial scales, etc. To enhance the vitality and resilience of their city-regions in the face of these changes, governments are urged to adopt a more proactive style. Traditional static land-use regulation, urban maintenance and the delivery and management of public services are not sufficient responses to new demands. These demands require the transformation of bureaucratic approaches and the involvement of skills, knowledge and resources that are often external to the traditional administrative apparatus. Neither can the aforementioned developments, demands, challenges and opportunities be tackled adequately with purely market-based solutions, nor by extrapolating from the past and the present simply by relying on economic growth or by keeping to vested interests, concepts, discourses and practices (Sachs and Esteva 2003; Mishan 1967; Hamilton 2004).

All this calls for more strategic forms of spatial planning. Strategic planning starts from the position that societies are not prisoners of their past and therefore carry responsibility for their future. They are doomed to find alternatives to currently dominant practices and discourses. No clear definition of strategic spatial planning exists in the literature. We therefore propose to see strategic spatial planning not as a single concept or procedure, but as a method for collectively re-imagining the possible futures of particular places and translating these into concrete priorities and action programmes (Albrechts 2004, 2006a; Healey 2004). Strategic spatial planning is often opposed to government-led forms of master or blueprint planning, which are mainly pursued through passive land-use control and zoning (Carmona *et al.* 2009; Van den Broeck 2004; Carmona and Burgess 2001; Albrechts 2006b). Land-use planning dominated planning practice and theory throughout most of the post-war period and is based on the idea that spatial development should be guided by modernist planning principles of functional separation (zoning), a preconceived plan or blueprint that results from a rational-comprehensive technical analysis of all the necessary data and the rational application of the modernist principles of functionalism. The effectiveness of land-use planning predicated a strong state able and willing to intervene in spatial development and to exert strict control and regulation of land use. This distinction between strategic and land-use planning should be treated carefully, however, as it can obscure the fact that the latter was sometimes inspired by strategic planning efforts, but operated on the belief that land-use and zoning plans were adequate and sufficient instruments to implement strategic visions. This assumption has since been problematised for reasons that will become clear in the following paragraphs and gave rise to the problematic that is central to this book.

During the 1970s, land-use planning fell into disrepute for failing both to live up to its grand promises and to respond to rapidly changing societal needs (Carmona *et al.* 2009). This perceived failure expressed the dwindling belief in the capacities of human beings to shape socio-spatial reality and is commonly attributed to a naïve modernist belief in the complete transparency of socio-spatial reality and the human possibilities of predicting and planning the development of society (Lindblom 1959), a central state lack of instruments and resources to steer spatial development and meet the – often unrealistic – goals laid down in land-use plans (in particular during times of fiscal austerity) and the limited attention paid to how unequal power structures and conflicting interests shape the planning context (Van den Broeck 2004). All this problematised the linear and quasi-automatic nature of the process from planning to implementation as assumed by rational-comprehensive planning. The neutral position of the planning professional who deployed technical expertise to mediate between competing societal interests and arrive at a singularly rational and optimal solution was challenged from various angles, not least by increasingly vocal demands from civil society (Davidoff 1965) for participation and consultation in the planning processes. The latter, combined with the criticism of the neoliberal right of the overly bureaucratic and centralised nature of the state institutions involved in spatial planning, further eroded the power of centralised state bureaucracies on which the effectiveness of rational-comprehensive planning and land-use control and regulation was predicated.

The emergence and consolidation of neoliberalism in the late 1970s and 1980s initially led to a retreat from planning altogether and a preoccupation with realising projects, but in the 1990s strategic spatial planning underwent a revival

(Albrechts 2004, 2006b; Healey 1997, 2007). This renewed form of strategic spatial planning rediscovers the need for providing spatial development that is sustainable in both social and ecological terms and combined with a long-term perspective, whether laid down in a strategic plan or not. This long-term perspective does not specify a fixed end state but operates as a flexible framework for sustainable spatial development. It combines this long-term perspective with a strong 'action orientation' and an increased sensitivity to the multiplicity of actors involved in strategic planning processes. It is with this rejuvenated concept of strategic spatial planning, particularly with its action orientation and focus on social innovation, that the chapters in this book are concerned. The action orientation implies an interest in planning instruments, the governing of land-use conflicts, ways of integrating various spatial claims and the operationalisation of spatial quality and sustainability, whereas social innovation draws attention to the coupling of the transformation of space and the transformation of social relations in space and to the satisfaction of local needs. Socio-spatial innovation happens through co-production, that is, the involvement and empowerment of multiple actors in the planning process, and particularly, but not only, non-conventional actors and disadvantaged groups. Responding to the challenges listed at the beginning of this chapter requires both the translation of long-terms visions into concrete actions and the structural transformation of the social relations of power in order to tackle the overpowering dominance of the market and to manage institutional reform.

We thus define strategic spatial planning here as a transformative and integrative, (preferably) public sector-led socio-spatial process through which visions, coherent actions and means for implementation and co-production are developed, which shape and frame both what a place is and what it might become (adapted from Albrechts 2006a: 1152; see also Healey 1997, 2007). The structural transformation of socio-spatial reality, a theme explored further in Part I of this book, cannot but be selective, given that budgetary means and human and institutional capacity are limited. Hence, a strategic approach to spatial planning entails choosing certain goals and places above others. This selection should not be read in sectoral terms, hence the reference to 'integrative' within the definition. However, an integrative focus on a limited set of goals and places entails cooperation, in horizontal as well as vertical terms, between different parts of the government as public responsibilities for socio-spatial reality are strongly compartmentalised in different government departments and public agencies. Co-production implies a specific focus on how spatial transformation may facilitate social innovation both in the substantive sense of improving the satisfaction of local needs and in the process sense of involving non-conventional, grassroots and disadvantaged actors and groups. The place focus of strategic planning and design (see Part II) provides a promising basis for public–public cooperation as well as cooperation between the government and civil society and private sector actors (a 'government-led-but-negotiated form of governance', cf. Albrechts 2004, 2006b; Healey 2007; Kunzmann 2000) and puts spatial quality and sustainability, the foundational values of spatial planning and design practice, centre stage in strategic planning efforts (see Part II and Chapter 9).

Indeed, the increasing social, cultural and political diversity of contemporary societies and the expanding reach of private market-based actors bring to the fore the governance (instead of narrow 'government') question in strategic spatial planning (Healey 2007; Salet and Gualini 2006). Salet and Gualini refer to 'framing', by which they mean 'the different ways in which individual agents can be held together' (Salet and Gualini 2006: 3). For them the strategic dimension in planning

> lies in the *transcendence of individual horizons* in scope and time . . . and in the *selection of symbols* that enable the reproduction of a joint direction for a possible future of cities that directly and indirectly might be shared by an unspecified number of individual agents.
>
> (Salet and Gualini 2006: 3; italics in the original)

The stress on the selection of symbols, an activity central to design (see Part II), is also supported by Albrechts (2006b), who refers to the visioning or visualisation of what a place could or should be in the future as one of the five core dimensions of strategic spatial planning, while Healey (2004) argues that representation is an important part of the persuasive capacity of strategic planning.

Although the core business of spatial planners is about 'qualifying space' (Loeckx and Shannon 2004), with sustainable spatial development as a necessary component of spatial quality, turning these core values into more concrete and operational (action-oriented) terms thus requires a focus on the active forces of spatial innovation and transformation. While operationalising their core values in concrete processes of spatial development, strategic planners are frequently confronted with, and challenged by, other actors pursuing different interests such as increasing land rents and profits, upgrading the mobility infrastructure, providing legal certainty, maintaining the status quo and increasing the space available for economic activities. In the planning process the gap between planning expert rationalities and knowledge and multiple social and spatial rationalities and knowledge is reflected in the dynamic 'criss-cross' relations between visioning, decision-making, co-production and implementation (Van den Broeck 1987, 2004; Albrechts 2007).

To combine the aims of re-imagining the future of particular places, structural transformation, social innovation and action orientation, a four-track approach was designed to operationalise strategic spatial planning (Albrechts *et al.* 1999; Van den Broeck 2004; Albrechts 2007; see also Van den Broeck 1987 for a three-track approach). This four-track approach, which is presented in greater detail in the introduction to Part II of this book, distinguishes four different trajectories interwoven in a strategic spatial planning process. The first track focuses on designing alternative futures and aims for structural socio-spatial transformation. The second track is concerned with addressing problems in the short term and working towards the desired future by taking actions in the here and now (action orientation). The third track is about involving all actors relevant in either giving substance to spatial quality and/or sustainable spatial development and land use in particular places, or providing institutional, material or ideological support to strategic planning processes (action orientation and social innovation). The fourth track is about empowering socially disadvantaged groups and non-conventional actors to participate in strategic planning processes, a goal that we will refer to as social innovation in this book.

STRATEGIC PLANNING THROUGH STRATEGIC PROJECTS

This book is mainly concerned with the concrete interrelationships between the first track (i.e. strategic planning in the sense of designing alternative futures and developing long-term visions) and the second, third and fourth tracks (i.e. the short-term actions, the relevant actors and planning instruments needed to implement strategic visions and co-production). Implementation, social innovation and political decision-making is still too often a black box for spatial planners and designers (Albrechts 2006a; however, see Salet and Gualini 2006 for some interesting work in this regard). More research is needed that connects plan-making to decision-making, implementation and social innovation. This book looks towards 'strategic projects' as concrete vehicles of strategic planning efforts and a way to bridge this gap.

The idea of strategic projects as a particular approach to steering spatial development is rooted in the 'urban project' tradition in southern Europe (Meijsmans 2007). The urban project as a concrete urban intervention was nurtured in the urban design and architecture tradition. Morales (1989) claims that the 'urban project' constitutes what he calls 'another modern tradition'. According to him, the tradition of functionalist urban planning associated with the international architecture platform CIAM (Congrès Internationaux d'Architecture Moderne), which held that it was both possible and desirable to eradicate the existing spatial structure of cities and replace it with a new, more rational urban structure, has been identified with the whole history of modern urban planning and has erased all references to the urban project as an alternative modernist tradition. Against the 'horizontal coherence of a general program' championed by functionalist urban planning (Morales 1989: 9), the urban project develops its interventions starting from the specific potential of a particular place in which to fashion its interventions and mitigates the requirements of modern public infrastructure with concern for its aesthetic. Different functional and spatial parts of the urban structure are treated as the object of so many different urban projects. Unlike a land-use plan, a project is only an intermediate step, not an end state (De Meulder *et al.* 2004). For Morales, the urban project recovers the intermediate scale of operation of urban design, which has been crushed between the general rules of urban planning and the architecture of individual buildings that ignores its broader urban context.

The crisis of traditional land-use planning, as derived from modernist functional planning principles, led to the rediscovery of the urban project tradition and a rethinking of the discipline of urbanism. Because of its successful application to Spanish urban renewal policy (Meijsmans 2007) during the 1980s and 1990s, it was increasingly perceived as containing important elements of a new approach to steering spatial development. Three factors are generally seen as central to the success of strategic urban projects (and they apply to strategic spatial projects more generally) (De Meulder *et al.* 2004). First, although strategic projects target urban or spatial fragments rather than the city or any other spatial system in its totality, they aim for a structural impact and catalysing effect on the larger urban region or spatial system. For Albrechts, they 'aim at transforming the spatial, economic and socio-cultural fabric of a larger area through a timely intervention' (2006a: 1492). The proclaimed leverage effect of strategic projects is crucial to the mobilisation of projects in planning trajectories in a strategic way and links the first and second trajectory in the four-track approach of strategic planning.

Second, strategic projects are based on strong interdependencies between a range of different, sometimes competing, actors and interests tied to a particular area (Carmona and Burgess 2001). For Albrechts the 'territorial focus seems to provide a promising basis for encouraging levels of government to work together (multi-level governance) and in partnership with actors in diverse positions in the economy and civil society' (2004: 749). De Meulder *et al.* (2004) concur with this point of view and argue that projects mediate difference and have the capacity to tie together multiple actions and actors. For Salet (2007), the framing effect of strategic projects is a core institutional innovation of the project mode of planning, but he warns at the same time that there is frequently a gap between the integrative ambitions of strategic projects and their actual outcomes. Third, because of their focus on the intermediate scale, both time-wise (medium-term perspective) and in terms of their spatial focus, strategic projects are deemed to be more feasible (De Meulder *et al.* 2004). This focus on the intermediate scale goes well with the selective nature of strategic spatial planning. It also allows spatial planners and designers to seize upon local opportunities (unanticipated market developments, voids, unexpected shifts in policy attention and resources, the emergence of new actors and social dynamics in particular areas, etc.) that suddenly emerge and require swift action.

The project mode of planning is often criticised for furthering a shift away from managerial towards entrepreneurial modes of urban governance (Harvey 1989; Swyngedouw *et al.* 2002; Carmona *et al.* 2009; Carmona and Burgess 2001). Swyngedouw *et al.* (2002) argue that large-scale urban development projects are often used as vehicles for generating future urban growth and improving the competitive position of cities in international urban networks. For Carmona, project-based forms of strategic planning signal a move away from a planning agenda firmly focused on controlling and limiting development towards more flexible and proactive strategies for competitive urban development (Carmona *et al.* 2009). Indeed, on the basis of comparative research on thirteen large-scale urban development projects in twelve European countries, Swyngedouw *et al.* (2002) conclude that these projects are increasingly being used to consolidate an elite-driven development agenda that implies the redirection of public investment away from social goals to the upgrading and beautifying of the built environment and infrastructure. As part of a shift towards a more entrepreneurial mode of urban governance, strategic projects increasingly help to undermine a universalistic spatial development agenda by the concentration of development resources and policy attention on a number of privileged areas. Projects also make it possible for real estate actors to pick and choose those areas in which rent extraction can be maximised with a minimum of costs, at least from their side. The frequent lack of integration of projects into the wider urban planning system contributes further to this.

As Meijsmans argues:

> if a project-based approach wants to be more than 'proposing what could be done' or 'surfing the waves' of what is in the process of being done, a wider strategy is needed. If not, a project-based approach will only serve as a convenient vehicle for facilitating private-market project developers.
>
> (Meijsmans 2007: 8)

This wider strategy is precisely what the aforementioned four-track approach offers. By embedding strategic projects in long-term visions shaped by values of diversity, social justice and equality (the aim of the third and fourth strategic planning tracks), the danger of cherry-picking only the most competitive parts of an urban region, or any other spatial system, for redevelopment can be averted. A strong articulation between the first (visioning) and the second track (action) also makes for more integrated forms of spatial development as more attention is being paid to how particular projects fit into a long-term spatial development vision for the wider area. The third track further ensures that projects are co-produced with all the relevant actors and are not solely driven by, and responsive to, elite interests, while the fourth track pays particular attention to empowering non-conventional actors and disadvantaged social groups, making sure that the social concerns that were at the heart of the post-war universalistic spatial development agenda are not lost.

The strategic planning approach adopted in this book does not reduce spatial planning to strategic projects, but mobilises strategic spatial projects as a vehicle to reinforce the action orientation of planning, paying careful attention to how it relates to the long-term visions for the wider area, the co-production of specific actions with a variety of actors and the promotion of social innovation (i.e. strategic projects integrated in a co-productive four-track approach). Within this approach, strategic spatial projects are then meant to make concrete abstract and broad long-term visions by connecting them to local opportunities, transformative and innovative action and means for implementation and co-production, with socially inclusive spatial transformation as a clear aim. Strategic projects operate 'horizontally' by bringing different policy sectors together within the same spatial vision and have a selective focus on a limited number of structural issues. In short, they have the potential to revive the strategic dimension of spatial planning.

The contributions in this book analyse and document the capacity of strategic spatial projects to translate transformative visions into strategic projects and bridge the gap between planning and design, on the one hand, and decision-making, co-production and the implementation of plans and policies, on the other. Each contribution develops its own theoretical perspective to deal with one or more of the strategic spatial planning concerns mentioned in this chapter and applies it to strategic spatial projects in diverse areas (urban and rural areas and strategic economic locations) within and beyond Belgium. In each of these cases sustained attempts have been made to develop, translate and implement transformative visions through strategic projects in complex, multi-actor contexts. The six empirical research-based chapters in this book are organised into three parts, with each addressing and assessing one particular way in which the action orientation and transformative and socio-spatially innovative nature of strategic planning can be reinforced through strategic projects. These three parts are concerned with spatial transformation through social innovation, design and spatial quality, and social and spatial sustainability. Each of these parts also carries an introduction, in which the specific focus of the chapters in that part is briefly developed and related to the overall theoretical approach set out within it, together with a commentary, in which a leading scholar critically reviews the research chapters from the point of view of the aims set out in the introduction and reflects on what the research conclusions mean for planning and design theory and practice.

We will now, for the convenience of the reader, briefly present the content of the six research chapters. The first part of the book is concerned with the transformation of space through social innovation, and vice versa. It explores to what extent strategic projects facilitate the involvement of grassroots and non-conventional actors within spatial planning processes and address their needs and aspirations. Both chapters mobilise (more or less explicitly) an institutionalist mode of analysis and analyse the institutional work carried out by strategic projects, thus taking a critical look at the action orientation of the projects and the planning instruments used from a socio-spatial innovation perspective. In Chapter 3, Barbara Van Dyck discusses the process of voicing and contesting spatial claims in industrial 'brownfield transformation projects' from the viewpoint of social innovation in strategic projects. She shows how these brownfields are spaces that embody tensions between a predetermined historical function and a relatively indeterminate future, and argues that it is precisely the indeterminate status of brownfields that creates opportunities for both the appearance and the subsequent confrontation of a variety of spatial claims, which, it is argued, may eventually contribute to social innovation through spatial planning processes. Van Dyck develops this argument through a case study on the strategic reconversion project on the brownfield site, Angus Locoshops, in Montreal (Canada). She examines how differing spatial claims on this previously industrial site gained voice, and to what extent the confrontation between them generated new and socially innovative relationships. Van Dyck analyses the strategic project from an institutional perspective as a governance device through which conflicting claims on spatial planning and development are negotiated, coordinated and operationalised. She questions the impact of these socially innovative governance relations on the capacity of the local community to influence spatial interventions that would work to their benefit. The case study reveals that the strong involvement of civil society groups in spatial development opens up opportunities to go beyond the confines of property development-led projects and take more account of local economic development in strategic projects. It also shows how the exposure of civil society groups to property dynamics generates tensions and forces adaptation, new relationships and choices.

In Chapter 4 Van den Broeck looks at planning instruments in strategic projects and assesses their socio-territorial innovation capacity. He claims that, although planning practitioners and academics are well aware that planning instruments are shaped by the societal context from which they emerge and in which they operate, more conceptual and empirical work is needed to enrich our understanding of the co-evolution of planning instruments and socio-political configurations. To that end, Van den Broeck develops an understanding of instruments as strategically selective ensembles of technical tools, social practices and institutional procedures and rules. His approach moves beyond the idea that planning instruments need to be adapted to their societal context to become more effective and argues that planning instruments are constitutive of, and not just constituted by, their societal context. He argues that making explicit the social and political processes through which planning instruments come into being or are reformed will help us to understand how strategic planning instruments can be made more socially innovative. From this perspective and on the basis of the case study Schipperskwartier in Antwerp (Belgium), where significant attempts have been made to move beyond physical planning and to integrate social concerns, the author analyses the strategically selective nature of the instruments deployed in this strategic project, in which actors attempt to structurally inscribe their interests in these instruments, how they do so and with what effects.

The second part of the book revolves around the role of design in strategic projects and concomitantly deals with spatial quality as one of the core values of spatial planning and design. It starts from the hypothesis that design (in a broad sense), because of its place focus and creative and imaginative capacities, is particularly well versed to reinforce the action orientation of strategic planning by operationalising spatial quality, and to involve a multitude of actors and their spatial claims in strategic projects (although the chapters in this part stop short of explicitly addressing social innovation in spatial design processes). In Chapter 6, Marleen Goethals and Jan Schreurs address the question of the operationalisation of spatial quality in strategic projects, which they argue is an important precondition for an effective debate and wide-ranging agreement on strategic spatial projects. The authors start with the 'dimensions of performance' outlined in *Good City Form* by Kevin Lynch (1984), together with findings from environment behaviour research, to provide terms that adequately grasp the concept of spatial quality and which, importantly, can be shared by all stakeholders. Goethals and Schreurs claim that, of all the different dimensions of spatial quality, 'experiential value' is probably the most difficult to communicate and operationalise. To clarify 'experiental value' as one of several performance dimensions of spatial quality, they analyse the argument processes involved in design decisions by designers and actors in exemplary urban renewal projects: the Ville-Port strategic urban project in Saint-Nazaire (France) and the strategic urban projects for the redevelopment of the railway station neighbourhood and the Korenmarkt and Braunplein central city squares in the Flemish cities of Roeselare and Ghent respectively (Belgium). They then follow up on this by analysing the way in which project-specific shared terms for the abstract concept of spatial quality, and more specifically for expe-riential value, come into being and highlight the vital role that design processes play in this. The latter is based on the observation of design processes in the aforementioned strategic projects in Roeselare and Ghent.

In Chapter 7, Elke Vanempten focuses on the issue of the integration of differ-ent spatial claims, voiced by different actors, and the associated land uses and functions, in strategic projects in 'rurban' areas. The highly fragmented nature and chaotic mix of urban and rural elements in the fringes of urban areas ('rurban' space) call for a more qualitative integration and interweaving of diverse spatial claims, land uses, functions and interests. Vanempten argues that a sector-based approach and regulatory planning instruments are inadequate for carrying integra-tion through in any meaningful way, because these, amongst other factors, tend to privilege procedural integration and sideline substantive concerns. Vanempten returns to the substantive concerns of spatial design and planning with space and its integrative qualities, and puts a place focus central to the question of inte-gration in strategic 'rurban' projects. She then argues that urban and landscape design are promising mediums through which to establish place-focused forms of integration because of the ways in which design builds creatively on the mul-tiple and relational potentialities of space in general, and landscape in particular. Integration through design implies identifying the different layers that structure a particular 'rurban' landscape, by paying attention to what is valuable in the existing landscape and carefully adding a new layer when relevant. Vanempten empirically tests her argument on how design can use landscape as a medium and means for integration in two strategic project case studies in 'rurban' areas: Parkbos in Ghent (Belgium) and Parc de la Deûle near Lille (France).

The third and last part of the book is dedicated to the question of social and spatial sustainability in strategic projects. Here again, the transformation of the broad and strategic vision of sustainable development into concrete actions such as strategic projects requires its operationalisation. This operationalisation has to be sensitive both to the relative autonomy of space, hence the need to develop a specifically spatial reading of sustainable development, and to the diverging and often conflicting understanding of what constitutes sustainable spatial develop-ment in particular places. In Chapter 9, Stijn Oosterlynck, Trui Maes and Han Verschure describe how sustainable development became a central concern in spatial planning and design. They observe, however, that, although sustainable development has become widely accepted in spatial planning and design, the concept is still somewhat elusive and in need of clarification and operationalisa-tion, especially if it is to be put into practice in strategic spatial projects. The authors call for more recognition of the active role that man-made space can play in making development sustainable. They support this argument by distinguishing three important components of sustainable land use, namely careful land use, multiple land use and reachability–accessibility–permeability; they refer to different strategies to implement these components and analyse various tools to assess sustainable land use in strategic spatial projects.

In Chapter 10, Tom Coppens focuses on social sustainability. Given the multiple and often conflicting claims on space, conflicts and community protest are frequent features of strategic urban projects and are often important barriers to project implementation. Coppens argues that in order to make strategic projects socially sustainable, spatial planners need a better understanding of conflicts, how and why they emerge, why they escalate and persist and how they come to an end. To answer these questions, he develops an interactionist perspective on conflicts, which explains them by analysing the particular perception and conflict behaviour of parties in the course of their interaction with adversaries. Coppens proposes distinguishing four stages in land-use conflicts, namely latent conflict, emergent conflict, conflict escalation and conflict de-escalation, and argues that each of these stages has a particular interaction pattern with its own distinct internal logic and development. He suggests that transformation from one conflict stage to another is caused by changes in the conflict parties, the conflict issues or the relations between the conflict parties. He then applies this approach to a case study of community conflict around a major strategic project for the redevelopment of a railway station area in Ghent (Belgium). The main conclusion from this analysis is that interaction patterns between adversaries do indeed play an important role in determining whether or not conflicts emerge and escalate, and hence that it matters how spatial planners act in the face of protest to develop constructive outcomes for land-use conflicts in strategic projects.

REFERENCES

Albrechts, L. (2004) 'Strategic (spatial) planning re-examined', *Environment and Planning B*, 31: 743–758.

Albrechts, L. (2006a) 'Bridge the gap: from spatial planning to strategic projects', *European Planning Studies*, 14: 1487–1500.

Albrechts, L. (2006b) 'Shift in strategic spatial planning? Some evidence from Europe and Australia', *Environment and Planning A*, 38: 1149–1170.

Albrechts, L. (2007) 'Bridge the gap: taking a provocative stand'. Paper presented at the International Conference 'New concepts and approaches for Urban and Regional Policy and Planning?', 2–3 April 2007, Leuven.

Albrechts, L., Leroy, P., Van den Broeck, J., Van Tatenhove, J. and Verachtert, K. (1999) *Opstellen van een methodiek voor geïntegreerd gebiedsgericht beleid*, Leuven/Nijmegen: K.U.Leuven and K.U.Nijmegen.

Carmona, M. and Burgess, R. (eds) (2001) *Strategic Planning & Urban Projects. Responding to Globalisation from 15 Cities*, Philadelphia: Coronet Books.

Carmona, M., Burgess, R. and Badenhorst, M. (eds) (2009) *Planning through Projects. Moving from Master Planning to Strategic Planning*, Amsterdam: Techne Press.

Davidoff, P. (1965) 'Advocacy and pluralism in planning', *Journal of the American Institute of Planners*, 31: 544–555.

De Meulder, B., Loeckx, A. and Shannon, K. (2004) 'A project of projects', in A. Loeckx, K. Shannon, R. Tuts and H. Verschure (eds) *Urban Trialogues. Visions_Projects_Co-Productions*, Nairobi: UN-Habitat.

Hamilton, C. (2004) *Growth Fetish*, London: Pluto Press.

Harvey, D. (1989) 'From managerialism to entrepreneurialism: the transformation in urban governance in late capitalism', *Geographiska Annaler B*, 71: 3–17.

Healey, P. (1997) 'The revival of strategic spatial planning in Europe', in P. Healey, A. Khakee, A. Motte and B. Needham (eds) *Making Strategic Spatial Plans. Innovation in Europe*, London: UCL Press.

Healey, P. (2004) 'The treatment of space and place in the new strategic spatial planning in Europe', *International Journal of Urban and Regional Research*, 28: 45–67.

Healey, P. (2007) *Urban Complexity and Spatial Strategies. Towards a Relational Planning for Our Times*, London: Routledge.

Kunzmann, K. (2000) 'Strategic spatial development through information and communication', in W. Salet and A. Faludi (eds) *The Revival of Strategic Spatial Planning*, Amsterdam: Royal Netherlands Academy of Arts and Sciences.

Lindblom, C. E. (1959) 'The science of "muddling through"', *Public Administration Review*, 19: 79–88.

Loeckx, A. and Shannon, K. (2004) 'Qualifying urban space', in A. Loeckx, K. Shannon, R. Tuts and H. Verschure (eds) *Urban Trialogues. Visions_Projects_Co-Productions*, Nairobi: UN-Habitat.

Lynch, K. (1984) *Good City Form*, Cambridge, MA: Massachusetts Institute of Technology.

Meijsmans, N. (2007) 'Exploring a project-based approach to the urban region'. ENHR 2007 International Conference 'Sustainable Urban Areas', Rotterdam.

Mishan, E. (1967) *The Costs of Economic Growth*, London: Staple Press

Morales, M. d. S. (1989) 'Another modern tradition. From the beak of 1930 to the modern urban project', *Lotus*, 62: 6–32.

Sachs, W. and Esteva, G. (2003). *Des ruines du développement*, Paris: Le Serpent à Plumes.

Salet, W. (2007) 'Framing strategic urban projects', in W. Salet and E. Gualini (eds) *Framing Strategic Urban Projects. Learning from Current Experiences in European Urban Regions*, London: Routledge.

Salet, W. and Gualini, E. (eds) (2006) *Framing Strategic Urban Projects. Learning from Current Experiences in European Urban Regions*, London: Routledge.

Swyngedouw, E., Moulaert, F. and Rodriguez, A. (2002) 'Neoliberal urbanisation in Europe: Large-scale urban development projects and the new urban policy', *Antipode*, 34: 542–577.

Van den Broeck, J. (1987) 'Structuurplanning in de praktijk: werken op drie sporen', *Ruimtelijke Planning*, 19, II.A2.c.: 53–119.

Van den Broeck, J. (2004) 'Strategic structure planning', in A. Loeckx, K. Shannon, R. Tuts and H. Verschure (eds) *Urban Trialogues. Visions_Projects_Co-Productions*, Nairobi: UN-Habitat.

PART I

SPATIAL TRANSFORMATION THROUGH SOCIAL INNOVATION

CHAPTER 2

TRANSFORMATIVE PRACTICES

WHERE STRATEGIC SPATIAL PLANNING MEETS SOCIAL INNOVATION

LOUIS ALBRECHTS

In the introductory chapter to the book it was argued that the problems, developments, challenges and opportunities that society is facing 'question' traditional planning approaches, established governance discourses and strategic projects. Questioning in this context is understood with respect to the need for a transformative agenda. There is indeed ample evidence that the problems and challenges confronting society can be tackled and managed adequately neither with the neo-conservative perspective nor with the intellectual technical–legal apparatus and mindset of traditional planning.

Socially innovative governance initiatives require a democratic polity that can encompass the realities of difference, inequality, etc. (see González and Healey 2005; Huxley 2000). Their core is a democratic struggle for inclusiveness in democratic procedures, for transparency in government interventions, for accountability, for the right of all citizens to be heard and to have a creative input in matters affecting their interests and concerns at different spatial scales and for reducing or eliminating unequal power structures between social groups and classes (see also Friedman and Douglas 1998). It is a plea for a type of governance that expands practical democratic deliberations rather than restricts them; that encourages diverse citizens' voices rather than stifles them; that directs resources to basic needs rather than to narrow private gain. This type of approach uses socially innovative governance to present real political opportunities, learning from action not only what works but also what matters. Through the involvement of non-traditional actors (and especially weak actors) in institutional sites beyond traditional elite arenas, with a more socially focused content than is usual in dominant approaches and the involvement of these actors in socially and politically relevant actions, some degree of empowerment, ownership or acceptance is sought for them (see Friedmann 1992; González and Healey 2005). In the introduction it was also argued that socially innovative strategic projects have a capacity for mobilizing actors, developing discourses and (structurally) changing practices. These projects are strategic with respect to their capacity to transform the spatial, economic and socio-cultural fabric of a larger area through a timely intervention. Strategic projects aim to integrate the agendas of different policy sectors and the private sector and to empower some non-traditional actors and discourses, thus opening space for new ideas. In this way strategic projects become meeting places for strategic spatial planning and socially innovative initiatives. They may become breeding grounds for experimentation, reflective learning and transformative practices.

TRANSFORMATIVE PRACTICES: NATURE AND CHARACTERISTICS

Transformative practices focus on the structural problems in society; they construct images/visions of a preferred outcome and how to implement this (see Friedmann 1987). Transformative practices simply refuse to accept that the current way of doing things is necessarily the best way; they break free from concepts, structures and ideas that persist only because of the process of continuity. Transformative practices focus on new concepts and new ways of thinking that change the way resources are used, (re)distributed and (re)allocated, and the way the regulatory powers are exercised. Change is looked upon as a subtle process of becoming; a 'creative advance' (Chia and Tsoukas 1999: 17) in which past events, integrated into the events of the present, are absorbed by future events in endless processes of flux and transformation (Hillier 2007: 74). In this way transformative practices become the activity whereby (taking into account structural constraints) that which *might become* is 'imposed' on that which *is,* and it is 'imposed'[1] for the purpose of changing what *is* into what *might become.* *Becoming* – understood as creative experimentation in the spatial (see Deleuze and Guattari 1987) – privileges change over persistence, activity over substance, process over product and novelty over continuity (Chia 2002: 866). This means a shift from an ontology of *being,* which privileges outcome and end-state, towards an ontology of *becoming,* in which actions, movement, relationships, process and emergence are emphasized (Chia 1995: 601; Chia 1999: 215). So I argue for thinking in terms of the *heterogeneous becoming* of institutional transformation, the *otherness* of institutional outcomes and the *immanent continuity* of institutional traces. The transformative invents, or creates, practices – in relation to the context and to the social and cultural values to which a particular place/society is historically committed – as something new rather than as a solution arrived at as a result of existing trends. We have to be aware that transformative practices are also needed to cope with an ongoing reproduction of unwanted discourses, concepts, strategies, policies and practices.

The spectrum for transformative practices cannot be so open that anything is possible, as if we could achieve anything we wanted to achieve (see Ozbekhan 1969; Berger 1964; Ogilvy 2002). Conditions and structural constraints on *'what is'* and *'what is not'* possible are placed by the past and the present. These conditions and constraints have to be questioned and challenged in the process, given the specific context of place, time and the actors involved. So, in order to imagine the conditions and constraints differently, we need to deal with history and to overcome history. This defines the boundaries of a fairly large space between openness and fixity.

There are ample arguments for reconsidering absolute faith in economic growth (Mishan 1967; Hamilton 2004), for living interculturally (Landry 2000; Sandercock 1998, 2003), for reacting against existing and persistent inequalities (Harvey 2000) and for creating a more sustainable society (Sachs and Esteva 2003). In order to (even partially) implement new strategies and policies, society needs to mobilize all necessary resources in such a way that these new strategies and policies develop the power to 'travel' and 'translate' into an array of practice arenas, and so that they transform these arenas, rather than merely being absorbed within them. This implies changes in governance institutions and agency that aim to contribute to sustainability and spatial quality in an equitable and socially just way (see also González and Healey 2005). Change is always subject to degradation as soon as the stimuli associated with a change effort are removed (see Kotter 1996, 2008); it is therefore important that change truly 'sticks' through its institutionalization into the structure, systems, social norms, shared values and, most of all, culture. Only those ideas and ways of thinking that accumulate sufficient power to become routinized may then 'sediment' down into the cultural ground, which sustains ongoing processes and feeds into new processes (Hajer 1995; Albrechts and Liévois 2004; Healey 2005: 147–148; Healey 2006: 532). Transformative change rarely occurs in instant revolutions. It is change that actually evolves in many small ways to produce an emergent pattern that, retrospectively, comes together and becomes evident in what history may then describe as 'a transformative moment' (Chia 1999: 212; Healey 2005: 158; Healey 2006: 541). Change is the sum of a great number of acts (individual, group, institutional), re-perception and behaviour change at every level. Transformative practices take decision-makers, planners, institutions and citizens out of their comfort zones (see also Kotter 1996) and compel them to confront their key beliefs, to challenge conventional wisdom, and to look at the prospects of new ideas and to consider 'breaking out of the box'. This is needed, as many actors (planners, citizens, institutions, politicians) are content with the status quo because they are afraid, often irrationally, of the consequences of change (Albrechts 2005a,b; Kotter 2008). Beliefs and expectations matter just as much as what we perceive as reality. How much change are citizens and society at large (and, ultimately, the voters) really ready to take?

Moreover, not everyone (individual planners, groups, institutions, the political class, citizens) wants to give up power associated with the status quo. All the usual forms of resistance to change (and definitely to structural change) are present. Real transformation takes time and dedication and therefore risks losing momentum if there are no short-term goals to meet and actions to celebrate (see Kotter 1996, 2008). Until changes sink down deeply into the culture, which for a city/region may take a considerable time, new strategies remain fragile and subject to regression (see Kotter 1996; Albrechts 1999). Taking one step at a time is important as most actors will not go on the long march unless they see compelling evidence within reasonable periods of time that the process is producing acceptable results. Indeed, short-term results can build the credibility needed to sustain efforts over the long haul and help to test a vision against concrete conditions (see Kotter 1996; Kotter and Rathgeber 2005). But we may not maximize short-term results at the expense of the future. It means that we have to move from episodic to continuous change (Kotter 2008: 17). The challenges facing our society and the subsequent call for transformative practices urge the planning community to reflect on its role and place.

WHAT ARE THE CONSEQUENCES OF OPENING UP FOR SOCIAL INNOVATION?

The transformative agenda challenges traditional planning approaches, vested concepts, existing knowledge, conventional wisdom and practices, and the attitudes and skills of planners. A focus on becoming forces planning to develop an alternative set of conceptual lenses for understanding the inherently creative nature of the change processes occurring in institutional renewal and transformation (see Chia 1999: 211; Hillier 2007). This leads to and establishes the contours of a social–innovative type of spatial planning that opens up potentialities for people-to-come (Hillier 2007: 232) and is based on the capacity of human beings – as a response to problems, challenges and potentials – to create, improve and reshape their places with the aid of knowledge (scientific as well as local), innovation and transformative practices that work with history and overcome history. This requires a climate that is conducive to new ideas in planning practices, to alternative visions and governance structures.

Planning practices have to be understood as unequal encounters between different spatial visions, spatial logics, urban narratives, spatial languages, conflicting claims held by different groups about the same place, and which are all embedded in the context (political, economic, cultural, social, power) of a concrete time, scale and space (see González and Healey 2005; Albrechts 2004). The context forms the setting of the planning process but also takes form and undergoes change in the process (see Dyrberg 1997). Places possess a distinctive spatiality as agglomerations of diversity locked into a multitude of relational networks of varying geographical reach. The interaction of actors is located in specific institutional arenas where ideas are expressed, strategies played out, decisions made and power games fought out (González and Healey 2005: 2061).

Visions confront our most deeply ingrained beliefs about what is important and why. They help to fight complacency and reveal how things can be different and truly better by shifting the unthinkable into the realm of the possible. They provide a motivation to take action in a specific direction and help to frame actions of different actors. Visions create integrated images that articulate the shared hopes and aspirations of places (a geography of the unknown; see Albrechts 2004); that stimulate sectors, organizations, groups who might be networked and collaborative to network with others to find out how their joint future(s) might look and to describe a transition from the present to a future state. Hence the need to shift from analysis, which seeks to discover a place that might exist, towards planning and design, which creates a place that would not otherwise be. This is somehow in line with Habermas' knowing (understand challenges and options available) and steering (capacity to take action to deal with challenges) (Habermas 1996). The steps required to deliver and to implement the wished-for spatial outcome vary according to the underlying structure. At the end we have to come back to what 'is' to present ideas, concepts that are solid, workable and of testable value. Visions must be looked upon as contextual, conscious and purposive actions to represent values and meanings for the future. The importance of the context is illustrated by the fact that some concepts (sustainability, spatial quality, private ownership) and instruments do mean quite different things to different actors (see also Hajer 1995). A consequence of the need for transformative practices is that 'more of the same' – be it more market, more technology or just keeping to vested concepts, discourses and (governance) practices – is not suited to the provision of the answers needed. This means that society as a whole needs to structurally transform its attitudes to the natural and built environment and to its relationships with others (especially 'the other'). In some places the process of 'discourse structuration' and its subsequent 'institutionalization' become perhaps more important than the plan as such (see Albrechts 1999, 2003a,b; Albrechts and Van den Broeck 2004; Hajer 1995). In this way new discourses may become institutionalized, embedded in norms, in ways of doing things, attitudes and practices, and provide a basis for structural change. From there a shared stock of values, knowledge, information, sensitivity and mutual understanding may spread and travel through an array of regional, provincial and local government arenas, sector departments and consultants. New approaches and new concepts can be sustainably embedded by way of institutionalization (see Healey 1997; Gualini 2001). To construct alternative strategies for the future, one needs both the solidity of the analysis that seeks to discover a place that might exist and the creativity of the making of a place that would not otherwise be. The active participation in the construction of visions may generate trust as participants in the process are likely to find that – and to understand why – some visions present a future that some of them would like to inhabit, whereas other possible futures are considered highly undesirable. The process helps the participants to think more broadly about the future and its driving forces and to realize that their own actions may move a place towards a particular kind of future. Moreover, it can become a learning process if it looks to the future in an open way, if it integrates the knowledge of what might happen with an understanding of the driving forces and a sense of what it means to a place and its citizens. As a collective process it is based on a trust in creativity from below, the wisdom of crowds (Surowiecki 2005). It focuses on the collective intelligence of the group as being greater than the intelligence of the individual.

Linking strategic spatial planning with socio-spatial innovation allows us to raise governance issues that go beyond established discourses and practices of technical/legal regulation and a mere technical-rational use of instruments. The socio-cultural and political context needs to be structurally embedded in planning (process, content, instruments used). This refers to changes in governance relating to current and historical relations of dominance and oppression (see also Young 1990). It involves a dynamic interaction between actors in the process rather than a unidirectional flow. The broad involvement of non-conventional actors is needed for their substantive contribution, their procedural competences and the role they might play in securing acceptance, in getting basic support and in providing (a kind of) legitimacy. This type of approach uses public involvement to present real political opportunities, learning from action not only what works but also what matters. The process allows participants to step away from entrenched positions and identify positive futures that they can work at creating. It allows for a high degree of ownership of the final product and illustrates that citizens do have a responsibility for the(ir) future.

Through the involvement of citizens (and especially weak groups) in socially and politically relevant actions some degree of empowerment, ownership or acceptance is sought for these citizens (see Friedmann 1992). Places must be creative with mutual understanding between cultures and ideas of equity (this is nothing less than a claim to full citizenship; see Sandercock 2003: 98). Interculturalism (Landry 2000) builds bridges, helps foster cohesion and conciliation and produces something new out of the multi-cultural patchwork of places (Landry

2000) so that views of the place of minority groups, or the otherwise socially excluded, are taken into account and their ideas brought to change planning, political decision-making and implementation.

Underlying all of this is a strong belief in the capability of human beings to construct (within limits) their places. This includes organizing the capacity (political, intellectual, socio-cultural and technical) of a civil society to deal in a fair and challenging way with its quality of life (see the discussion on capabilities[2] in Nussbaum and Sen 1993), good governance structures and the legitimacy to deal adequately with the challenges, problems and potentials facing its places. I fully realize, however, that this includes a clear and persistent call upon the civil society for renewed civic engagement. Civic engagement facilitates the use and understanding of the full complexity of places, and it helps to broaden the scope of the answers, and the likelihood of implementation. In a new governance culture the construction of arenas (who has to be involved, and what issues must be discussed), their timing (links to the strategic momentum), the definition of which arenas seem fixed and what issues in each seem fixed, the awareness that fixed may be a relative term in some contexts, all need careful reflection and full attention.

The two cases in this chapter document a capacity to translate (although not fully translated) a transformative vision into action. In doing so they go beyond the confines of traditional ways of doing (by giving voice to a variety of spatial claims and by looking at instruments as strategically selective ensembles of technical tools, social practices, institutional procedures and rules) by integrating social concerns into their strategic project. They illustrate that broadening the scope of traditional spatial planning towards social innovation opens up different perspectives. The cases show how action is mobilized to open up institutional opportunities and expand somehow the space for innovative actions, and how far this lets in new non-conventional actors (trade unions, non-governmental organizations, local inhabitants, etc.) and generates different, more socially focused, visions and practices, logics, claims and local knowledge. In this way non-conventional actors add to an understanding of the daily life conditions of citizens and workers, and give voice and some power to non-traditional actors to raise their issues and concerns (Albrechts 2002; González and Healey 2005). The cases also show the resistance encountered in the struggles to expand and institutionalize.

NOTES

1   Although 'imposed' may refer to a top-down jargon, I use the term very deliberately. As soon as directions based on an emancipatory practice are agreed upon they must be imposed to achieve action.

2   With the term 'capabilities' Sen (1993: 30) tried to explore a particular approach to well-being and advantage in terms of a person's ability to do valuable acts or reach valuable states of being. The expression was picked to represent the alternative combination of things a person is able to do or be – the various 'functionings' he or she can achieve.

REFERENCES

Albrechts, L. (1999) 'Planners as catalysts and initiators of change. The new Structure Plan for Flanders', *European Planning Studies*, 7 (5): 587–603.

Albrechts, L. (2002) 'The planning community reflects on enchancing public involvement: views from academics and reflective practitioners', *Planning Theory & Practice*, 3 (3): 331–347.

Albrechts, L. (2003a) 'Planning and power: towards an emancipatory approach', *Environment and Planning C*, 21 (6): 905–924.

Albrechts, L. (2003b) 'Planning versus politics', *Planning Theory*, 2 (3): 249–268.

Albrechts, L. (2004) 'Strategic (spatial) planning reexamined', *Environment and Planning B*, 31: 743–758.

Albrechts, L. (2005a) 'Creativity in and for planning', *DISP*, 169 (3): 14–25.

Albrechts, L. (2005b) 'Creativity as a drive for change', *Planning Theory*, (4) 2: 247–269.

Albrechts, L, and Liévois, G. (2004) 'The Flemish Diamond: urban network in the making', *European Planning Studies*, 12 (3): 351–370.

Albrechts, L. and Van den Broeck, J. (2004) 'From discourse to facts. The case of the ROM project in Ghent, Belgium', *Town Planning Review*, 75 (2): 127–150.

Berger, G. (1964) *Phénoménologie du temps et prospective*, Paris: PUF.

Chia, R. (1995) 'From modern to postmodern organizational analysis', *Organization Studies*, 16 (4): 579–604.

Chia, R. (1999) 'A "rhizomic" model of organizational change and transformation: perspective from a metaphysics of change', *British Journal of Management*, 10: 209–227.

Chia, R. (2002) 'Time, duration and simultaneity: rethinking process and change in organizational analysis', *Organization Studies*, 22 (6): 863–868.

Chia, R. and Tzoukas, H. (1999) 'On organizational becoming: rethinking organizational change', Working Paper No 99/12, Colchester: Department of Accounting, Finance and Management, University of Essex.

Deleuze, G. and Guattari, F. (1987) *A Thousand Plateaus: Capitalism and Schizophrenia*, Minneapolis: University of Minnesota Press.

Dyrberg, T. B (1997) *The Circular Structure of Power*, London: Verso.

Friedmann, J. (1987) *Planning in the Public Domain: From Knowledge to Action*, Princeton, NJ: Princeton University Press.

Friedmann, J. (1992) *Empowerment. The Politics of Alternative Development*, Oxford: Blackwell.

Friedmann, J. and Douglas, M. (1998) 'Editor's introduction', in M. Douglas and J. Friedmann (eds) *Cities for Citizens*, Chichester: John Wiley and Sons.

González, S. and Healey, P. (2005) 'A sociological institutionalist approach to the study of innovation in governance capacity', *Urban Studies*, 42 (11): 2055–2069.

Gualini, E. (2001) *Planning and the Intelligence of Institutions*, Aldershot: Ashgate.

Habermas, J. (1996) 'Normative content of modernity', in W. Outhwaite (ed.) *The Habermas Reader*, Cambridge: Polity.

Hajer, M. (1995) *The Politics of Environmental Discourse*, Oxford: Oxford University Press.

Hamilton, C. (2004) *Growth Fetish*, London: Pluto Press.

Harvey, D. (2000) *Spaces of Hope*, Berkeley: University of California Press.

Healey, P. (1997) *Collaborative Planning, Shaping Places in Fragmented Societies*, London: Macmillan.

Healey, P. (2005) 'Network complexity and the imaginative power of strategic spatial planning', in L. Albrechts and S. Mandelbaum (eds) *The Network Society: A New Context for Planning?* New York, Routledge.

Healey, P. (2006) 'Relational complexity and the imaginative power of strategic spatial planning', *European Planning Studies*, 14 (4): 525–546.

Hillier, J. (2007) *Stretching Beyond the Horizon*, Aldershot: Ashgate.

Huxley, M. (2000) 'The limits of communicative planning', *Journal of Planning Education and Research*, 19 (4): 369–377.

Kotter, P. (1996) *Leading Change*, Boston: Harvard Business School Press.

Kotter, P. (2008) *A Sense of Urgency*, Boston: Harvard Business School Press.

Kotter, P. and Rathgeber, H. (2005) *Our Iceberg Is Melting*, New York: St Martin's Press.

Landry, Ch., (2000) *The Creative City: A Toolkit for Urban Innovators*, London: Earthscan.

Mishan, E. (1967) *The Costs of Economic Growth*, London: Staple Press.

Nussbaum, M. and Sen, A. (eds) (1993) *The Quality of Life*, Oxford: Clarendon Press.

Ogilvy, J. (2002) *Creating Better Futures*, Oxford: Oxford University Press.

Ozbekhan, H. (1969) 'Towards a general theory of planning', in E. Jantsch (ed.) *Perspectives of Planning*, Paris, OECD.

Sachs, W. and Esteva, G. (2003) *Des ruines du développement*, Paris: Le Serpent à Plumes.

Sandercock, L. (1998) *Towards Cosmopolis. Planning for Multicultural Cities*, Chichester: John Wiley and Sons.

Sandercock, L. (2003) *Cosmopolis II. Mongrel Cities in the 21st Century*, London: Continuum.

Sen, A. (1993) 'Capabilities and well-being', in M. Nussbaum and A. Sen (eds) *The Quality of Life*, Oxford: Clarendon Press.

Surowiecki, J. (2005) *The Wisdom of Crowds*, New York: Anchor Books.

Young, I. (1990) *Justice and the Politics of Difference*, Princeton, NJ: Princeton University Press.

CHAPTER 3

MULTIPLE VOICES, COMPETING SPATIAL CLAIMS

SOCIAL INNOVATION AND THE TRANSFORMATION OF THE ANGUS LOCOSHOPS BROWNFIELD SITE (MONTRÉAL)[1]

BARBARA VAN DYCK

INTRODUCTION

Urban brownfield sites are industrial, harbour, railway or military 'idle' spaces. Although they constitute landed property, they are rarely suitable for generating short-term financial profit because of issues of contamination, complex owner-ship, peripheral location, etc. Private developers ignore them, or put the land on hold until a more lucrative period. Public authorities intervene to remove invest-ment barriers for a variety of reasons, such as public health, security, image, environmental degradation, marginalization, densification strategies and eco-nomic development concerns. Likewise, many academic and policy debates discuss brownfields chiefly as a rational management problem, in which the main issue becomes the 'removal' of the brownfield. Yet I argue here that, from a social innovation perspective on strategic spatial planning, the definition of policy prob-lems should focus more on substantive questions concerning the nature of the brownfield transformation project, the actors involved and the project's role in inclusive territorial development.

Examples show that brownfields occasionally give rise to experimental prac-tices that challenge conventional property-led urban development practices (TransEuropeHalles 2001). Civil society actors, such as residents, socio-cultural and community-based organizations, artists and intellectuals, find ways of express-ing their views and engaging in the transformation of abandoned spaces in ways that fit their logic and modes of action (Bouchain 2008). Such initiatives ques-tion predominant physical urban transformation practices, such as redevelopment based on remove and replace practices and undemocratic modes of governance. Instead, practices emerge in which no clear boundaries exist between those who imagine, direct, implement, use or benefit from a project; new ways of 'bridging the gap between planning and implementation' become possible.

These new practices emerge, as this chapter shows, when marginalized or hith-erto unheard spatial claims are expressed not as particular complaints directed at technocratic procedures, but rather as constructive forms of contestation, which generate public debate about strategic economic projects, constitute new social relationships and change the way in which assets are valued. To demonstrate this, I draw on the body of scholarship on the concept of *social innovation* (Moulaert *et al.* 2005; Fontan *et al.* 2005a; Klein and Harrisson 2007; MacCallum *et al.* 2008), which develops helpful analytical approaches for studying the transformation of social relations to benefit socially excluded or less well-resourced social groups. My analysis deals with the dynamics that shape the translation of multiple and competing spatial claims into a strategic project by focusing explicitly on the social relations forged during the transformation of brownfields.

To demonstrate how the interaction of competing spatial claims leads to a creative reconfiguration of social relations, the chapter focuses on the claims that emerged in the Angus Locoshops brownfield project in Montréal. However, in order to develop an analytical framework for the study of social innovation in brownfield transformation projects, the theory on brownfields, on strategic projects and on social innovation is outlined first. Based on the analytical framework then developed, I explore the emergence of a variety of spatial claims in the Angus Locoshops project; how these gained a voice; and to what extent the confrontation between them generated new social relationships. The brownfield transformation project therefore is analysed from an institutional perspective as a governance device through which conflicting claims on spatial planning and development are negotiated, coordinated and operationalized. Finally, the chapter draws conclusions on the relationship between the interaction of competing spatial claims, including those of civil actors, and spatial development and social innovation capacity.

BROWNFIELD TRANSFORMATION PROJECTS FROM A SOCIAL INNOVATION PERSPECTIVE

BROWNFIELD TRANSFORMATION PROJECTS AS GOVERNANCE DEVICES

In contrast to a rationalist managerial view that supposes linear causal relations,[2] an institutionalist view sees strategic projects as devices that coordinate social actors and their actions and thus impact on social relations (for a more elaborate account of institutionalism in planning theory, see pp. 53–58 in Chapter 4 in this volume). Strategic projects emerged as part of a wider shift in urban governance. Moulaert *et al.* (2003) demonstrate how such projects – which they refer to as large-scale urban development projects – are an important ingredient in the strategic turn in urban governance. They are strategic spatial interventions that bundle public and private investments into specific locations to achieve policy objectives and goals from different policy sectors at different levels (Albrechts 2006). Moreover, strategic projects are characterized by greater involvement of private actors and civil society in urban decision-making (Van Den Broeck and Verschure 2004). Thus, strategic projects as governance devices exemplify new socio-political formations. Brownfield transformation projects are particular forms of strategic projects focused on the redevelopment of brownfield sites.

In strategic spatial planning, brownfields have a particular status because they remain undetermined for a shorter or longer period because of speculation or investment barriers. According to Groth and Corijn (2005), this explains why such places allow for the emergence of non-planned or spontaneous urbanity, and thus the generation of 'other' social relationships. Ambrosino and Andrès (2008) also link the development of creative and political spatial processes to the existence of a temporal indeterminate status of land ('le temps de veille'). This, they argue, is not simply the moment between the abandoning of a site and its re-use, but the moment at which the strategies of different actors are revealed. It gives an opportunity for the emergence of civil society actor plans in parallel (or not) with the planned interventions of authorities or private landowners.

Obviously, private landowners imagine other possible futures for their (buildable) land than those envisaged by planning authorities, neighbouring residents or shop owners. The web of emerging interests is complex, yet the identification of and distinction between exchange-value and use-value interests provides a strong explanatory power. Classic writings in urban political economy (Harvey 1973; Logan and Molotch 1987) give detailed accounts of the role of exchange and use value in shaping individual and collective claims in the production of space. They show that the nature of land value differs according to the frame of reference of the claimants. For brownfields this is particularly relevant. The availability of temporary undefined space often stimulates different actors to formulate visions and spatial strategies to revalue the site, in a way that matches individual or collective interests. If several actors then manage to translate their vision into a spatial claim, competing claims emerge. I aim to demonstrate here that the way and extent to which strategic projects accommodate different spatial claims both define, and are defined by, the nature of the brownfield transformation project. Drawing on approaches that see strategic projects as governance devices, a brownfield transformation project is defined here as an ensemble of actors, their strategic actions and the resources they mobilize, the interactions among the actors involved and the mechanisms coordinating all these, which jointly generate the capacity to induce change in, and through, brownfield spaces.

A SOCIAL INNOVATION PERSPECTIVE

Strategic projects are increasingly dominated by the principles of market-driven reforms and a drive towards improving the competitiveness of urban economies; as a result, they tend to reinforce existing relations of power, social exclusion and polarization in cities (Moulaert *et al.* 2003; Paloscia 2004; Bornstein 2007). They are criticized for producing physical, social and economic results that testify to 'wrong choices, missed opportunities and unequal benefit shares' (Gualini and Majoor 2007: 297). Furthermore, some authors stress the hybridity of rationalities and regulatory processes in shaping projects, and emphasize the capacity of projects to institutionalize collective agency within a diffused power context, because of their mobilizing capacity, the creation of common goals and language, and a definition of the rules of the game (Avitabile 2005; Pinson 2009).

In social innovation literature and related perspectives, it is argued that, in a context in which resources are scattered and governance beyond government arrangements becomes common practice for policy-making and implementation, openings for more radical development alternatives are created (Moulaert 2000; Leitner *et al.* 2006). Focusing on civil society involvement and social economy initiatives, they assess the shaping of alternative urban development trajectories that go beyond assisting strategies of roll-out neoliberalism, and defend the assets of local communities (Fontan *et al.* 2003a). The social innovation perspective argues that mainstream globalization discourses, as well as strong versions of path-dependency (Mendell 2002; Graefe 2004), tend to underestimate, albeit in very different ways, the ability of actors to contest and transform existing institutions. Furthermore, it is argued that opportunities exist for alternative regeneration pathways, especially in old industrial zones, which are typically confronted with marginalization and absence of social services and economic investment, as well as an abundance of idle space.

With regard to governance, this literature focuses on innovation in social relations; on an increase in socio-political capability and access to resources (Gerometta *et al.* 2005); and on how shifting spatial arrangements create the conditions for different types of social innovation (Novy *et al.* 2008). The mobilization of a combination of exogenous and localized resources is identified as a crucial factor in triggering local initiatives and turning them into collective actions (Klein *et al.* 2009). According to Klein and colleagues (2009), this mobilization generates the dynamics necessary to create the conditions for partnerships and local empowerment, which in turn generate a recurring knowledge-building cycle. This process, according to the authors, is what generates the power to change institutional structures and so create social innovation. Nevertheless, in the literature, social innovation is rarely linked to strategic projects as governance devices.

Consequently, and as a part of an effort to address this gap, I aim to analyse how strategic projects can give rise to social innovation in urban governance relations.

BRIDGING THE GAP: BROWNFIELD TRANSFORMATION PROJECTS AND SOCIAL INNOVATION

As will be shown, established brownfield practices are challenged when actors seize on physically visible opportunities for reclaiming space through experimental spatial interventions. The very presence of unoccupied, unallocated buildings and land presents opportunities to respond to unaddressed needs (such as affordable work space), or to establish new links and relations leading to participation in urban governance or entry into the labour market. Approaching brownfield transformation projects from a social innovation perspective thus implies studying how they foster both the reproduction and the transformation of social relations. To demonstrate this, I will identify the various spatial claims that emerge in the transformation process of an urban brownfield site to explain the spatial strategies, resource mobilization processes and alliances despite differentiated interests that shape the brownfield transformation project.

Based on the Angus case study (Montréal), I will give a detailed account of the dynamics of conflict and cooperation within the framework of a brownfield transformation project. The spatial strategies and resource mobilization processes of the Angus brownfield transformation project characterize urban renewal dynamics in an advanced capitalist society. Nevertheless, the project is an interesting case study from a social innovation perspective because of the particular arrangement of territorial actors who engaged with its transformation. On the basis of the Angus Technopôle case study, Fontan *et al.* (2005a) and Klein *et al.* (2008) prove their thesis of social innovation in the form of a 'third generation' type of community initiative that is neither an exclusively social and endogenous based project nor an exclusively business-oriented one, but a project that merges both dimensions as elements of the plural economy. The research presented here builds upon earlier work of Fontan *et al.*, yet adds new insights: first, the project has evolved since their analysis; and, second, the case is analysed from a governance perspective, which stresses how the brownfield transformation is part of the production trend of large-scale and emblematic urban development projects, and therefore adds new questions about the socially innovative nature of the project.

The case study is based on twenty in-depth interviews with civil, private business, political and public sector actors conducted between May 2007 and September 2008, and on the analysis of press articles as well as archive documents that actors involved in the project provided. The extensive research on the case conducted by Fontan *et al.*, who themselves played an important role in the early years of the project, has been another important source of primary data (Fontan and Klein 2004; Fontan *et al.* 2005a; Klein *et al.* 2008). The interviews were transcribed and coded with qualitative research software for references to spatial claims, spatial concepts mobilized, resources activated, interactions and relations with other actors and innovations and impact of the project itself. In the following section, I develop an analysis of the transformation of the Angus Locoshops, which focuses on the confrontation, negotiation and coordination of competing spatial claims that emerged from the brownfield and the social relations it created. In line with the literature on social innovation, I present a case study that stresses the creative reconfiguration of social relations through a brownfield transformation project.

A CENTURY OF ANGUS LOCOSHOPS: FROM INDUSTRIAL AVANT GARDE TO DERELICTION AND FORWARD TO NEW ECONOMIC VIBRANCY

The Angus Locoshops are located in an industrial neighbourhood east of the inner city of Montréal. The Canadian Pacific Railway (CPR) established the shops in 1904 for the production and maintenance of its locomotives and rolling material. The shops were exemplary for the new large-scale production and labour processes of industrial capitalism. The CPR and its immense Angus shops (500 m long on 92 ha of land), employing up to 10,000 workers in its heyday during World War II, directly induced the urbanization of what is today the borough of Rosemont-Petite-Patrie. The Angus workers, often residents of the neighbourhood, passed long hours on the industrial site and depended on it for wages to sustain their families. In turn, the shops in the neighbourhood depended on the workers' purchasing power for their prosperity. For the CPR the Angus site was the location of long-term investments in productive infrastructure and skilled human labour to enable the accumulation of capital.

The railway industry was crucial to the rise of Montréal as a political and economic centre of Canada, but was equally important in its decline during the late nineteenth and early twentieth centuries (Linteau 2000; Dickinson and Young 2003). Nevertheless, for Montréal itself, the railway industry remained important throughout the twentieth century, yet from the 1950s the number of workers in the Angus shops gradually decreased until the final shutdown in January 1992. As part of a general trend towards deindustrialization and decentralization of population and economic activity to the suburbs, the factory's closure contributed to the decline of eastern Montréal (Dickinson and Young 2003). It left behind vast buildings and 50 ha of contaminated land (the other half of the earlier abandoned area was redeveloped during the 1980s). In the last years before closure only a thousand jobs remained. Yet, the closure of the Angus sites was a serious symbolic slap for east Montréal, which had lost many industrial activities in the previous decade.

The closure of the factories led to a breakdown in long-standing social relations, such as the Angus workers' community, which in itself had already suffered adverse economic effects (job disappearances and decreasing purchasing power). Moreover, the image of the neighbourhood further declined and put off new investment. However, not all social relationships disintegrated in and beyond the neighbourhood. The president and chief operating officer of Desjardins Venture Capital (part of the largest financial cooperative group in Canada), Louis Roquet, who was heavily involved himself in the brownfield transformation project, remembers that:

> I used to hang around in my father's business next to the Angus site in the 1950s, and that day after day I would be impressed by the thousands of men going in and out the factory when the bells rang; all of them wearing the same blue overall, and carrying black metal lunchboxes.
>
> (Louis Roquet in interview with author, September 2008)

The emotional link with this particular place partially accounts for the drive to be passionately involved in the transformation of the Angus site. Also the community associations felt closely connected with Angus' history and future. In fact, in Québec the crises of Fordism in the 1970s and 1980s gave rise to a very active social movement engaged in the development of enabling instruments (finance, training, business services and research) for the social economy and local development sector (Mendell 2006).

One of the main concerns of this movement was the creation of accessible and qualitative jobs (Lamoureux 2008), aiming to reverse the weak development capacities in territories hit by high unemployment. The establishment of community development corporations, or the Corporations de Développement Economique Communautaire (CDECs), in different neighbourhoods of the city emerged from this movement. The CDECs brought together local businesses, union representatives, shopkeepers and community groups with the objective of revitalizing their neighbourhoods. As Fontan and colleagues (2003a) explain, the CDECs had been created by social activists and community organizations concerned about the unemployment and poverty that affected a large part of the population in several of Montréal's districts, and they were considered important local economic development players by a state looking for solutions in the fight against these ills. The CDECs received public funding and mandates to improve the employability of the local populations, and to support local entrepreneurship

(Fontan *et al.* 2003a). Gradually some of the CDECs took up different roles in the revitalization processes. The CDEC Rosemont-Petite-Patrie (CDEC-RPP) initiated discussion and became a leading partner in the transformation of the Angus site to ensure that it would contribute to improvement of the socio-economic situation in the neighbourhood, rather than realization of shareholder benefit.

The Société de Développement d'Angus (SDA) is the organization born out of the CDEC-RPP to take up this role. After long negotiations, the CPR, the landowner, sold 23 ha, which was about half the remaining site, to the SDA, which became developer and manager of what is today Angus Technopôle (Figure 3.1). The CPR initially also favoured selling the second half of the land, but because of new environmental regulations and unfavourable property market conditions, it acted as developer 'by default'[3] for housing projects on the remaining 23 ha. Even if this was not the fastest way to mobilize the capital bound up in the site, as a large multinational the CPR had the financial assets to finance a development of this size, including soil remediation works. In consultation with the SDA, the CPR

Figure 3.1   Transformation of the Angus brownfield site (Rosemont-Petite-Patrie, Montréal) into (1) Technopôle – 23 ha, (2) residential zone – 23 ha and (3) commercial zone – 4 ha. Parks constitute 10% of the total new development. Source: Adapted from Google Earth (top); photos 1, 2 and 3 by author (bottom).

also attracted some commerce. The city of Montréal and the CPR handled and co-financed infrastructure development on the entire site, and the city of Montréal assumed the main costs and responsibilities for the establishment of the parks.

In 2008, the vast Locoshop continues to exist, partly mutated and re-used successfully as a modern industrial mall and as a supermarket, and partly mutilated to make way for a new road and overabundant parking space. The soil is decontaminated up to legal standards. Seven other industrial malls were constructed and constitute the Angus Technopôle. It hosts forty-four (many high-tech-related) companies, which are a mixture of both profit-making and non-profit-making organizations. One major and several smaller neighbourhood parks have been established. About 1,400 housing units have been constructed and are inhabited, mostly by well-off residents seeking the quietness of the suburbs while being close to the city centre (Le Bel *et al.* 2005). A social economy catering service, child care, service flats for elderly people and a child centre for palliative care have also been established. Several pieces of the site await development as part of the Technopôle.

To provide an understanding of the project dynamics, Table 3.1 gives an overview of the main actors and some important dates. The following paragraphs focus on the various spatial claims and the related resource mobilization processes that made collective action possible within a context of dispersed resources. The first part focuses on the voicing of claims that both confronted and aligned interests

Table 3.1   Key moments and key actors in the transformation of the Angus Locoshops brownfield site

Key moments	Key actors
1904 – Implantation of the Angus factories 1970s – First closure of part of the Angus factories 1992 – Final closure of the Angus factories and start of the CDEC mobilization for jobs 1994 – Public assembly on zoning and first agreement between the CPR and the CDEC 1995 – Start of housing and commercial project 1998 – Agreement between the CPR and the SDA on concept of the industrial project and first land acquisition 1999 – Creation of Insertech (a social economy enterprise for work training in computer repair) 2000 – Opening of the restored Locoshop 2008 – To be completed: part of the Angus Technopôle	Canadian Pacific Railway (CPR): landowner 1904 until early 2000s, developer housing and commerce (1995–2006) Organized civil society (CDEC-RPP, IFDEC, SDA, Insertech): driving force Angus Technopôle State actors (local authority, provincial and national authorities): mediation, financial support of the SDA and finance infrastructure and parks Residents Rosemont-Petite-Patrie: Angus Locoshop workers, referendum support Technopôle Social economy-related financial structures (Fondation, Desjardins)

and visions; the second zooms in on the mobilization processes from the moment a local compromise was negotiated and project implementation started.

ANGUS TRANSFORMATIVE DYNAMICS AND CHANGING RELATIONS

VOICING CLAIMS

Logan and Molotch's (1987) 'growth machine' paradigm explains how growth coalitions mobilize with the promise that growth benefits all through trickle-down effects, and so succeed in trading off the use value of the majority for the exchange value of a few. This frequently makes territorial social conflicts invisible. By contrast, in the Angus case, territorial social conflicts were made visible. This is often the case when the functions, ownership status or user rights of land are temporarily undefined, or suddenly changed. Direct appropriation through occupation or squatting of underused landed property is an obvious means of giving voice to otherwise unheard actors and claims. This did not happen on the Angus site, but community activists did not wait for the last employee to be sent home before starting to brainstorm on possible futures for this large piece of urban land. Civil actors steered and triggered public debate to such an extent that it became impossible to ignore the existence of a collective claim: land development for jobs.

DEVELOPING VISIONS

The central claim for jobs was not unique to the transformation of the Angus Locoshops, but part of a larger social movement in Montréal that organized itself around the issue of industrial reconversion (Fontan et al. 2005a,b). The symbolic, economic and social importance of the Locoshops in the history of the neighbourhood, as well as their size and appearance, transformed them into a central, and also personal, target for community activists. The site's future was imagined as 'a structuring element of an industrial corridor along the railway-line, providing 2000 high quality jobs related to the new economy, accessible to the East Montreal inhabitants' (Ville de Montréal 1990: 47). The city council, at that time headed by the Montréal Citizens' Movement, was preparing its first master plan. The civil actors' visioning, which imagined how the Angus site might regain its strategic character in the economic development of Rosemont-Petite-Patrie, was a welcome input to the plan.[4] A vast consultation process, the well-developed communitarian milieu, comprising community actors and urban movements that had promoted local economic development in Montréal since the 1980s, and good relations between this milieu and the politicians and officials in charge of the

master planning process ensured that the city of Montréal included the consolidation of the industrial vocation of the land along the railway in its final first master
plan (Ville de Montréal, 1992).

The civil actors had a vision. The initial ideas were discussed among community activists mainly from IFDEC, an institute for popular education and community
development, and CDEC-RPP. CDEC-RPP then started to mobilize (see Table
3.2). However, few believed that the CDEC would succeed in mobilizing the
resources needed to acquire and develop the land. Nor did the statutes and mission of CDEC allow such actions. Consequently, the SDA, a non-profit developer,
was established.

First CDEC, and later SDA, worked hard to make the western part of the
Angus Locoshops visible, attracting policy interest and public and private funding

Table 3.2 Organization of the key civil society actors involved in the transformation of the
Angus Locoshops

Key organization or key players	Organizational form	Function	Mobilization
IFDEC, researchers, active community, CDEC (late 1980s–early 1990s)	Professional associations, activists and researchers interact and exchange informally	Development of strategies of alternative development	Community organizations and urban movements, local political arenas
CDEC-RPP (early 1990s–1996)	Professional community organization; link with research collective	Initiation of the Angus Technopôle project and set-up of social economy enterprises (e.g. Insertech)	Wide mobilization in the local community (vote on zoning plan, public finance campaign, etc.), in the Montréal business and research milieus, in local and supra-local political arenas
SDA (1996–2004)	Not-for-profit developer	Development of the Angus Technopôle	Mobilization in local business milieus, in political arenas, international exchange with civil society industrial reconversion initiatives
SDA–Fondaction partnership (since 2004)	Not-for-profit developer in formal partnership with a pension fund	Development of the Angus Technopôle and expansion to other projects	Mobilization in local business milieus, international ethical capital

to redevelop the site while preserving heritage and incorporating the values of local development.

The first ideas and strategies developed informally around kitchen tables and in bars towards the end of the 1980s before the factory closed down. Furthermore, in December 1988 IFDEC Montréal co-organized a conference, entitled 'Le local en Action', which discussed ideas and experiences of community economic development practices (CED – for the North Americans) and local territorial development (for the Europeans). Creating partnerships between private business, labour movements, community movements and institutional or public actors was identified as an essential tool for the future of local development (conference report ANDPL and IFDEC 1989). These partnerships would generate new social relations and modify actor mentality and behaviour (conference report ANDPL and IFDEC 1989). Influenced by such meetings, ideas developed for the Locoshops' future. Much was uncertain; however, it became clear that jobs, job training and the environment should be the main issues. Within this setting, partnerships for local development emerged and organized around old industrial space.

The local authorities were well connected with, and aware of, the push for jobs within the community movement. Moreover, the city administration, as well as a small number of heritage activists, were concerned with the preservation of Angus heritage. CPR's request to demolish the Angus shops was rejected; it had to seek new uses for the remaining built structures, acting in concert with the city.[5] Finally, a feasibility study for the Technopôle project stressed the value of the Locoshops, and provided a further stimulus for its re-use.

The landowner, the CPR, did not imagine a future for the area. At the time of the Angus closure, the CPR's decision-making centre was no longer anchored in Montréal, and the company restructuring strategy aimed at the valorization of its vacant and underused property.[6] The Angus site was perceived merely as a cost and a liability. The CPR therefore directly approached the city officials with a proposal for a residential development project.

It is remarkable that the desires of the different actors (landowner, civil society actor and local authority) became visible before the definition of a formal project and that the actual existence of a brownfield induced local interactions between the different actors. The CDEC was the driving force in making spatial claims heard widely, using public debate and perseverance as its principal tools. The CPR, in contrast, would not consider the community as an interlocutor, and preferred direct negotiation on development plans with the city administration. Whereas these first steps in voicing claims consisted mainly of informal visioning processes without open confrontation, a second step, and therewith the first confrontation of claims, consisted of challenging the private ownership model and its supposed rights.

CLAIMING LAND THAT IS NOT YOURS

The concept of property was central to the alignment of claims and the transformation of these into tangible results. This was the case for the landowner,
who wanted to sell ownership rights to capitalize on the land value, as well as
for the civil actor, whose claim for the physical space was crucial to realizing the
reconversion for jobs project. In fact, the main asset of brownfields is the availability of space. At the same time, access to space is crucial to gaining autonomy
whatever the activity envisaged. By convention, land ownership and zoning are
central concepts in defining which activities can take place at a particular location and who has access or not and under which conditions. Blomley (2003: xiv)
graphically describes what we associate with landed property: 'a restricted area,
with boundaries and where in and out depends on whether you are granted the
permission, or not'. The division of land into privately held, demarcated plots creates one of the basic institutions of capitalist social relations, a system of inclusion
and exclusion. Furthermore, zoning regulations both protect and limit the freedom
granted through property rights.

In the definition of the Angus brownfield transformation project, both zoning
and the imagination of landownership, although as a collective property owned
by the local community, have been of strategic importance. In imagining a future
for the land and translating this into a plan, community activists contested the
traditional ownership model and prevented the landowner from 'quietly enjoy[ing]
its land'. In fact, whereas the property model has encouraged us to ignore the
claims and aspirations of non-landowning actors, local activists here questioned
the legitimacy of the model by claiming ownership of the land for the benefit of the
community and using this as a local development lever in the form of a community
land trust. Thus, if CPR, owner of the Angus site, initially expected to operate
its quasi-monopoly to control 'its space', CDEC confronted this with a counter-
claim: the long-standing relationship of workers with the Angus site justified the
community's fight for jobs rather than acceptance of 'losing the space' by its
transformation into residential space.

FORCING NEGOTIATIONS

A third crucial element in voicing claims processes is the creation of active negotiations forums between different stakeholders. Aware of the existing claims, the
local planning department, led by an ex-social activist, forced a dialogue between
the competing interests. CPR, the landowner, wanted to realize a residential and
commercial project and so increase the amount of land rent. However, a zoning

change was needed to develop the programme, and, as stated in the regulations, this had to be publicly approved by a community assembly. The legal force of zoning thus became a crucial instrument in forcing negotiations, because the community had the power to reject the demand for change of land use, and so block CPR's project. Consequently, CPR, under pressure from the city administration, started to negotiate with CDEC as an intermediary for the community.

In the meantime, CDEC had realized the importance of mobilizing the community with an alternative vision. Through intensive relations with local media, CDEC succeeded in transforming its own vision into a locally shared one and an empowering planning instrument. Community support guaranteed CDEC's power during negotiations with the CPR. However, after almost two years of negotiations without satisfactory results, the city council acted strategically and fixed a date (4 May 1994) for the community assembly to vote for the zoning revision of the Angus shops. The extra pressure led to a first agreement in 1994, and a refinement in 1998. The CDEC/SDA was granted preferential rights to gradually buy 23 ha for the development of a Technopôle. For the CDEC this achievement was a way of recognizing and remunerating the workers' sweat and energy poured into the site for almost a century. In exchange, CDEC would mobilize the community to support a zoning modification for the eastern part of the site.

Hence, different voices were heard (through visioning processes and claiming land) and confronted (through negotiations), so that conflicts settled down before the project machine became fully functional. These dynamics were fundamental to the emergence of a project that started from lived concerns (in contrast to a fully planned project that receives a flavour of participation afterwards). Yet the official planning moments (change of zoning and confirmation of industrial allocation in the master plan) are what generated official legitimacy for the strategic project. The CDEC/SDA project assumed a space of hope in the local milieu for democratization of urban space and economic development (SDA 2000). The project therefore was confronted with the challenge of integrating social, economic and political dimensions.

PUTTING THE PROJECT MACHINE INTO MOTION

The Angus brownfield transformation project can be understood as the articulation of a variety of interacting mobilization processes and the negotiation of competing spatial claims voiced by actors after the Angus complex became available for new uses. The project itself, continuously driven by the civil actors, became an established institution and mobilizing force. The chapter goes on to explore the main resource mobilization processes and their impact on social relations, grouping them into three categories: conducting studies and external expertise, generating public debate to gain public attention and mobilize funds, and social entrepreneurship and organizational innovation.

THE MOBILIZING ROLE OF STUDIES AND EXTERNAL EXPERTISE

From the moment of the early brainstorming exercises, the leading CDEC employees were surrounded by academics and activists mobilized through personal networks. Personal contacts with the city hall influenced the master plan, and forced the landowner into negotiations with the community-based organization. During the negotiations, the employees were assisted by volunteer engineers and lawyers. Later, after obtaining virtual ownership over the land, studies were fundamental to the mobilization of financial resources. In fact, the conduct of studies was a precondition for public support. Such expert studies are generally accepted tools in public and private actor milieus in the preparation of a formal project.

Consequently, the fact that a community-based actor agreed to comply with this more formal language and method of approach generated trust and further support. Indeed, 'the study phase appeared to be crucial, not necessarily in its outcome', Christian Yaccarini[7] remembers, 'but as a process and as a tool in generating legitimacy'. Throughout the project this technique of local project leadership combined with external expertise became a crucial way to steer content and approach and build support. For example, when the SDA was set up, its board of directors included several influential players from the Montréal business milieu. They brought in their personal knowledge and networks, and generated the trust that facilitated access to public and private funds.

GENERATING PUBLIC DEBATE

The generation of public debate was another key mobilizing process. The strategic use of the press and the involvement of non-conventional players to influence public opinion and disseminate a vision have been reported in other cases (e.g. Albrechts 2001). The CDEC/SDA was extremely successful in that respect. Headed by a social entrepreneur (a leader with powerful political skills), the organization ensured the near impossibility of denying the collective claim on Angus. Not only was press attention pursued on every possible occasion, but articles frequently also included sharp comments or strategic statements. By such methods, public debate constructed legitimacy. A project such as the Angus Technopôle is not born at one particular moment, yet one could refer to a 'strategic project' from the moment the informal actors were able to influence the public debate. It is at this moment that spatial claims became claims shared by many.

Residents and community-based actors strongly supported the CDEC, and for politicians it became useful to be actively involved in the project.

The Angus site generated think-tank and negotiation coalitions, large-scale resident mobilization and the emergence of media and local entrepreneurs; all these led to public debate and increased the visibility of spatial claims. Visibility became strategic not only in the redevelopment of a concrete parcel of land, but also important ideologically. Press articles and interviews reveal that the debate became symbolic of the role that civil actors could play in economic regeneration. Furthermore, strategic visibility assured access to public and private resources at various scales. Long-lasting support from individual politicians at all relevant scales assured access to public funds through programmes and cheap loans, as long as 'results' were delivered.[8] Political support at the local level was also crucial in formally legitimizing the claims of the community-based organizations. In addition, creative financing mechanisms contributed to public debate and project ownership. For example, a public finance campaign (golf tournament, Angus beer, lottery, etc.), which symbolically sold land, did not directly raise large amounts of cash. Yet the large number of politicians, businessmen, unionists, urban elite and residents involved in the campaign demonstrate its importance in mobilizing people around the project.

Public debate and the confrontation of overlapping and conflicting spatial claims resulted in a variety of opportunistic coalitions. They range from ephemeral cooperation to long-lasting coalitions to pragmatic formal agreements between the civil society and the private actor, and between the private actor and the local government.

EMERGENCE OF A NOT-FOR-PROFIT DEVELOPER: SOCIAL ENTREPRENEURSHIP AND ORGANIZATIONAL INNOVATION

The goals striven for by the civil society actor imposed the development of a new organization, which was able to assume the role of project leader, handle the articulation of different logics and processes, and connect desires, visioning, and planning and implementation practices.

The CDEC traditionally favoured connections between local economic actors, and assisted in development programmes, but would not normally act as developer. Besides the fact that it lacked the culture for doing this, it would be organizationally difficult. The SDA was established to overcome these problems, and had to play a crucial role in translating a locally shared vision into actual spatial interventions. The not-for-profit developer therefore functions as a private developer but aims for community development instead of financial profit.

The SDA had a plan; it negotiated potential ownership rights and achieved legitimacy, but it still had to mobilize the resources to actually develop the Tech-nopôle as envisaged. Therefore, the SDA constructed a network of connections, which linked it directly to favourable decision-making chains (Fontan *et al.* 2004). Focusing on converging interests and compromises, alliances were forced to ensure finance and the development of an attractive concept that would attract viable, innovative companies that also had a social mission.[9] Further, the SDA offered assistance and services to the companies implanted on the site. Hence, the civil society actor plays a role not only in the creation of jobs, but also in creating the conditions necessary to attract companies. Finally, the SDA wanted to be a 'pole of local governance, based on partnership and an implication with the community in the realization of projects' (Fontan and Yaccarini, 1996: 35 [authors' translation]). This implied an overall programme that aimed at the integration of physical, institutional, economic, ecological and social change programmes. To realize its mission, the SDA was forced to cooperate closely with a financially stronger party. Since 2004, therefore, Fondaction, a union-related financial institution working in venture capital for the development of Québec's economy, has been a development partner.

INNOVATIVE GOVERNANCE ARRANGEMENTS

INTERPRETING HETEROGENEOUS CLAIMS AND THEIR CONSEQUENCES ON THE COALITION FORMATION

The above paragraphs show that the actors in the Angus project framed their claims differently according to the relations they had with the site, or the way in which they perceived it. The Angus shops were a symbol of modernity and settled prosperity, but also a symbol of changing economic geographies and a problematic socio-economic situation. Furthermore, the Angus shops were propertied space, to be prepared for another round of capital accumulation. The undefined status of the brownfield became an opportunity for the amplification and confrontation of spatial claims (Figure 3.2). The case also shows that the different spatial claims led to contestation as well as partnerships. This was not necessarily because the claims were shared, but because voicing claims made common interests (such as economic development) visible, and therefore forged coalitions. Initial conflict and a context of distrust thus gave way to more collaborative situations, yet with strongly divergent interests.

The capacity of the SDA executive director to understand and deal with the various spatial claims and link across established groups has been a key resource in fostering innovation in governance relations. It was at the root of the involvement of the cooperative financial institutions and higher-level government tiers,

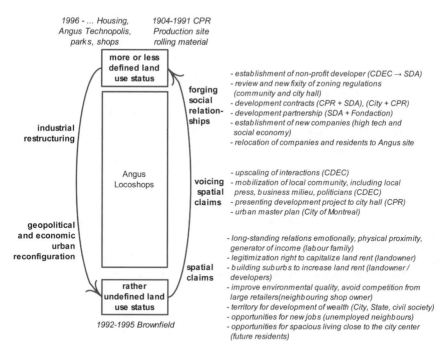

Figure 3.2   Brownfield transformation dynamics for the Angus Locoshops.

which provided development resources. By understanding different spatial logics, confronting and combining them, he successfully generated trust among persons in business, academic and political milieus to the extent that they were ready to engage in exchanges across their traditional environment, trespass against formal rules and adapt to other ways of thinking in the interest of the common Angus project. The community leader, as well as Rosemont's current mayor and former community activist, were able to translate languages and concepts and act as bridge figures between the community and the urban elites. Yet, as will be shown, this bridging and 'scale-jumping' (Smith 2006) also resulted in weakened relations with other community associations.

SOCIAL INNOVATION?

The Angus case shows the extent to which a civil society actor can become involved in, drive forward and shape the redevelopment of a brownfield. The interaction of spatial claims related to the Angus Locoshops resulted in a brownfield transformation project that coordinated an ad hoc governance arrangement, which generated the capacity for action in a context of dispersed resources. Although it was initially based on community development logics and local resources, the register of action shifted to connect to higher-scale networks and politico-economical perspectives. The particular governance arrangement and the strong interconnection between a community organization and labour union-related risk capital makes it an interesting case study from a social innovation perspective.

The public actors assumed a mediating role. The strategic role of the local government explains part of the success of the unusual negotiations between a civil society actor and a large private developer. Furthermore, the alliances between the civil society actor and the Montréal cooperative business milieu on the SDA board of councillors, who joined forces for local economic development, are crucial. Despite their different backgrounds and different relationships with the Angus site, the Montréal business personalities were ready to support the SDA because of the nature of the project (fostering economic development and job creation), and because of the leadership capacities of the civil society actor.[10] The coalition of private expertise supporting the civil society actor enabled communication with the private developer on shared terms. The combination of skilled civil society actors endowed with an entrepreneurial and political spirit, businessmen interested in assuming societal responsibilities and looking for personal challenges, public actors with an activist trajectory and the CDEC culture led to a situation in which informal actors acquired visibility and legitimacy in the public debate on economic and urban revitalization of east Montréal's industrial tissue.

LOWERING INVESTMENT BARRIERS OR CONTROLLING RESOURCES FOR SOCIAL CHANGE?

The fact that brownfield revitalization fitted in with the CDEC's mission of economic community development added to its credibility and support. The CDEC/SDA primarily wanted to bring economic development to Rosemont-Petite-Patrie to benefit its residents. Dewar and Deitrick (2004) indicate two principal rationales for community organizations to do so: first, to control economic resources to benefit weaker social groups and to redirect economic opportunities to impoverished neighbourhoods; and, second, to deal with market barriers in low-income areas. The CDEC/SDA showed leadership by demonstrating the potential for economic investment in a difficult area and by controlling economic resources (land, property development and management of a business park). The early strategies developed by the SDA explicitly emphasize business development, job training and broad community building (e.g. Comité de relance Angus 1997).

The SDA became a strong organization on the economic reconversion scene, but gradually detached from neighbourhood and community development when communication and cooperation with the neighbourhood decreased as well as with its involvement in setting up social economy enterprises. Upscaling of the SDA through partnership with public and private actors empowered it as an organization, but increased the gap with other community-based groups that continued to work at the neighbourhood level. Moreover, it is easier to mobilize for 'jobs' than for 'social change'. The message of investment in jobs and economic revitalization successfully mobilized residents and public and private business actors, and led to new social networks. Besides functioning as a platform for new initiatives (such as the social economy enterprises on site), the private sector alone would not have imagined the Angus project; nor would it have assumed the risk if the civil society actors had not provided the audacity and strategic skills and set an example in overcoming economic barriers to investment in the neighbourhood. The civil society actor combined the concept of a traditional business park with community development through job training and insertion programmes, standard adoption of ecological building techniques, transport reduction initiatives and mixed spatial development.

The Angus project was initiated and led by an organization that had emerged from the community. The community, however, has very little control over the SDA. Its resource base depends partly on its own functioning, but also on public funding and private capital. This partly confirms Stoecker's (1997) doubts about the community development corporation model as a viable alternative for urban development. Yet a project of this size would not have been possible without an external financial base. Financiers invested in the project because of shared or complementary missions of economic development, rather than for expectations of short-term profit. However, a decrease in community-articulated agendas and the concentration on establishing economic activities indicate that the SDA responded first to a funder's interest and only then to its social agenda. It shifted from a comprehensive social, economic and physical agenda towards economic/physical-centred development activities. Since the start of the implementation works, SDA communications and year reports stress its role in property and economic development. It sees its role as creating the conditions for a business location where public and private sector are willing to make new investments that will benefit the neighbourhood. However, labour training programmes, mediating activities in local governance or direct cooperation with the surrounding neighbourhood currently have no priority. A community group thus gained power to act in guiding investment in its neighbourhood, but to what extent such dynamics indeed improve socio-economic equity remains an open question.

The project exemplifies a territorial mode of coordination in which the SDA leadership had the capacity to establish favourable conditions by generating public debate, setting up an impressive network and holding together all complex relationships and partnerships. Yet, if socially innovative governance arrangements mean democratic decision-making structures in which residents, users, etc. also have an important say throughout a large part of the transformation processes, the Angus governance arrangement would not qualify as such. The success of the Angus transformation, as has been shown, is based on social entrepreneurship, that is, local leadership and the ability to mobilize and combine a large range of resources to realize an appealing vision. Angus was not subject to the pressure of short-term financial profit, and therefore had the means to do something different, and to allow slower planning processes. Property rights on the Angus site generate power over access and the activities taking place there and influence the flows passing through the space. These in turn influence the social relationships constructed throughout the space (e.g. mixing social economy activities with a traditional profit economy in the long term generates new business communities sharing the values and logics of a plural economy; Klein *et al.* 2008). The co-presence of these activities and the people they attract generates new interactions and initiatives.

LEARNING AND INSTITUTIONALIZATION?

Social innovation refers not only to finding new ways of addressing locally perceived needs, but also to the learning and institutionalization of new practices (Fontan *et al.* 2004). One crucial impact of the Angus project is that it started to travel. Relations were forged around a particular brownfield, but continue to exist in relation to other, sometimes far away, spaces. The SDA project travels in four ways. Primarily in Montréal, but also beyond, the project is regularly perceived as best practice (e.g. Leite 2008; US Green Building Council 2008). Community groups also refer directly to the Technopôle as an example of what is possible or desirable, even if not necessarily evident. Second, the case was noticed by researchers with an interest in how traditional ownership and governance structures could be challenged and successfully contested (Fontan *et al.* 2005a,b; Klein *et al.* 2008). Third, the partnerships with private corporations and politicians were a means to gaining support for the SDA project, but led in the long run to the travelling of events and ideas. During interviews, several politicians and private actors referred to their involvement in the Angus project as an experience from which they learned personally and which led to the questioning of their working practices. Finally, financial resources were not abundant in 2006 and no major developments were in prospect, so looking outwards became a necessity. The Technopôle buildings paid for themselves, but they do not generate income to run the SDA. The knowledge collectively built up over the last fifteen years through the development of the Angus project is now used outside the physical boundaries of the site. Time will prove whether or not this change marks the shift from the SDA as an organization 'with a cause' into an urban not-for-profit developer (Van Dyck 2010).

CONCLUSION

The case study of Angus Technopôle shows the possibility of connecting conflicting and overlapping spatial claims and going beyond purely profit-oriented property-led urban development in strategic projects. The case suggests a project approach that starts *from* places and the aspirations of the local community, in contrast to projects that are implemented *on* strategic locations. The analysis shows the opportunities that strategic projects generate for co-productive spatial strategies. Yet, even if the brownfield transformation project is based on socially innovative partnerships, the analysis also shows how, paradoxically, these progressive approaches contribute both to the transformation as well as to the reproduction of established social relations.

The Angus case illustrates the opportunities that a community land trust can generate for the realization of an industrial project combining the social economy and high-tech-based economic development. Moreover, it directed eyes towards industrial green space in the city centre. The social innovation in social relations is most evident in the upscaling of organized civil society actors. Community actors and urban movements, in partnership with risk capital, give rise to a new form of corporatism, which in the long run may provide changes in governance regimes (see also Klein and Tremblay 2009). In addition, the case shows the difficulty of going beyond learning effects within a very restricted group to wider empowerment. I would like to call therefore for renewed interest in combining the project approach with complementary strategies for resource redistribution, rather than betting solely on the implementation of strategic projects to realize planning goals. Furthermore, this case suggests that so-called 'socially innovative' strategic projects share many similarities as governance devices with current neoliberal large-scale urban development projects. Both are based on socially innovative partnerships, piloted by small autocratic organizational forms, and are spatially selective, and their impact on larger urban development processes and social inclusion is not monitored. Therefore, it raises questions about the capacity of socially innovative strategic projects to break away from the urban growth machine. The main difference with the Angus project is that, because of the types of actors involved and their behavioural rationales, a variety of endogenous as well as exogenous resources were mobilized. The result is a project in which financial profit and property development are catalysts, but not the aim. The analysis thus points to the benefits of including civil society actors in urban development coalitions. It showed how the open confrontation of spatial claims led to the settling down in space of a locally negotiated compromise with an eye to the diversity of spatial uses. Nevertheless, questions have to be asked concerning how and to what extent this steers resource allocation away from economic growth strategies and towards improving the living conditions and development capacities of weaker social groups in society.

NOTES

1 The author would like to thank the Centre de recherche sur les innovations sociales à l'Université de Québec à Montréal, and Jean-Marc Fontan and Jean-Louis Klein, in particular, for sharing their reflections and providing access to key sources during the fieldwork. The author would also like to acknowledge the valuable contribution of editor Stijn Oosterlynck, who reviewed earlier versions of this chapter.
2 See, for example, the overview of definitions for a project in the *Wideman Comparative Glossary of Project Management Terms v3.1* (http://www.maxwideman.com).
3 Interview with Pierre St-Cyr, former project manager for CPR, Montréal, 24 May 2007.
4 Interview with André Lavallée, current mayor of Rosemont-Petite-Patrie, officer in charge of the master plan in the early 1990s and Angus community activist in the 1970s, Montréal, 4 June 2007.
5 Interviews with Elaine Gauthier, advisor at the city Department of Territory and Heritage Valorization, 8 September 2008, and with André Lavallée, current mayor of Rosemont-Petite-Patrie, officer in charge of the master plan in the early 1990s and Angus community activist in the 1970s, Montréal, 4 June 2007.
6 Interview with Pierre St-Cyr, former project manager for CPR, Montréal, 24 May 2007.
7 Interview with Christian Yaccarini, director of the SDA, former CDEC employee and community activist, Montréal, 31 May 2007.
8 Interview with Martin Cauchon, state secretary at the Economic Development Agency of Canada for the Regions of Québec (1996–2002), Montréal, 10 September 2008.
9 Interview with Juan-Luis Klein, researcher and former SDA advisor, Montréal, 31 May 2007.
10 Interview with Léopold Beaulieu, Fondaction chairman and SDA councillor since 1995, Montréal, 16 August 2009.

REFERENCES

Albrechts, L. (2001) 'From traditional land use planning to strategic spatial planning: the case of Flanders', in L. Albrechts, J. Alden and A. Da Rosa Pires (eds) *The Changing Institutional Landscape of Planning*, Aldershot: Ashgate Publishing.
Albrechts, L. (2006) 'Bridge the gap: from spatial planning to strategic projects', *European Planning Studies*, 14 (10): 1487–1500.
Ambrosino, C. and Andrès, L. (2008) 'Friches en ville: du temps de veille aux politiques de l'espace', *Espaces et sociétés*, 3 (134): 37–51.
ANDPL and IFDEC (1989) 'Le local en action'. International conference report on local development conference, Montréal, 1988. Montréal: ANDPL–IFDEC.
Avitabile, A. (2005) *La mise en scène du projet urbain. Pour une structuration des démarches*, Paris: L'Harmattan.

Blomley, N. (2003) *Unsettling the City*, New York: Routledge.

Bornstein, L. (2007) 'Confrontation, collaboration and community benefits: lessons from Canadian and U.S. cities on working together around strategic projects'. Paper presented at 43rd ISOCARP congress, Antwerp, September 2007.

Bouchain, P. (2008) 'Faire face et réunir', in *La Friche la Belle de Mai. Marseille. Un espace capital dans une capitale européenne*, Marseille: SFT.

Comité de Relance Angus (1997) *Rosemont-Petite-Patrie, S'organiser localement pour l'emploi, Plan stratégique d'adaptation de la main-d'œuvre*, Montréal: CDÉC Rosemont-Petite-Patrie.

Dewar, M. and Deitrick, S. (2004) 'The role of community development corporations in brownfield redevelopment', in *Recycling the City. The Use and Reuse of Urban Land*, Cambridge, MA: Lincoln Institute of Land Policy.

Dickinson, J. and Young, B. (2003) *A Short History of Quebec*, 3rd edn, Montréal: McGill Queen's University Press.

Fontan, J. M. and Yaccarini, C. (1996). 'Le project Angus: une expérience novatrice de mobilization locale au Coeur de Montréal'. *Economie et Solidarité* 28 (1): 31–42.

Fontan, J. M., Hamel, P., Morin, R. and Shragge, E. (2003a) 'The institutionalization of Montreal's CDECS: From grassroots organizations to state apparatus?', *Canadian Journal of Urban Research*, 12 (1): 58–77.

Fontan, J. M., Klein, J. L. and Lévesque, B. (2003b) *Reconversion économique et développement territorial*, Québec: Presses de l'Université du Québec.

Fontan, J. M. and Klein, J. L. (2004a) 'La mobilisation du capital socioterritorial: le cas du Technopole Angus', *Revue internationale d'action communautaire*, 52: 139–149.

Fontan, J. M., Klein, J. L. and Tremblay, D. G. (2004b) 'Innovation and society: broadening the analysis of the territorial effects of innovation', Research Note No. 2004-07A, Canada Research Chair on the Socio-Organizational Challenges of the Knowledge Economy, Télé-université/Université du Québec à Montréal.

Fontan, J. M., Klein, J. L. and Tremblay, D. G. (2005a) *Innovation socioterritoriale et reconversion économique: le cas de Montréal*, Paris: L'Harmattan.

Fontan, J. M., Klein, J. L. and Lévesque, B. (2005b) 'The fight for jobs and economic governance: The Montreal model', in P. Booth and B. Jouve (eds) *Metropolitan Democracies: Transformations of the State and Urban Policy in Canada, France and Great Britain*, Aldershot: Burlington.

Gerometta, J., Haussermann, H. and Longo, G. (2005) 'Social innovation and civil society in urban governance: strategies for an inclusive city', *Urban Studies*, 42 (11): 2007–2021.

Graefe, P. (2004) 'Welfare regimes and the third sector: rendering path dependency contingent?'. Paper presented at the International Conference of the Society for Third Sector Research, Toronto, July 2004.

Groth, J. and Corijn, E. (2005) 'Reclaiming urbanity: indeterminate spaces, informal actors and urban agenda setting', *Urban Studies*, 42 (3): 503–526.

Gualini, E. and Majoor, S. (2007) 'Innovative practices in large urban development projects: conflicting frames in the quest for "New Urbanity"', *Planning Theory & Practice*, 8 (3): 297–318.

Harvey, D. (1973) *Social Justice and the City*, Baltimore: Johns Hopkins University Press.

Klein, J.L. and Harrisson, D. (2007) *L'innovation sociale: émergence et effets sur la transformation des sociétés*, Quebec: Presses Universitaires du Quebec.

Klein, J. L. and Tremblay, D. G. (2009) 'Social actors and their role in metropolitan governance in Montréal: Towards an inclusive coalition?', *GeoJournal*, online, March 2009, DOI: 10.1007/s10708-009-9270-0.

Klein, J. L., Fontan, J. M. and Tremblay, D. G. (2008) 'Local development as social innovation: the case of Montreal', in P. Drewe, J. L. Klein and E. Hulsbergen (eds) *The Challenge of Social Innovation in Urban Revitalization*, Amsterdam: Techne Press.

Klein, J. L., Tremblay, D. G. and Bussières, D. (2009) 'Social economy-based local initiatives and social innovation: a Montreal case study', *International Journal of Technology Management* 51 (1): 121–138.

Lamoureux, D. (2008) 'Québec 2001: un tournant pour les mouvements sociaux québécois?', in *Québec en mouvements*, Montréal: Lux Editeur.

Le Bel, P. M., Desjardins Rivard, J. and Driant, C. (2005) 'Le développement résidentiel Angus: Mixité sociale? Qualité architecturale?', *Urbanité*, October: 11–13.

Leite, C. (2008) 'Reinventing Sao Paolo at the sustainability age'. Online editorial of the Instituto de Arquictecura tropical, issue sustainability Red. Available at: http://www.arquitecturatropical.org/EDITORIAL/INDEX.htm.

Leitner, H., Peck, J. and Sheppard, E. S. (2006) *Contesting Neoliberalism: Urban Frontiers*, New York: Guilford Press.

Linteau, P. A. (2000) *Histoire de Montréal depuis la confédération*, 2nd edn, Montreal: Boreal.

Logan, J. and Molotch, H. (1987) *Urban Fortunes: The Political Economy of Place*, Berkeley: University of California Press.

MacCallum, D., Moulaert, F., Hillier, J. and Vicari, S. (2008) *Social Innovation and Territorial Development*, Aldershot: Ashgate Publishing.

Mendell, M. (2002) 'The social economy in Québec. Discourse and strategies', in A. Bakan and E. MacDonald (eds) *Critical Political Studies: Debates and Dialogues for the Left*, Montréal: McGill Queens University Press.

Mendell, M. (2006) 'The social economy in Quebec'. Paper presented at Balta Meeting, Alberta, 2006.

Moulaert, F. (2000) *Globalization and Integrated Area Development in European Cities*, Oxford: Oxford University Press.

Moulaert, F., Swyngedouw, E. and Rodriguez, A. (2003) *The Globalized City*, Oxford: Oxford University Press.

Moulaert, F., Martinelli, F., Swyngedouw, E. and González, S. (2005) 'Towards alternative model(s) of local innovation', *Urban Studies*, 42 (11): 1969–1990.

Novy, A., Hammer, E. and Leubolt, B. (2008) 'Social innovation and governance of scale in Austria', in D. MacCallum, F. Moulaert, J. Hillier and S. Vicari (eds) *Social Innovation And Territorial Governance*, Aldershot: Ashgate Publishing.

Paloscia, R. (2004) *The Contested Metropolis: Six Cities at the Beginning of the 21st Century*, Basel: Birkhäuser.

Pinson, G. (2009) *Gouverner la ville par projet. Urbanisme et gouvernance des villes européennes*, Paris: Les Presses.

SDA (2000) *Plan d'action Société de Développement Angus 2000–2001*, Montréal: Dépot Légal Bibliothèque Nationale du Québec.

Smith, N. (2006) 'Scale', in R. Johnston, D. Gregory, G. Pratt and M. Watts (eds) *The Dictionary of Human Geography*, 4th edn, Oxford: Blackwell Publishing.

Stoecker, R. (1997) 'The CDC model of urban redevelopment: a critique and an alternative', *Journal of Urban Affairs*, 19 (1): 1–22.

TransEuropeHalles, F. (2001) *Les fabriques: lieux imprévus*, Besançon: Imprimeur.

US Green Building Council (2009) USGBC in the news details 02/09/2009, 'Leed for neighborhood development'. Online. Available at: http://www.usgbc.org/News/USGB-CInTheNewsDetails.aspx?ID=3968.

Van Den Broeck, J. and Verschure, H. (2004) 'Urban development by co-production', in A. Loeckx, K. Shannon, R. Tuts and H. Verschure (eds) *Urban Trialogues. Localising Agenda 21, Visions, Projects, Co-productions*, Nairobi: UN-Habitat.

Van Dyck, B. (2010) 'Social entrepreneurship in urban planning and development in Montréal', in G. Baeten and T. Tasan-Kok (eds) *Contradictions of Neoliberal Planning: Cities, Policies, And Politics*, Dordrecht: Springer (forthcoming).

Ville de Montréal (1990) *Rapport de la concertation sur les enjeux d'aménagement et de développement. Faites votre ville*, June 1990, Montréal: Ville de Montréal.

Ville de Montréal (1992) *Plan d'urbanisme 1992: Réussir Montréal*, Montréal: Ville de Montréal.

CHAPTER 4

ANALYSING SOCIAL INNOVATION THROUGH PLANNING INSTRUMENTS

A STRATEGIC-RELATIONAL APPROACH

PIETER VAN DEN BROECK

PLANNING INSTRUMENTS AS A PERSPECTIVE

Over the last decade, the social sustainability of strategic urban flagship projects has been questioned. Indeed, strategic urban projects, particularly in the form of large-scale urban development projects, have been criticized for promoting gentrification and social polarization, focusing one-sidedly on profit-oriented development and bypassing democratic control (Bornstein 2007; Moulaert *et al*. 2003; Swyngedouw *et al*. 2004). The question is, however, whether strategic projects are inherently neoliberal and autocratic or whether they can also be inclusive, emancipatory and innovative in socio-territorial terms. In this chapter, I want to argue for the latter. I will do so by taking planning instruments as the entry point into an analysis of how strategic urban projects generate socio-spatial transformation. The dynamic relation between planning instruments and their societal context will be crucial to this analysis.

Planning practitioners and academics have long been aware that planning instruments are shaped by the societal context from which they emerge and in which they operate (Albrechts *et al*. 2001; Booth *et al*. 2007; European Commission 2000; Vigar *et al*. 2000). On the other hand, large parts of planning theory and practice focus on methods to bring about change in society (Albrechts 1999, 2005; de Caluwe and Vermaak 2005; Healey *et al*. 1997). In this chapter I want to argue that there is a need to connect the two perspectives and examine more carefully the dynamics of both planning instruments and their societal context, drawing in particular on institutionalist planning theory. Indeed, planning instruments do not automatically emerge in response to changes in society, nor do they directly and unproblematically lead to changes in society. In this chapter, I will develop a conceptual framework that moves beyond a simple dualism between 'planning instruments' and (societal) 'context'. The framework starts from a sociological perspective on planning instruments in which these are analysed not just as technical means to predefined ends, but as social undertakings. It will explicitly address socio-political concerns about who is benefiting from planning instrument-induced societal changes, and who attempts to change planning instruments and how, for what reasons and with what consequences for their socio-political content and meaning. This chapter aims to show that planning instruments in strategic projects allow for different answers to these questions, and that, more specifically, they can be vehicles for both socio-territorial innovation and market-driven and real estate-led urban transformations.

In the second part of the chapter I develop the leads in institutionalist planning theory for analysing spatial planning instruments and expand the theory with a dialectical approach based on sociological institutionalism and on Jessop's strategic-relational approach. I then operationalize this approach for planning instruments, using concepts from political theory and from science and technology studies. Planning instruments are defined as the technical core of institutional frames, interacting dialectically with individual and collective actors and relevant social groups. Hence, socio-political content and meaning are structurally embedded within planning instruments. In the third part of the chapter the development and mobilization of planning instruments in one particular strategic project, 'First Quarter', in the city of Antwerp, is analysed from the strategic-relational institutionalist perspective outlined in the previous section. I examine the interplay between planning instruments, their institutional frames, the individual and collective actors and the relevant social groups involved in order to assess how socio-territorial innovation capacities are differentially embedded in the planning instruments mobilized in different episodes of the strategic project. The final section concludes that the strategic-relational institutionalist perspective on planning instruments and strategic projects is necessary for the analysis of the complexity of their dynamics, for the evaluation of their socio-territorial innovation capacity and to orientate planners towards embedding objectives of socio-territorial innovation into future planning instruments.

THE INSTITUTIONALIST APPROACH

Institutionalist planning theory is an appropriate starting point for an analysis of the interactions between planning processes, instruments and their societal context. Alongside and complementary to planning process theories,[1] variously labelled as planner–client oriented, subject centred and/or instrumentalist,[2] institutionalist planning theorists have developed a more social science-oriented planning theory. Proponents of this, over the last fifteen years, have focused on the role of institutions in/for planning, both formal (organizations, legal rules and procedures) and informal (values, conventions and behavioural codes), in structuring action in social contexts (Mandelbaum 1985; Fainstein 2000; Gualini 2001; Hajer 2003; Healey 1997, 1999, 2005; Innes 1995; Moulaert 2005; Saey 1995a,b; Verma

2007). Inspired by sociological institutionalism,[3] institutionalist planning theory moves beyond the study of planner behaviour, planning methods and planning effects. It draws attention to both the planning practices and the complex institutional dynamics connected to a place, including changes in social relations and ways of collective decision-making. It acknowledges that planning operates in a changing institutional frame and realizes its goals of transformation and project implementation only when accompanied by institutional changes (Gualini 2001; Hajer 2003; Healey 1999, 2005; Healey et al. 2003). As Gonzalez and Healey put it:

> This infusion of ideas shifts attention, in the discussion of policy processes, from the design of projects and policies and the potential impact on material outcomes, to the design of the institutional infrastructure which frames what projects and policies emerge and to impacts on identities, knowledge resources and cultural assumptions/mores as well as material outcomes.
>
> (Gonzalez and Healey 2005: 2057)

To analyse the dynamics of planning instruments and their societal context, I adopt an institutionalist perspective here perceiving planning as embedded in an 'institutional field'. Rather than focusing on institutions in planning, this means seeing planning as an institutionalized practice, as 'a set of practices itself subject to processes of institutionalization' (Gualini 2001: 51), guided not only by a technical rationality but also by a multiplicity of social rationalities. Following Jessop (2001), this entails using institutionalism in ontological terms, rather than seeing institutions as one amongst several other possible themes of investigation in the planning field. Following Berger and Luckmann's (1967) social constructivist perspective on social reality and Jessop's (2001) strategic-relational approach, I see an 'institutional field' as consisting both of actors and their practices and of institutions expressed and examined in terms of each other: institutions in terms of action and action in terms of institutions. Jessop's strategic-relational perspective as applied to institutions involves examining how – at any given time – particular institutions may privilege (but not determine) some actors, some actions, some strategies, etc. over others ('structurally inscribed strategic selectivities'), and the ways – if any – in which actors take account of this differential privileging when choosing a course of action ('structurally oriented strategic calculation'). Over time, actors reproduce or reorganize institutions reflexively, that is, to different extents, taking into account structural constraints and windows of opportunity. Institutions select or privilege some actors' strategies and tactics recursively, that is, time and again responding to actors' strategic behaviour in a more or less consistent way. The entire interaction between actors and institutions can be referred to as reflexively–recursively dialectal. More or less the same idea is expressed by authors such as March and Olson and Hodgson, who go beyond making a distinction between institutional evolution and institutional design by acknowledging how institutional design itself is part of the process of institutionalization (Buitelaar *et al.* 2007). This process itself *is guided by institutions*, and this leads 'to the conundrum of infinite regress in which institutions are revolving as both explananda and explanans' (Buitelaar *et al.* 2007: 894, referring to Hodgson 1993). Because 'institutional development follows a "logic of social appropriateness" rather than a "logic of instrumentality"' and 'institutions are devised and adopted principally because of their social appropriateness and legitimacy' (Buitelaar *et al.* 2007: 894, referring to March and Olsen 1989), institutional design should be seen not as opposed to institutional evolution, but as an integral part of it.

Broadening institutionalist planning theory along the lines suggested above has implications for the concept of 'planning instruments'. Instead of examining these instruments as the means to predefined ends, they can be analysed as *institutions* in their own right (see also Lascoumes and Le Galès 2007). In so doing, a planning regulation or a structure plan or a development convenant becomes a more or less coherent, interconnected set of formal and informal routines, conventions, organizational procedures, rules, sanctioning mechanisms, etc. These have to be seen as social facts resulting from reciprocal typifications of the routinized behaviour of interacting individuals; they structure the interactions between relevant actors and both enable and constrain collective action (Berger and Luckmann 1967; Moulaert and Jessop 2006). The social rationality that informs them can include, but is never limited to, a technical rationality which links instruments to policy goals in a linear fashion. A zoning plan, for example, changes land values, creates a relationship between spatial design and the juridical–administrative complex, organizes new relationships between different actors (owners, government, users, sectoral groups, etc.) and is mobilized in struggles over land uses and land values.

To situate different forms of planning and planning instruments in the reflexive–recursive dynamics of institutional fields, I apply Jessop's strategic-relational approach to planning instruments, considering planning instruments as a technical core embedded in an 'institutional frame' (for a similar reasoning, see Bijker 1995; Lascoumes and Le Galès 2007; Mazza 2002). Following Bijker (1995), I define this technical core as the actors' criteria that give definition to a planning instrument as a 'working' device (as opposed to 'non-working'). An 'institutional frame' is an institutional ensemble related to a specific planning instrument, or group of planning instruments, that privileges certain actors, uses and outcomes over others, and hence structures the institutional field in which planning processes are unrolled (Figure 4.1). In addition to the technical dimension (planning instruments), and following Bijker (1995), Healey (2007), Healey *et al.* (2003), Hajer (2003) and Mazza (2002), I distinguish a cognitive (knowledge systems), socio-political (social relations and governance configurations) and discursive (production of meaning) dimension within the institutional frame. While strategically (or unconsciously) producing and reproducing planning instruments and their institutional frame, different individual and/or collective actors become embedded in, and structured by, the instruments cum institutional frame. They become part of the dynamics that sustain planning instruments and their operation and therefore become its 'relevant social group' (Figure 4.1). Because instruments and their institutional frames are selective, they include certain actors but exclude others, who, as a consequence, attempt to transform or even abolish these instruments and/or their institutional frames, or create completely new ones. From a strategic-relational institutionalist perspective, planning is thus not a monolith 'operating within institutions' (Verma 2007: 1), but an institutionalized practice the different forms of which are struggled over by many individual and collective actors, who, in the process, organize themselves into different relevant social groups. Following Bijker (1995: 273), I define each complex of a relevant social group (individual and collective actors included) and the related institutional frame (technical, cognitive, socio-politicial and discursive elements included) as a 'socio-technical ensemble'.

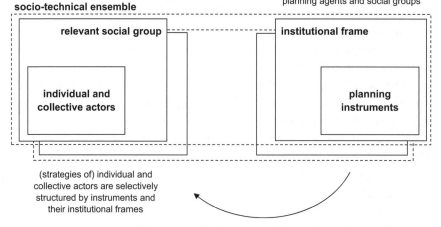

Figure 4.1 Dialectical relationships between actors, relevant social groups, planning instruments and institutional frames at a given time. Source: author inspired by Jessop (2001) and Bijker (1995).

By distinguishing planning actors, relevant social groups and their practices and strategies (Figure 4.1, left-hand side), and planning instruments and their institutional frames (Figure 4.1, right-hand side), I suggest that we should look at planning processes and instruments from the perspective of both agency and institutions. To avoid a one-sided actor-oriented view, the practices of planning actors – strategic with respect to planning instruments and institutional frames – have to be seen as pre-structured by these also. Equally, to avoid a deterministic perspective, the planning instruments and institutional frames – strategically selective with respect to the practices of planning actors (i.e. to varying degrees leaving room for different strategies and actors) – have to be analysed as resulting from previous actions of planning actors and relevant social groups who embed their values and interests in the instruments and their institutional frames.

The complexity of reflexive–recursive dialectical processes over time can be abstracted, expressing a reflexive–recursive shift from moment t1 to moment t2 (Figure 4.2), thereby changing the planning actors, relevant social groups and their strategic calculations, on the one hand, and the planning instruments, institutional frames and their strategic selectivities, on the other. These shifts by no means follow each other in a linear pattern, but may or may not happen. Rather they exhibit a route of bifurcations, power struggles, missed opportunities, dead ends, choices with no return, etc., path dependent on previous institutionalization processes through which planning instruments received their specific forms, in specific times and in specific places.

Finally, the strategic-relational institutionalist perspective outlined above raises a number of questions: how particular individual and collective actors succeed or fail to imbue their values and interests into planning instruments and their institutional frames; how planning instruments and institutional frames embody compromises between different values and interests and concomitant power relations and who dominates these compromises; how these structurally inscribed values and interests in turn inform the behaviour of different planning actors and who benefits from this. Planning instruments are thus deeply socio-political not only because of actors' attempts to manipulate instruments and the political struggle over the choice of planning instruments, but also in their very (strategically selective and institutional) nature. This socio-political perspective on planning instruments enables both a more critical position concerning them and an evaluation of how this affects the socio-territorial innovation capacity of strategic projects. Following Moulaert and others on social innovation – which is defined as a change in social relations (i.e. the process perspective), fulfilling basic needs for all, and especially for disadvantaged groups (i.e. the content perspective) – I will analyse the extent to which particular planning instruments promote fundamental spatial and social transformations. The latter include transformations of the spatial

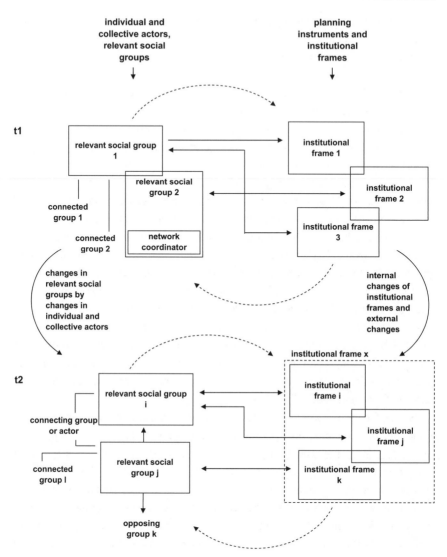

Figure 4.2 Reflexive–recursive institutional dynamics over time. Source: author.

governance system to include disadvantaged social groups in open-ended planning processes that allow for collective learning (Fontan and Klein 2004; Moulaert
et al. 2007; Moulaert 2009; Moulaert and Nussbaumer 2005).[4] This analysis will
enable us to take up Mazza's challenge, 'to try to unfold the political content of
technical issues' (Mazza 2002: 23).

PLANNING INSTRUMENTS, INSTITUTIONAL
DYNAMICS AND SOCIO-TERRITORIAL INNOVATION IN
THE 'FIRST QUARTER' IN ANTWERP (BELGIUM)

METHODOLOGY AND CASE STUDY

I will now use the strategic-relational institutionalist approach to analyse the recent transformations in the 'First Quarter' in the city of Antwerp, which includes the red light district ('Schipperskwartier'). The 'First Quarter' is an area north of city hall and south of the oldest docks. In the last thirty years it has been transformed from a run-down area where crime and prostitution ran rife into a quiet residential place. Window prostitution is now concentrated in three small streets to the north, the so-called 'zone of tolerance'. The 'First Quarter' is one of the oldest quarters in the city. Its recent transformation was occasioned through a rich set of experiments with planning instruments and changes in institutional frames, most notable among these being urban renewal, community development, prostitution policy and urban development. Altogether this makes it a very interesting case study in which to analyse the institutional dynamics of planning instruments. The second reason for the selection of this particular case is that it demonstrates the overt struggles between different planning actors, the way in which the consequent compromises are embodied in instruments and the persistence of social issues (related to the presence of prostitution). All this highlights the importance of looking at the socio-political content of planning instruments, particularly with regard to socio-territorial innovation.

For the empirical research, I pursued a critical constructivist case study research strategy (Yin 2003). The main primary and secondary data are based on semi-structured in-depth interviews with key actors,[5] policy documents and reports, scientific articles and books, laws and regulations, research carried out by students, minutes of meetings, press articles, websites,[6] site visits and informal talks. The aim of the case study is theoretical abstraction, not statistical generalization. The empirical data were used to build a valid explanation of how planning instruments operate in strategic projects and how they might be more or less socio-territorially innovative.

Similar to Bijker (1995) on the social construction of technology and Palier (2007) and Bezes (2007) on policy instruments, I keep planning instruments at the heart of the analysis. Methodologically, I use a double 'snowball method' to identify the relevant actors and instruments and to gradually reconstruct the dynamics of planning instruments, their institutional frames and relevant social groups (Table 4.1). My research starts from the instruments identified and mobilized by different kinds of participants (not just public ones) in the implementation

of the strategic project. These relate therefore to spatial policy, planning, participation and collective decision-making, implementation, design and spatial
organization, project management, communication and legitimation. They are part
of the mobilization of collective resources for transforming an area. I then follow
all relevant leads (the 'snowball' method; see Bijker 1995: 48) to the individual
and collective actors who mobilize these instruments, on the one hand, and to the
institutions that structure actors' practices in using the instruments, on the other
(therefore 'double snowball'). The dimensions of actors and institutions shown
in Table 4.1 provide a heuristic to track empirical pathways on both the actor
side (actors and biographies, bridging actors, networks, coalitions, etc.) and the
institutional side (technical, cognitive, socio-political and discursive elements).
On this basis, I then reconstruct the history of the reflexive–recursive dialectics

Table 4.1 Operationalization of relevant social groups and institutional frames

Categories of the analytical framework	Possible empirical tracks
Relevant social groups	Planning actors and their biographies – positions, roles, strategies, interests
	Bridging actors, embedded in multiple institutional frames
	Collective actors
	Networks, (discourse) coalitions, urban regimes
	Consultation fora
	Inclusion of actors in relevant social groups
	Practices and strategies of the former
Institutional frames	
Technical elements/core (= planning instrument)	Goals, key problems, problem-solving strategies
	Actors' criteria of what defines the planning instrument as a 'working device'
Cognitive elements related to the planning instrument	Implicit knowledge
	Test procedures of planning instruments
	Design methods and criteria
	Instrument for which the new instrument is seen as a substitute
	Current theories concerning the instrument
Socio-political elements related to the planning instrument	Formal rules, procedures, laws, regulations
	Social and socio-economic mechanisms
	Political balance of power, parties
	Financial resources, their conditions and socio-political basis
	Organizational and governance configurations: positions, roles and interplay of public, civil, private and hybrid actors
	Collective decision-making mechanisms concerning the instrument
Discursive elements related to the planning instrument	Exemplary projects in which the instruments have been used
	Meanings attached to the instruments by different actors
	Terms of policy discourse (vocabularies, story lines, generative metaphors, epistemic notions)

of planning instruments and the related socio-technical ensembles (see Figures 4.3–4.6).

My case study spans a period of roughly twenty-five years starting around 1984, when changes in the socio-technical ensembles of urban renewal, social housing, community development and semi-tolerated prostitution first became apparent. I distinguish four important episodes; each is characterized by specific reflexive–recursive dialectics between and within different socio-technical ensembles. I give a brief overview of the dialectics within the main socio-technical ensembles in each episode, as well as the crucial factors of change between this and the previous one. The overview is then used to assess the socio-territorial innovation capacity of the mobilized instruments and their institutional frames, from both a process perspective (dynamics of institutionalization and de-institutionalization) and a (socio-political) content perspective (socially innovative qualities of the instruments and their institutional frames). I start my analysis with a brief history of the period before the actual case study.

PREHISTORY – GROWING TENSIONS IN A FRAME OF URBAN RENEWAL, SOCIAL HOUSING, COMMUNITY DEVELOPMENT AND SEMI-TOLERATED PROSTITUTION

At the beginning of the 1980s, the 'First Quarter' in Antwerp was a poor and physically run-down area in which four relatively autonomous and sometimes conflicting socio-technical ensembles had formed: inner-city 'urban renewal', the building of 'social housing', 'community development' and a 'semi-tolerance of prostitution and nightlife'. This configuration faced important challenges. The various relevant social groups, namely the board of aldermen (operating within the institutional frames of 'urban renewal' and 'social housing'), social housing companies ('social housing'), residents and community workers ('community development') and prostitutes and visitors to the red light district ('prostitution and nightlife') all perceived different problems, envisaged different possible futures for the area and favoured different instruments. Because they also operated within different institutional frames, conflicts were frequent and compromises over a common problem definition and possible solutions were very unlikely to emerge. Moreover, in the 1980s the prostitution sector became entangled in international human trafficking and forced prostitution and expanded its activities further into the 'First Quarter' (De Stoop 1992), attracting other criminal activities in the process. In addition, the northward move of Antwerp harbour away from the 'First Quarter' meant that prostitution lost its historical harbour-related embeddedness in the area. The expansion of prostitution and criminal activities led to numerous conflicts with residents. Other factors later reinforced these tensions: the rise of the extreme right party Vlaams Blok from 1982 onwards and the arrival of upper-class residents and offices on the quayside around 1985.

These developments in the 'First Quarter' added to the long history of degradation of Antwerp's historical centre, which had involved diverse attempts to 'clean up' the city centre and eject its low-income inhabitants (Migom 2004). During the 1980s and 1990s, the number and acuteness of the conflicts between residents, the prostitution and criminal sectors, city hall, etc. gradually intensified; this became one of the main driving forces behind the continuous shift in planning actors, relevant social groups, planning instruments and institutional frames analysed below.

SOCIAL WORK, SOCIO-POLITICAL ACTIVISM AND PUBLIC SAFETY POLICY (1984–1997)

The disintegration of the institutional frame of 'urban renewal', caused by changes in the subsidy system, the withdrawal of community development workers from the 'First Quarter', the common conviction that enough social housing had been built, the tensions described previously and the entry of new actors onto the scene, initiated the reflexive–recursive development of new socio-technical ensembles, such as 'social work', 'socio-political activism' and 'public safety policy' (Figure 4.3). First, in reaction to the rising abuse and poverty of prostitutes in the 'First Quarter' and influenced by previous initiatives in community development, the Antwerp artist-teacher Patsy Sörensen and others founded a lobby group for prostitutes, the non-governmental organization Payoke. This group began developing instruments to assist prostitutes, using techniques such as making direct contact, offering legal, financial and administrative support and providing hiding places when required. These instruments were gradually elaborated into Payoke's systems of direct support to prostitutes, of health-care initiatives and of aid to victims of human trafficking, under the common institutional frame of prostitution-oriented 'social work'. This work included, for example, a new law on human trafficking passed by the Belgian parliament in 1995 after ten years of lobbying by Payoke and its partners. At the same time, a relevant social group developed centred around Payoke; this included prostitutes and social welfare organizations, and operated within the institutional frame of prostitution-oriented 'social work'. Eventually this was formalized in 1998 through the integration of Payoke into the formal structures of Flemish social work. Second, Payoke tried to create a more constructive awareness of prostitution, a higher degree of public acceptance, and a better social and juridical status for prostitutes by mobilizing three groups of instruments: (1) the establishment of a neighbourhood centre to initiate neighbourhood-oriented activities, rooted in Sörensen's contacts with community

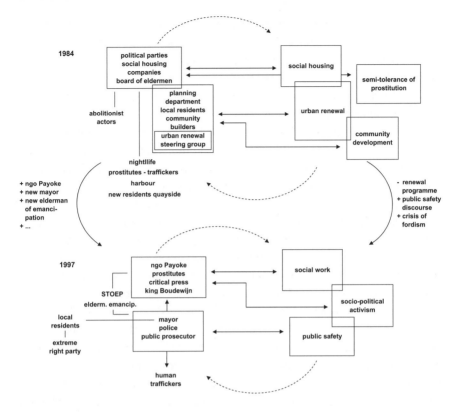

Figure 4.3 Institutional dynamics in the first episode (1997–2001) in the 'First quarter'.

workers and in the institutional frame of 'community development' present in the previous episode; (2) the development of activist instruments aimed at the emancipation of prostitutes (lobbying, networking, attracting media attention, organizing actions against the city and against criminals in the world of prostitution), inspired by a frame of 'neo-regulationism';[7] and (3) the launching of Sörensen's party political career, which got her onto the board of aldermen in 1995 and raised Payoke's political impact. As a result, Payoke's network became quite a large relevant social group, its instruments predominantly supported by the institutional frame of 'socio-political activism'. The fact that in 1992 the Belgian king Boudewijn showed his interest in the fight against human trafficking and forced prostitution was a great help in reinforcing this frame. A third frame, oriented towards 'public safety', came about after the new social-democrat mayor, elected in 1994, activated national laws on public safety intended to create local cooperation between different police forces and justice departments. Public safety had been a federal, regional and urban concern since the second half of the 1980s, and in the 1990s this resulted in new laws on police, justice and public safety. In addition, the mayor also activated her local competences in order to protect public space and to shut down unsafe buildings. In this way a set of planning instruments developed, together with a corresponding institutional frame of 'public safety', which included procedures for cooperation between the mayor and her cabinet, the public prosecutor and three police departments and the department of local building inspection. These were mobilized by the mayor to close down a number of brothels near to city hall. Paralleling the previous episode, a relevant social group developed, which included the mayor, her cabinet, different police divisions and the department of the public prosecutor.

The development of instruments embedded in the institutional frames of 'social work', 'socio-political activism' and 'public safety' favoured the actions of the relevant social groups around Payoke (support to prostitutes, lobbying, etc.) and the mayor's cabinet (e.g. closing down prostitution houses, cooperation with the police and the justice department), and undermined the previously dominant socio-technical ensembles of 'urban renewal', 'social housing', 'community development' and 'semi-tolerance of prostitution'. Looking at socio-territorial innovation from a content perspective, we see, on the one hand, that the instruments and institutional frames of 'social work' and 'socio-political activism' initiated by Payoke empowered strategies from actors connected to prostitution. On the other hand, in a climate of neo-racism, criticisms of justice and public safety policies from different governmental levels and the instruments and institutional frame of 'public safety' mobilized by the mayor and her cabinet favoured rather repressive strategies from the city and the police. However, a compromise was reached because of the work of the city's administration of social affairs, the bridging role of Sörensen both as a local politician and as chairperson of Payoke and the involvement of the mayor and her cabinet in public safety as well as in social affairs. This compromise was most clearly expressed in a document produced by the consultation group STOEP (1991), which took into account the interests, visions and instruments of Payoke, the city and the police, and was institutionalized in the next episode. It prepared the ground for a long-lasting impact on prostitutes' conditions in the red light district: the issue of prostitution was placed high on the political agenda, the notion of the concentration of prostitutes in a particular area was introduced, a basis for improved health and working conditions was created, and for the first time the public safety approach targeted no longer the prostitutes themselves but the people exploiting them. This is all the more important as the position of prostitutes in a specific area – as an extremely weak group subject to direct abuses of power and exploitation – is an indicator for socio-territorial innovation that was realized in parts of the process.

EMERGENCE AND PROFESSIONALIZATION OF A 'PROSTITUTION POLICY' (1997–2001)

In 1997, a consultant who had assisted in the development of prostitution policies in a number of Dutch cities contacted alderman Sörensen, attracted by her
work and position regarding prostitution, and in 1998 he was commissioned by
the board of aldermen to write a prostitution policy plan. In the same period, the
city recruited a prostitution officer, closed down the former consultation group
STOEP, and created a new consultation group, BOP, in which only municipal
public organizations were represented, and from which Payoke was consequently
excluded. After approval of the prostitution plan (Seinpost adviesbureau 1999)
by the board of aldermen, the newly created prostitution service involved a range
of city administration and police departments, and organized them in a 'steering
committee on prostitution policy'; this involved developing new instruments and
implementing the prostitution policy plan, and subsequently the committee developed into a new relevant social group. In the beginning Payoke still supported
the municipality's actions, mainly through alderman Sörensen's bridging position.
After 1999, however, Sörensen left the board of aldermen to become a member
of the EU parliament and Payoke withdrew from active lobbying for the rights of
prostitutes and concentrated on social welfare actions for victims of human trafficking. Payoke was excluded from policy-making, thus making the relevant social
group more homogeneous and mainly public sector based. The growing network
of individuals and groups dealing with Antwerp prostitution, which originated in
the previous episode, was further consolidated, especially in formal professional
terms, but the grassroots movements from whose actions it originally emerged
gradually lost control over it. In terms of instruments and institutional frames,
'socio-political activism' was marginalized and replaced by 'professional strategic planning' (Figure 4.4). Consequently, the institutional frame of 'prostitution
policy' emerged out of the professionalization of the previous instruments, institutional frames and relevant social groups and the marginalization of socio-political
activism. This configuration hosted an extensive but more or less consistent amal-
gamation of elements from the previous institutional frames of 'social work' and
'public safety', and the new institutional frame of 'strategic planning'. BOP and
the steering committee supervised the preparation of the Antwerp prostitution
policy plan, created action plans and introduced (Dutch) ideas on property development. The compromise between 'social work' and 'public safety' included the
demarcation of a 'zone of tolerance' of three streets in the 'First Quarter', where
property owners could lease windows for prostitution under strict conditions and
under the surveillance of a new police office. Outside this area the police closed
down all prostitution houses in 2001 (about 150 windows in fourteen streets)
after city council approval of two new city regulations on prostitution in 2000

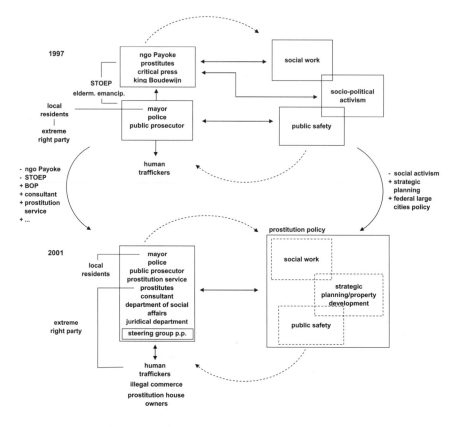

Figure 4.4 Institutional dynamics in the second episode (1997–2001) in the 'First quarter'.

(Stad Antwerpen Gemeenteraad 2000a,b), following federal public safety policies and the introduction of municipal administrative penalties. Linked to Belgian
and Flemish welfare policies, the establishment of specialized health care for
prostitutes improved working and health conditions in the 'zone of tolerance'.
Finally, the creation of a neighbourhood centre integrated some of the social
department's traditions in community work into 'prostitution policy'.

Seen from a process perspective, professionalization was an important element
of socio-territorial innovation in the second episode. Indeed, professionalization
proved necessary in definitively dismantling the early 1980s instruments and
institutions of an ambiguous 'semi-tolerance of prostitution', in order to establish
the 'prostitution policy' as a new set of instruments and institutional frame and
to consolidate the relevant social group. The introduction of methods of process
planning and management and the centralization of decisions in the public sector
proved instrumental here. From a content perspective, despite the reshuffling of
the relevant social group and the introduction of new instruments and associated

institutional frame, the same socio-territorial innovation capacity as in the first episode was more or less preserved, although now facilitated by different city and police services. The different instruments and institutional frames favoured the rise of new community networks, safe and healthy working conditions for prostitutes and public safety for existing and new residents. Excluded from the relevant social group reproducing these instruments and institutional frames were owners of prostitution houses, pimps, black market dealers and other criminals exploiting prostitutes and the neighbourhood, as these were deliberately opposed by the city, police and justice department. Because of public professionalization, however, the impact of grassroots-based strategies decreased, as expressed by the shift in Payoke's activities in 1999. Public sector instruments and practices, by interacting directly with prostitutes and thus bypassing grassroots groups, increasingly replaced community development instruments and practices. In short, the new instruments and stabilizing institutional frame of 'prostitution policy' largely preserved a socio-territorially innovative content created in the previous episode, on the one hand, but shifted the direct impact of disadvantaged groups to a more indirect one, filtered by a public sector logic, on the other.

PROSTITUTION POLICY AND SPATIAL RESTRUCTURING IN A 'SOCIAL URBAN DEVELOPMENT' (2001–2004)

The redevelopment of the neighbourhood around the 'zone of tolerance' as announced in the prostitution policy plan, early initiatives in property development, communication and spatial planning[8] in the previous episode (1999–2000) and the regeneration of the central train station area (where prostitution was an issue) by the city planning department increased the contacts between the different administrations and aldermen of social affairs and urban planning. Actors with skills and instruments in the fields of planning and property development were also subsequently involved in the regeneration of the 'First Quarter'. From 2002 the city planning and development service increasingly guided the 'First Quarter' transformation process, initially in close cooperation with the prostitution service (part of the department of social affairs), and involved a whole range of city administrations in a physical restructuring process (Figure 4.5). In order to manage an increasing number of urban development actions, and as one of their instruments, the planning and development service created a steering committee, Schipperskwartier. This contributed to a shift in the relevant social group for the instruments mobilized in the 'First Quarter'. Also, existing and future inhabitants of the area were integrated into the relevant social group in order to gain support for the city's actions. Evidently, the Antwerp planning and development service mobilized its instruments and institutional procedures and practices as

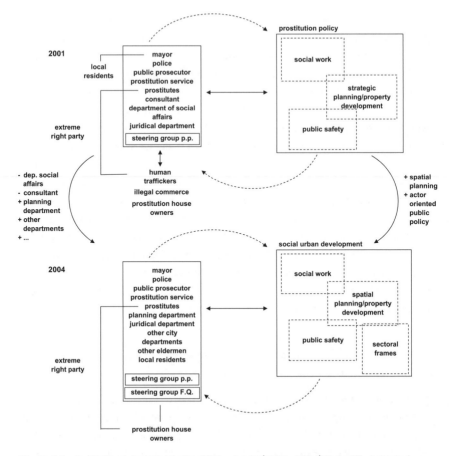

Figure 4.5   Institutional dynamics in the third episode (2001–2004) in the 'First quarter'.

developed in previous years but recently influenced by (Dutch) public policy and property development. These included spatial analysis, the making of action plans (e.g. Stad Antwerpen dienst prostitutiebeleid and Stad Antwerpen planningscel 2002a,b), process design and the implementation of physical actions. Consequently, the planning and development service and the prostitution service supervised the refurbishment of the three prostitution streets (also pedestrianizing them), the purchase and transformation of a number of former prostitution houses into dwellings, the financial and logistic support of a large number of private renovations in the area, the transformation of an old port warehouse into a medium-scale housing project in cooperation with the private sector, the refurbishment of ten streets and two public squares outside the 'zone of tolerance' and the financial support of touristic and artistic projects. They cooperated with other city administrations to mobilize and adapt, for example, instruments of the housing department and the department of tourism. In addition, extensive communication programmes helped gain public support.

In the third episode, the city planning department, social housing and other residents in the area, new owners investing in their properties and other city administrations got involved in the physical restructuring of the 'First Quarter'. These new actors added instruments and institutional frames of physical planning and middle-class housing policy to the existing institutional frame of 'prostitution policy' and thus created a wider institutional frame of 'social urban development'. The latter retained the social goals regarding prostitution in a central position. This was due to close cooperation within the city administration between the prostitution service, the planning department and other departments, political support from the mayor and different aldermen and, importantly, the conditions tied to federal funding mechanisms through which most of the regeneration was financed and which stimulated a mixed social, economic and physical approach. Over time the physical approach grew more dominant and public decision-making was further centralized to facilitate implementation, visible physical transformation and management of the increasing complexities. This inevitably threatened the socio-territorial innovation capacity of the regeneration process. Despite the increased diversity of the instruments and institutional frame of 'social urban development', the strategies they privileged were largely public, even more than in the previous episode. Early private investments were incorporated into the public logic of enforced renovation of prostitution houses, renovation subsidies for renovated dwellings, public communication strategies, police control, public health policy, etc. Besides public organizations, the predominant instruments and institutional frame in this episode also privileged local strategies, especially those of residents living in the existing social housing and those with enough money to invest in the renovation of houses, while at the same time incorporating these actors in the relevant social group. In addition, the city's large investments in the area attracted new residents. As a consequence, and despite continuing community work, disadvantaged residents such as prostitutes and the less well-off were increasingly excluded from the relevant social group of the instruments mobilized in the regeneration process.

INSTITUTIONALIZATION OF URBAN DEVELOPMENT, CITY MARKETING, COMMUNITY WORK AND PROSTITUTION MANAGEMENT (2004 – NOW)

In this episode newly involved city administrations, a strengthened social democrat–liberal political coalition and private actors, all facilitated by the previous shift towards physical restructuring, deconstructed and transformed the institutional frame of 'social urban development' into separate institutional frames of 'urban development', 'city marketing', 'community work' and 'prostitution management' (Figure 4.6). In 2004–2005 prostitution policy became completely formalized and professionalized, led by the (one) prostitution officer and the public safety department. Grassroots involvement in prostitution policy disappeared. In 2003, using new federal legislation on municipality competences, the city started up the semi-autonomous development agency (VESPA) to execute the city's property development policy, thus strengthening the property development logic in strategic projects. Also in 2003, and upheld in 2006, the mayor, the board of aldermen and the balance of power changed quite drastically in Antwerp. The long tradition of Christian democratic–social democratic coalitions was definitively broken and a new generation of (young urban) politicians within the social democratic and liberal parties introduced neoliberal policies that had been present at the federal and regional level since 1999. At the same time, a new middle class moved into the

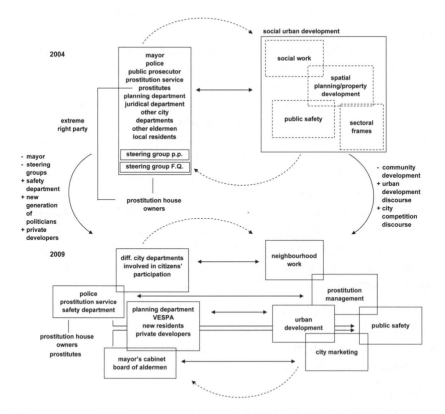

Figure 4.6   Institutional dynamics in the fourth episode (2004–2009) in the 'First quarter'.

area, offices around the 'zone of tolerance' expanded and upmarket restaurants and bars opened. Private developers were also closely involved in the regeneration strategy in this episode through cooperation in two larger housing and office projects. These administrative, political and private actors all deconstructed the relevant social group of 'social urban development' into different relevant social groups through the reorganization of the administration, the introduction of the aforementioned new actors and their connection to the new networks, etc. They also introduced Flemish and European urban development practice and discourse, promoting large-scale urban development projects, project management, public–private partnerships, semi-public development organizations, etc. Also, communication about the project was now centralized with the new mayor's cabinet, which progressively integrated the regeneration of the 'First Quarter' into a city marketing approach. Prostitution policy remained important for the 'First Quarter' but was reduced to the efficient management of the 'zone of tolerance'. Empowering sex workers, for example by pushing towards a new national law, no longer seems to be on the political agenda.

After twenty-five years of change in the 'First Quarter', 'neighbourhood work', 'prostitution management', 'urban development', 'public safety' and 'city marketing' have more or less stabilized as separate institutional frames. The private sector, real estate developers, new middle-class and upmarket residents, companies surrounding the red light district, a new generation of politicians and the new semi-autonomous property development company have become the new relevant social group of the dominant instruments used for the regeneration of the 'First Quarter'. Physical restructuring and management instruments and approaches were already evident in the third episode but then became dominant, supported by an international market-oriented and property development discourse. Through management of the 'zone of tolerance' and of the enforced renovations, the city prostitution policy became a management issue rather than an issue of the emancipation of a weaker group. The prostitution service was progressively reduced in size and increasingly sidelined. Previous efforts to reach prostitutes, to stimulate the formation of a lobby group of prostitutes and to influence their juridical and political position came to an end. As a result, the new institutional frame lost part of its socio-territorial innovation capacity and more and more favoured the strategies of private actors and affluent residents while public and grassroots impact decreased. However, like previous institutional frames, this one is not unambiguous. Community work, health support, police control and regulation of the quality of prostitution houses have been given a rather permanent character in order to continuously safeguard the position of prostitutes.

CONCLUSIONS

In this chapter, I have shown how a strategic-relational institutionalist perspective on planning instruments can be used to evaluate the socio-territorial innovation capacities of strategic projects. The analysis of the transformation process in the 'First Quarter' in the city of Antwerp from this perspective showed a different story from the official, policy-driven one that is mostly prevalent. Indeed, this transformation does not start simply with the making and approval of the city's 'prostitution policy plan' in 1999, nor is it a clearly managed, linear and unidirectional process with a clearly defined goal. New instruments are not just created at will, nor because they are better than previous ones. Planning instruments do not emerge after conscious choices because they technically 'work'. On the contrary, the process of socio-technical change proves to be a complex, path-dependent and path-shaping reflexive–recursive dialectic of actors in relevant social groups, and planning instruments in institutional frames, guided by multiple social rationalities rather than a technical one. Actors thus strategically create, transform and/or reproduce instruments and institutional frames, reflecting on the available instruments and to different extents being informed, constrained or empowered by them. Accordingly, institutions are selectively open to actors' strategies and tactics, depending on the specific interests that are embedded within them as a result of struggles and compromises between different actors. I have shown how the institutional frames of 'community building', 'urban renewal' and 'semi-tolerance of prostitution' made possible and encouraged Payoke's activist practices, which in turn produced the instruments and institutional frame of 'socio-political activism'. In the meantime the relevant social group, including – among others – the mayor's cabinet, responded to the federal safety discourse and developed the instruments and institutional frame of 'public safety'. Following a long period of action and debate, a compromise between the interests and values of both groups became embodied in 'prostitution policy'. This compromise had a long-lasting influence on the subsequent actions of the prostitution service, the planning department and others, even during later changes in actors and institutional frames. The relevant social group supporting and pursuing 'prostitution policy' – integrating the previous relevant social groups around Payoke and the mayor's cabinet – attracted the planning department, whose particular instruments and institutional frames impacted strongly on the socio-technical ensemble of 'prostitution policy' and transformed it into the qualitatively different socio-technical ensemble of 'social urban development'. Finally, instruments of physical restructuring and the associated institutional frames encouraged new coalitions between the city, its property development company, private developers and new residents, and the new institutional frames of 'urban development', 'city marketing' and 'prostitution management'.

Mobilizing instruments thus implies mobilizing their institutional frames, and the socio-political characteristics of both. Planning instruments *embody* socio-political characteristics, expressed in strategic selectivities favouring or constraining specific strategies of specific actors. Consequently, we can evaluate specific types of planning instruments (land-use planning, strategic planning, etc.) with respect to their socio-political characteristics. The question is who benefits from these instruments and in what time perspective. However, in order to evaluate the socio-territorial innovation capacity of land-use planning instruments, or strategic planning instruments, 'traditional', 'meeting-based' or 'modern event-based' consultation methods, etc., we must assess how instruments operate within a specific socio-technical ensemble rather than just focusing on instruments as ideal types.

The same is true for strategic projects in which, as the 'First Quarter' case study shows, different planning instruments are mobilized over time. Indeed, the case study analysis shows how different actor-related and institutional factors and their dynamics influence the socio-territorial innovation capacity in the four episodes of the regeneration process in the 'First Quarter'. Different ways in which power relations become structurally embedded in planning instruments and institutional frames, and different configurations of actors in relevant social groups that become structurally sustained, lead to differences in the socio-territorial innovation capacity of different episodes in the same strategic project. In the 'First Quarter' the recent shift towards more physical and property development-led instruments and institutional frames has reduced the socio-territorial innovation capacity of the project. This shift has been slowed down by the persistence of institutions of 'socio-political activism' focused on the emancipation of the prostitutes originating in the first episode and reflecting a compromise between the interests of Payoke and the prostitutes, and those of the mayor and the police.

Finally, the strategic-relational institutionalist perspective has implications for the position of planners in planning processes. Because they are part of the reflexive–recursive dialectics of socio-technical ensembles, planners' practices, including the coalitions they join and the design, choice and/or transformation of planning instruments, are technical, socio-political and socio-territorial (i.e. socio-technical) undertakings. The development of both coalitions and instruments should therefore always be acknowledged not only as a technical exercise, but also as informed by a socio-political position, expressed in the value-conscious choice of issues and actors for whom new instruments are developed (Van den Broeck *et al*. 2009). It is thus an important task to evaluate the literature (and my own conclusions in the 'First Quarter' case study) that critiques the influence of international neo-liberal ideologies on the predominant shift in planners' practices towards power-confirming activities, and to reactivate coalitions between planners, community developers, ecologists and the like, which are able to change political agendas. This should lead to more critical evaluations of current planning practices, instruments and institutional frames and to efforts to embed ecological and social values in new practices, instruments and institutional frames. As the case study shows, despite planners' expertise, this will occur in a field of many actors, with different interests and values and with different conceptions of planning. It is therefore a collective, strategic and political enterprise.

ACKNOWLEDGEMENTS

I am grateful to fellow researchers in the SP2SP project for discussions on planning and institutionalism, to the editors of this book for comments on earlier drafts of this chapter and to the teaching staff of the postgraduate module on European spatial planning in Newcastle for the critical perspective they offered on planning.

NOTES

1 Common examples of planning process theories are rational-comprehensive planning, incrementalism, mixed scanning, advocacy planning, radical planning, communicative planning, strategic spatial planning, etc. See, for example, Allmendinger (2002), Sandercock (1998) and Taylor (2005).
2 See, for example, Chapter 2 in Gualini (2001).
3 Within sociological institutionalism different theories exist, which focus, for example, on different sources of institutional change (Moulaert 2005; Moulaert and Mehmood 2009). Although not elaborated here, the authors mentioned in this chapter (Healey, Gualini, Moulaert, Jessop, etc.) highlight the importance of both macro-structural societal developments and human agency and interaction as sources of institutional change and consider institutions as having or gaining a certain operational autonomy from human agency over time. This excludes rational choice institutionalism (of, for example, Alexander or Webster).
4 Since social innovation not only *happens in* a spatial context but also *involves* the transformation of spatial relations and is spatially specific, spatially negotiated and spatially embedded (Moulaert 2009), assessing the social innovation capacity of planning instruments and institutional frames includes assessing their territorial (i.e. the localization of economic, social and political practices) and spatial (i.e. the spatial organization, the design, the spatial layout, . . . itself) dimensions. Although rarely brought to attention in social innovation literature, the transformation of the *spatial organization* of an area (the design, the spatial layout, etc.) is part and parcel of its socio-territorial transformation. In other words, the spatial capital of an area is part of its socio-territorial capital (Van den Broeck 2007). Since spatial organization is highlighted in other chapters of this book, this chapter will keep its focus on planning instruments.
5 For the purpose of this research, the author carried out forty-four interviews with thirty-three key actors (spring 2007, summer 2008, spring 2009). Additionally, researcher Maarten

Loopmans kindly placed eight interviews with eight additional actors (spring 2005) at the author's disposal. Filmmaker Terenja Van Dijk made available eleven interviews with six additional and five overlapping actors (spring 2007). The interviewees include two Antwerp mayors and a member of their cabinet, community workers, a private urban planner, (ex-) members of the Antwerp planning department, (ex-)members of the Antwerp department of social affairs, two Antwerp aldermen, historians, members of the grassroots organization Payoke, (ex-)members of the Antwerp prostitution service, members of the Antwerp juridical department, a private prostitution policy consultant, a member of the Antwerp property development service, residents of the 'First Quarter', a representative of a neighbourhood committee, representatives of action groups of prostitutes and property owners, the director of the Antwerp health house for prostitutes, members of the Belgian administration for large cities policy, members of the Antwerp service for regional subsidies management and a member of the Antwerp communication service. A full list of interviewees is available from the author.

6   Primary and secondary written sources include Antwerp policy documents regarding urban renewal, prostitution policy and urban development; different texts by the grassroots organization Payoke on prostitution; Payoke's yearly reports; books on prostitution and human trafficking; books on urban renewal in the Flemish region; texts on the history of the 'First Quarter'; scientific articles on urban regeneration in Antwerp; a protocol on the Antwerp public safety policy; preparatory texts by the Antwerp departments of social affairs and urban planning; decisions by the board of the mayor and aldermen; proceedings of a symposium on prostitution in Antwerp; minutes of meetings of all relevant consultation fora regarding prostitution policy and urban development; the Antwerp prostitution policy plan; minutes of the city council; the Antwerp city website; websites of action groups; conference papers by key actors; books by key actors; the Antwerp regulations on prostitution; laws on prostitution, public safety and political organization, etc. A full list of primary and secondary sources is available from the author.

7   A Belgian law from 1948 that forbids municipal regulation of prostitution, and which is seen as abolitionistic and aimed at banning prostitution, frames prostitution in Antwerp up to this day. By contrast, neo-regulationism sees voluntary prostitution as possible and therefore seeks a proper legal statute especially in the fields of work and health insurance. See, for example, Payoke vzw (1997).

8   For example, ideas on setting up a public–private property development company, renovation of an old city warehouse in the area to create a community centre, changing of the circulation of traffic to create an experimental car-free area, preparation of the building and management of the health house 'Gh@pro'.

REFERENCES

Albrechts, L. (1999) 'Planners as catalysts and initiators of change. The new structure plan for Flanders', *European Planning Studies*, 7: 587–603.

Albrechts, L. (2005) 'Creativity as a drive for change', *Planning Theory*, 4: 247–269.

Albrechts, L., Alden, J. and Da Rosa Pires, A. (eds) (2001) *The Changing Institutional Landscape of Planning*, Farnham: Ashgate.

Allmendinger, P. (2002) *Planning Theory*, Houndmills: Palgrave.

Berger, P. and Luckmann, T. (1967) *The Social Construction of Reality. A Treatise in the Sociology of Knowledge*, New York: Anchor Books.

Bezes, Ph. (2007) 'The hidden politics of administrative reform. Cutting French civil service wages with a low-profile instrument', *Governance*, 20: 23–56.

Bijker, W. (1995) *Of Bicycles, Bakelites and Bulbs. Toward a Theory of Sociotechnical Change*, Cambridge, MA: MIT Press.

Booth, P., Breuillard, M., Fraser, C. and Paris, D. E. (2007) *Spatial Planning Systems of Britain and France. A Comparative Analysis*, London: Routledge.

Bornstein, L. (2007) 'Confrontation, collaboration and community benefits. Lessons from Canadian and US cities on working together around strategic projects'. Paper presented at ISoCaRP conference, Antwerp, September 2007.

Buitelaar, E., Lagendijk, A. and Jacobs, W. (2007) 'A theory of institutional change: Illustrated by Dutch city-provinces and Dutch land policy', *Environment and Planning A*, 39: 891–908.

de Caluwe, L. and Vermaak, H. (2005) *Leren veranderen. Een handboek voor de veranderkundige*, Mechelen: Kluwer.

De Stoop, C. (1992) *Ze zijn zo lief meneer. Over vrouwenhandel, meisjesballetten en de bende van de Miljardair*, Leuven: Kritak.

European Commission (2000) *The EU Compendium of Spatial Planning Systems and Policies*, Brussels: European Commission.

Fainstein, S. (2000) 'New directions in planning theory', *Urban Affairs Review*, 35: 451–478.

Fontan, J.-M. and Klein, J.-L. (2004) 'La mobilisation du capital socioterritorial: le cas du Technopôle Angus', *Lien socials et Politiques*, 52: 139–149.

Gonzalez, S. and Healey, P. (2005) 'A sociological institutionalist approach to the study of innovation in governance capacity', *Urban Studies*, 42: 2055–2069.

Gualini, E. (2001) *Planning and the Intelligence of Institutions. Interactive Approaches to Territorial Policy-Making Between Institutional Design and Institution-Building*, Farnham: Ashgate.

Hajer, M. (2003) 'A frame in the fields. Policy-making and the reinvention of politics', in M. Hajer and H. Wagenaar (eds) *Deliberative Policy Analysis. Understanding Governance in the Network Society*, Cambridge: Cambridge University Press.

Healey, P. (1997) *Collaborative Planning. Shaping Places in Fragmented Societies*, Houndmills: Palgrave Macmillan.

Healey, P. (1999) 'Institutionalist analysis, communicative planning and shaping places', *Journal of Planning Education and Research*, 19: 111–122.

Healey, P. (2005) 'On the project of institutional transformation in the planning field. Commentary on the contributions', *Planning Theory*, 4: 301–310.

Healey, P., Khakee, A., Motte, A. and Needham, B. (1997) *Making Strategic Spatial Plans. Innovation in Europe*, London: UCL Press.

Healey, P., de Magalhaes, C., Madanipour, A. and Pendlebury, J. (2003) 'Place, identity and local politics. Analysing initiatives in deliberative governance', in M. Hajer and H. Wagenaar (eds) *Deliberative Policy Analysis. Understanding Governance in the Network Society*, Cambridge: Cambridge University Press.

Hodgson, G. (1993) *Economics and Evolution. Bringing Life Back into Economics*, Cambridge: Polity Press.

Innes, J. (1995) 'Planning theory's emerging paradigm. Communicative action and interactive practice', *Journal of Planning Education and Research*, 14: 183–189.

Jessop, B. (2001) 'Institutional (re)turns and the strategic-relational approach', *Environment and Planning A*, 33: 1213–1235.

Lascoumes, P. and Le Galès, P. (2007) 'Understanding public policy through its instruments. From the nature of instruments to the sociology of public policy instrumentation', *Governance*, 20: 1–21.

Mandelbaum, S. J. (1985) 'The institutional focus of planning theory', *Journal of Planning Education and Research*, 5: 3–9.

March, J. and Olsen, J. (1989) *Rediscovering Institutions. The Organizational Basis of Politics*, New York: The Free Press.

Mazza, L. (2002) 'Technical knowledge and planning actions', *Planning Theory*, 1: 11–26.

Migom, S. (2004) 'Van werf tot Ruckersplein. 200 jaar Vleeshuiswijk', in S. Migom, J. Veeckman and F. Auwera (eds) *Rondom het Vleeshuis. Geschiedenis van een verdwenen buurt*, Antwerpen: Pandora.

Moulaert, F. (2005) 'Institutional economics and planning theory. A partnership between ostriches', *Planning Theory*, 4: 21–32.

Moulaert, F. (2009) 'Social innovation. Institutionally embedded, territorially (re)produced', in D. MacCallum, F. Moulaert, J. Hillier, and S. Vicari Haddock (eds) *Social Innovation and Territorial Development*, Farnham: Ashgate.

Moulaert, F. and Nussbaumer, J. (2005) 'Beyond the learning region. The dialectics of innovation and culture in territorial development', in R. Boschma and R. Kloosterman (eds) *Learning from Clusters. A Critical Assessment*, Dordrecht: Springer.

Moulaert, F. and Jessop, B. (2006) *Agency, Structure, Institutions, Discourse.* Demologos Thematic Synthesis Paper 1. Demologos EU research project (unpublished).

Moulaert, F. and Mehmood, A. (2009) 'Spatial planning and institutional design. What can we expect from transaction cost economics?', in H. Geyer (ed.) *International Handbook of Urban Policy*, Vol. 2, Cheltenham: Edward Elgar.

Moulaert, F., Rodriguez, A. and Swyngedouw, E. (2003) *The Globalized City. Economic Restructuring and Social Polarization in European Cities*, Oxford: Oxford University Press.

Moulaert, F., Martinelli, F., Gonzalez, S. and Swyngedouw, E. (2007) 'Introduction: social innovation and governance in European cities. Urban development between path dependency and radical innovation', *European Urban and Regional Studies*, 14: 195–209.

Palier, B. (2007) 'Tracking the evolution of a single instrument can reveal profound challenges. The case of funded pensions in France', *Governance*, 20: 85–107.

Payoke vzw (1997) *Prostitutie, zoveel meer dan. . . Tien jaar Payoke*, Antwerp: Payoke.

Saey, P. (1995a) 'Omtrent de maakbaarheid van de samenleving door de ruimtelijke planning. Deel 1: er is maakbaarheid en er is maakbaarheid', *Planologisch Nieuws*, 15: 159–167.

Saey, P. (1995b) 'Omtrent de maakbaarheid van de samenleving door ruimtelijke planning. Deel 2: ruimtelijke ordening als maatschappelijk gebeuren', *Planologisch Nieuws*, 15: 279–299.

Sandercock, L. (1998) *Towards Cosmopolis. Planning for Multicultural Cities,* Chichester: John Wiley & Sons.

Seinpost adviesbureau (1999) *Beleidsplan prostitutie Antwerpen*, Antwerp, Stad Antwerpen (unpublished).

Stad Antwerpen dienst prostitutiebeleid and Stad Antwerpen planningscel (2002a) *Consensusnota. Visie van de stad met betrekking tot de gewenste ontwikkeling van het Schipperskwartier*, Antwerp, Stad Antwerpen (unpublished).

Stad Antwerpen dienst prostitutiebeleid and Stad Antwerpen planningscel (2002b) *Startnota. Schipperskwartier en omgeving*, Antwerp, Stad Antwerpen (unpublished).

Stad Antwerpen Gemeenteraad (2000a) Samenlevingsopbouw. Integrale aanpak prostitutie. Reglement geschiktheidsverklaring raamprostitutiepand: Jaarnummer 1322, Antwerp, Gemeenteraad Antwerp (unpublished).

Stad Antwerpen Gemeenteraad (2000b) Samenlevingsopbouw. Integrale aanpak prostitutie. Aanvulling van hoofdstuk IV van de code van de gemeentelijke politiereglementen: Jaarnummer 1323, Antwerp, Gemeenteraad Antwerp (unpublished).

STOEP (1991) *Project gedoogzone. Advies voor de stad Antwerpen inzake prostitutiebeleid*, Antwerp, Stad Antwerpen (unpublished).

Swyngedouw, E., Moulaert, F. and Rodriguez, A. (2004) 'Neoliberal urbanization in Europe. Large-scale urban development projects and the new urban policy', *Antipode*, 34: 542–577.

Taylor, N. (2005) *Urban Planning Theory Since 1945*, London: Sage.

Van den Broeck, P. (2007) 'Towards socially and spatially innovative planning tools? The case of the red light district in the city of Antwerp'. Paper presented at IIe Colloque International du CRISES 'Créer et diffuser l'innovation sociale. De l'initiative à l'institutionnalisation', November 2007, Montréal.

Van den Broeck, P., Vloebergh, G., De Smet, L., Wuillaume, P., Wauters, E. and De Greef, J. (2009) 'De sociale constructie van instrumenten. Toepassing op Vlaamse planningsinstrumenten', Final Report SP2SP, Brussels: IWT.

Verma, N. (ed.) (2007) *Institutions and Planning*, Amsterdam: Elsevier.

Vigar, G., Healey, P., Hull, A. and Davoudi, S. (2000) *Planning, Governance and Spatial Strategy in Britain*, Houndmills: Macmillan.

Yin, R. (2003) *Case Study Research. Design and Methods*, London: Sage.

COMMENTARY ON PART I

WHEN SOLIDARITY BOOSTS STRATEGIC PLANNING

FRANK MOULAERT

In his introduction to this first part of the book Louis Albrechts asserts that it is in 'transformative practices that strategic spatial planning meets social innovation'. Is that really so? And do the two case chapters in this part confirm this assertion? I will try to answer or at least qualify these questions, first by distilling the relationship between social innovation and strategic planning in theoretical terms, then by having a look at how the case studies address this relationship, and finally by exploring the common ground between social innovation and strategic transformative practice.

TRANSFORMATIVE PRACTICE AND SOCIAL INNOVATION

Albrechts, referring to Friedmann (1987), argues that:

> Transformative practices focus on the structural problems in society; they construct images/visions of a preferred outcome and how to implement this. Transformative practices simply refuse to accept that the current way of doing things is necessarily the best way; they break free from concepts, structures and ideas that only persist because of the process of continuity. Transformative practices focus on new concepts and new ways of thinking that change the way resources are used, (re) distributed and (re)allocated, and the way the regulatory powers are exercised.
> (Albrechts in this volume: p. 18)

The concept of social innovation, then, was introduced in social science spatial disciplines, some twenty years ago, simultaneously by the Centre de Recherches sur les Innovations Economiques et Sociales in Montréal, Québec (CRISES: http://www.crises.uqam.ca/pages/fr/; Lévesque 1989; Klein and Harrisson 2007) and the local development group at IFRESI in Lille, France (Poverty III Research Programme 1989–1993; Moulaert and Leontidou 1995). The definition of social

innovation as shared by the research teams refers to social innovation within territorial dynamics and defines it as the innovation in social relations geared towards
the implementation of a local development agenda meant to overcome socio-
cultural, socio-economic and socio-political alienation of (parts) of the population
in a neighbourhood or locality (Moulaert 2009). Social relations are considered as
spatially embedded not just locally, but within nested spatial scales. According to
the same conception of social relations, the local or neighbourhood refers not to
clear spatial confines, but to a social place, the definition of which hinges on the
use of the term 'community' and its spatial dialectics. In this respect, 'community'
seldom means a localised socially cohesive group but, rather, an ensemble of
groups sharing a limited set of collective ambitions and practice within a locality
articulated across wider spatial scales (Moulaert and Mehmood 2010). Important
in this definition is that social innovation is not 'imposed' but socially reproduced,
through community dynamics and through mediation with institutions and agents
'outside' the community, that it involves a process as well as collective action
and that it is ethically grounded. The last means that the ethics inspiring human
action is geared towards uniform human development, with a special focus on
fragilised population groups and taking into account limits of the political change
movements.

THE CASE STUDIES ON TRANSFORMATIVE PRACTICE AND SOCIAL INNOVATION

The two research chapters in this part have much to offer in facilitating communication between strategic spatial planning and social innovation. Space (physical
and social), an issue not touched upon in the introduction to this part, is a central
concern in the chapter by Barbara Van Dyck, who puts it at the heart of socially
innovative transformative practice: *physical space* as needed to implement a
local development agenda (the transformation of the Angus Locoshops brownfield site in Montréal) and *social space* where socially innovative relations are
both the catalysts and the outcome of the struggle between claims over physical
space. Van Dyck first explains the particular features of the Angus brownfield
site: it is not of particular *immediate* market-economic use but has value from a
medium-term real estate investment perspective. This more relaxed temporality
creates a relative openness enabling interaction between actors who are potentially interested in medium-term socio-economic initiatives. Thus, the Angus site
is not only physically 'open', but also economically (with no *immediate* economic
return pressure) and socio-politically (time space available for mediating interests
of interested partners) open. Of course, the Angus site and its social dynamics are part of the real world with its path dependency of opportunities but also

its cracks or interstitial spaces hosting hope for change. Although the Angus project 'shows the possibility of connecting conflicting and overlapping spatial claims and going beyond purely profit-oriented property-led development in strategic projects' (p. 47, this volume), it also provides evidence on how progressive approaches of negotiation about potentially conflicting spatial claims lead not only to the socially innovative transformation of established social relations, but also to their reproduction. A *progressive pessimistic* view of this outcome could be that the exquisite skills of progressive leadership (hosted by the SDA management) have been used to establish the governance structure needed to put the Angus economic territory back on the tracks of (medium-term) capitalist profitability. A *progressive optimistic* view in turn would picture the negotiation and governance-building process and its outcomes as a robust coalition between old and new types of actors who co-produced a development agenda in which both social and market economy criteria have been combined with more democratic socio-economic decision-making processes. The case is also 'real' in the sense that it shows that skilled leadership and availability of resources do matter.

In the case study of the Schipperskwartier in Antwerp, the social innovation perspective is considered a dual perspective, looking at transformative practice as progressive planning through the application of planning instruments, and also as a socially innovative transformation of institutional frames. The author of the case study, Pieter Van den Broeck, does not explicitly use the 'transformation concept', but, interpreting Albrechts' definition, it would be possible to apply it to Van den Broeck's framework. Van den Broeck has developed his own key concepts, which are relatively original but still need some maturation. He defines planning instruments 'as a technical core [of planning tools?] embedded in an institutional frame' and an institutional frame 'as an institutional ensemble related to a specific planning instrument, or group of planning instruments, which privileges certain actors, uses and outcomes over others, and hence structures the institutional field in which planning processes are unrolled'. According to Van den Broeck, different individual and or collective actors 'become embedded in, and structured by, the instruments cum institutional frame. They become part of the dynamics that sustain planning instruments and their operation and therefore become its "relevant social group"' (Chapter 4 this volume, p. 56). What Van den Broeck leaves out in his *theoretical framework* is the other direction of the interrelational causality, namely the strategic impact of social actors in the building of planning instruments and institutional frames through the social construction of movements, coalitions and strategies that will enhance them. In his case study he considers this part as integral to institutional dynamics; but the theoretical perspective remains asymmetrical on this 'historically primary' movement and puts too much stress on '. . . how particular individual and collective actors succeed or fail to imbue their values and interests into planning instruments and institutional frames' (Chapter 4 this volume, p. 57). Rereading the conclusions of this chapter only strengthens this observation – unless, of course, an institutional frame also refers to the ideology, cultural drivers and habitus of social movements such as Payoke? Relevant social groups, therefore, are groups of actors who reproduce an institutional frame, or contest it, with the objective of transforming or integrating it, or overturning and replacing it by an alternative frame. Within an alternative frame, similar 'planning instruments' may return, but their purposefulness and their socio-political meaning may drastically change.

SOCIAL INNOVATION: MORE THAN SOCIALLY TRANSFORMATIVE PRACTICES

Let us now return to the two questions we launched at the outset. Is it really the case that it is in 'transformative practices that strategic spatial planning meets social innovation'? And do the two case chapters in this part confirm this assertion?

To the first question the answer is 'contextual' and text critical. What does Louis Albrechts mean by 'meet'? Does he refer to an 'intersection' between the two approaches?

> The transformative agenda challenges traditional planning approaches, vested concepts, existing knowledge, conventional wisdom and practices, and the attitudes and skills of planners. . . . This leads to and establishes the contours of a social–innovative type of spatial planning that . . . is based on the capacity of human beings – as a response to problems, challenges and potentials – to create, improve and reshape their places with the aid of knowledge (scientific as well as local knowledge), innovation and transformative practices that work with history and overcome history. This requires a climate that is conducive to new ideas in planning practices, to alternative visions and governance structures.
>
> (Albrechts in this volume: p. 20)

This excerpt on the transformative agenda certainly shows a strong similarity to social innovation as a collective agency (Moulaert and Nussbaumer 2008; Klein and Harrisson 2007): when transformative action chooses explicitly for human development, then its collective agency goes unambiguously for socially innovative progress, according to explicit ethical terms (inclusion of marginalised groups and places, promoting social cohesion among groups and places, etc.). Basically, once these ethical grounds become shared between strategic planning and social innovation, other commonalities appear: socially innovative transformative actions need 'changes in governance institutions and agency that aim to contribute to sustainability and spatial quality in an equitable and socially just way' (Albrechts citing from González and Healey 2005); the institutionalisation of change into structure, systems, social norms, shared values and, most of all, culture; the development of 'an alternative set of conceptual lenses for understanding the inherently creative nature of the change processes occurring in institutional renewal and transformation' (Albrechts in this volume: p. 20); the development of visions for the future is a social learning process; and others.

But even in the case of shared norm systems there are also significant differences in approach, or should I say in the way Louis Albrechts and the social innovation authors (including the two case study authors in this part) understand the social innovation approach. Social innovation is less voluntarist than Louis Albrechts suggests: as social innovation is both process and action driven, socially innovative processes are an outcome not only of collective rationality but of institutionalisation processes as well; and following the socio-political cycles, institutionalisation may or may not sustain socially innovative practices and norm systems, as a regime theory perspective on social policy at the urban level shows (Moulaert *et al.* 2007).

The way in which Louis Albrechts distinguishes similarities and differences between the social innovation and strategic planning approaches also reveals some critical issues to be considered in the strategic planning approach itself: a strong confidence in visioning and the analysis of the conditions under which visions would materialise, but with less concern about the path dependency of the resources; a too sequential view of the relationships between visioning, action, structure, institutions and discourse whereas, for example, collective action and discourse may confirm the logic of institutions, contradict it or simply become frozen in their desire for innovation because of 'institutional regression' or 'ethical checking'.

AND THE CASE STUDIES?

The case studies provide several elements for building a meeting ground between strategic planning and social innovation, often going well beyond what is suggested by Albrechts in the introduction. Their authors' conclusions should be read as a call to enrich the strategic planning literature with that of social innovation and the structure agency institutions literature in social science. We should indeed not forget that the origins of strategic planning lie with military strategy-making, logistics and business administration. Far from arguing that these 'root' disciplines are naturally unethical, and that strategic spatial planning would not have materialised a major ethical corrigendum to the ethics of its 'root' disciplines, it should still be recognised that social innovation is founded on the fundamental ethical premise of 'inclusion' through opening up societal social relations for all communities and by putting the development of deprived groups and communities at the top of the political agenda. This fundamental ethical choice means that socially innovative strategies and change processes regularly enter into conflict with political regimes, and have to look for the cracks in the system 'to do their thing', whereas strategic planning, although not uncritical of conservative planning strategies and value systems, is usually sufficiently integrated into the planning system to be counted as part of it and, therefore, seldom has to fight for its survival as many social innovation initiatives must. The case studies show the dependency of socially innovative change strategies on local socio-political regimes, the role of collective ethics and action and the availability of 'residual' resources. In this way they are a wonderful mirror of the state of social cohesiveness of the urban societies in which they have materialised – with, as far as I am concerned, Montréal the big winner over Antwerp.

BIBLIOGRAPHY

Albrechts, L. (2004a) 'Strategic (spatial) planning challenged or the challenge of strategic (spatial) planning', *Planning Theory and Practice*, 5 (1): 62–63.
Albrechts, L. (2004b) 'Strategic (spatial) planning reexamined', *Environment and Planning B*, 31: 743–758.
Friedmann, J. (1987) *Planning for the Public Domain. From Knowledge to Action*, Princeton, NJ: Princeton University Press.
González, S. and Healey, P. (2005) 'A sociological institutionalist approach to the study of innovation in governance capacity', *Urban Studies*, 42 (11): 2055–2069.
Klein, J. L. and Harrisson, D. (2007). *L'Innovation sociale. Emergence et effets sur la transformation des sociétés*, Québec: Presses Universitaires du Québec.
Lévesque, B. (1989) 'Les cooperatives au Québec, un secteur stratégique à la recherche d'un projet pour l'an 2000', *Annals of Public and Cooperative Economics*, 60 (2): 181–215.
MacCallum, D., Moulaert, F., Hillier, J. and Vicari Haddock, S. (eds) (2009) *Social Innovation and Territorial Development*, Farnham: Ashgate.
Moulaert, F. (2009) 'Social innovation: institutionally embedded, territorially (re)produced', in D. MacCallum, F. Moulaert, J. Hillier, and S. Vicari Haddock (eds) *Social Innovation and Territorial Development*, Farnham: Ashgate.
Moulaert F. and Leontidou, L. (1995) 'Localités déintégrées et stratégies de lutte contre la pauvreté: une réflexion méthodologique post-moderne', *Espaces et Sociétés*, 78: 35–53.
Moulaert, F. and Nussbaumer, J. (2008) *La logique sociale du développement territorial*. Québec: Presses Universitaires du Québec.
Moulaert, F. and Mehmood, A. (2010) 'Analysing regional development and policy. A structural-realist approach', *Regional Studies*, 44 (1): 103–118.
Moulaert, F., Martinelli, F., González, S. and Swyngedouw, E. (2007) 'Introduction: social innovation and governance in European cities – urban development between path dependency and radical innovation', *European Urban and Regional Studies*, 14 (3): 195–209.

PART II

DESIGNING STRATEGIC PROJECTS FOR SPATIAL QUALITY

CHAPTER 5

SPATIAL DESIGN AS A STRATEGY FOR A QUALITATIVE SOCIAL–SPATIAL TRANSFORMATION

JEF VAN DEN BROECK

In this introduction to the second part, I want to explain the role of 'design', defined here in a broad – not purely physical – sense, and its importance in transformative processes linking planning and implementation, knowledge and creativity and relating actors. Spatial design is considered as an essential creative activity within planning processes and as a core capacity and skill of planners. It is a medium to integrate different fields of knowledge, visions, contexts and actors, an aspect which is developed in Chapter 7 on the integrative potential of design, and a co-productive way to define and share terms of spatial quality, which is explained in Chapter 6. In this introduction I try to define the meaning of 'spatial design' within a multi-track planning approach (see also Chapter 1) in order to situate the research questions addressed in the following two chapters within the broader debate on the role of design in strategic planning and projects. Spatial design, as defined in this introduction, is seen as a clue to relate the 'four tracks' with each other, as a key activity within a visioning process imagining possible futures and perspectives, as a practical way to position projects in a wider sphere in order to make them strategic, as the 'art' to materialise and make concrete futures and to create possible 'realities' that can be used as a source for learning, discussion, negotiation, decision-making and implementation.

DESIGN: A CREATIVE, TRANSFORMATIVE AND COLLECTIVE ACTIVITY

Design is the capacity and the artistry to create, to generate, to conceive, to represent, to diagnose, to read and to question possible futures, strategies, actions and projects in a proactive and co-productive way in order to use them for framing, social judgement, negotiation and decision-making. This is done in an interactive collective and individual process, and results in what Healey (2008: 18) calls 'collective sense-making' about social–spatial transformation and innovation.

In this definition 'design' has a broad meaning and cannot and may not be reduced to a purely aesthetic physical formalism creating an abstraction from social reality, nor reduced to the production of regular plans used for the (bureau-cratic/juridical) control of land use, nor linked with one specific spatial scale or discipline. Such reductions, often institutionalised in education and practice, are unfruitful, artificial and counter-productive if we accept that 'creating becomings' (Hillier 2008: 46) is the core task of planners and designers and that planning aims to transform and innovate space by spatial interventions and all kind of actions.

Different authors refer to the ambiguity within the discipline of planning between process (the how) and product (the what), and between scientific knowledge of a different kind and 'the practical art of acting to generate change' (Healey 2008: 12). Madanipour tries to overcome this tension by defining and broadening the urban design process as

> a multi-disciplinary activity of shaping and managing urban environments, interested in both the process of this shaping and the spaces it helps to shape. Combining technical, social and expressive concerns, urban designers use both visual and verbal means of communication and engage all scales of the urban socio-spatial continuum.
>
> (Madanipour 2007: 22)

Within a broad conception, 'design' is not merely a creative process deal-ing with the physical context and the design of artefacts. It deals also with the exploration of realities, the development, representation and exploration of visions, concepts, scenarios, metaphors and stories, the design of policies and processes, solutions, etc., looking for possible 'futures or becomings' in such a way that exchange of information, interpretation and integration of knowledge of a differ-ent kind, and visions are generated. As such, design and its products – different kinds of representations and images – become not only a medium for integration of content but also a way to confront values, visions and interests, to discuss and negotiate, and to deal with power structures. The (implicit) power of images and representations within such processes may not be underestimated. As a specific language revealing characteristics and qualities of existing spaces and places and their possible futures, these images and representations can easily be read and understood by people – at least when represented in a communicative way – and serve 'as a tool for negotiation and as a concrete frame for agreements' (De Meulder et al. 2004: 194).

Last but not least, 'design' is not a neutral activity because it expresses the values, interests and ambitions of individuals and groups. Within spatial plan-ning processes design proposals can express a future with new content, form and meaning; a future based upon such values as diversity, solidarity and equity. Design is a powerful tool that should be used as the art of creating and representing possible 'sustainable and qualitative becomings' and operatonalising them in a 'collective' and co-productive process, which 'integrates' different actors in an equal way.

DESIGN AND SPACE

Since the 1980s, a 'spatial turn' (Döring and Thielmann 2008) has been noticeable within various scientific disciplines, resulting in renewed attention to the concept of 'space', its definition, and the analysis and construction thereof. However, this pertains mainly to such disciplines as geography (Lefebvre 1974; Soja 1989), sociology (Löw 2001), anthropology, etc. Within 'design sciences' there has been only limited scientific research over the last decade, notwithstanding the great need for a more scientific approach to this discipline. One of the reasons for this may be that planning has been conceived merely as 'a practical art' up until now and not as a scientific discipline. Other reasons are the societal context and the methods used within the profession, which are aimed at laying down land uses and creating legal certainty. Within such a concept, space is seen as a 'neutral and sexless' consumer good. This opinion is also reflected in (older) UN literature, in which 'sustainable' spatial development is dealt with in two ways: on the one hand based on (technical) requirements regarding environmental quality (air, water, etc.) and, on the other hand, based on the requirement for (affordable) housing, equipment and infrastructure. In this context, space is seen as a 'neutral and unqualified' item (Loeckx and Shannon 2004: 160). Its only value is its 'use', which is expressed in terms of a price tag.

In contrast to this, our argument is based on the premise that space is not merely derived from social processes but has its own relative autonomy and, by its logic, also contributes to ordering, shaping and identifying human activities. Spatial developments are situated in an existing physical reality, either in an undeveloped area with a specific soil, relief, nature value and capital, or in a built-up area with historic–cultural capital. Each programme and project must integrate itself into an existing spatial context. The outcome is always a blend of existing and new elements, of 'old' and 'new' values. Space can thus be seen as a multi-layered representation of a cultural history within a spatial frame, a palimpsest.

Because of the intrinsic quality of space and its integrational capacity, this argument considers space itself as an important entry to, and the object of, spatial planning and design and, by extension, of the discipline. Space is the frame in which social, cultural, economic and ecological artefacts and activities can be integrated, in which their invisible relations can be materialised into a cohesive entity with its own new and individual significance. Spatial structure as the expression of relations and the shape of space as its materialisation (in fabrics, volumes, public space infrastructure, etc.) are the subject and medium of spatial quality and sustainable development.

Space thus has its own characteristics and its own logic, which have an instrinsic value and which can be used as a resource and opportunity for all types of human requirements, whether economic, social or cultural. The cases discussed in the following chapters demonstrate this. For example, spatial logic pertains to the adequacy of space to order diverse functions, to generate density, to allow for adaptability, to improve access, to optimise light and views and to minimise energy and maintenance requirements. Relative autonomy also pertains to space's formal appearance, spatial architecture that can generate meanings, impressions, associations, etc., as well as an individual and collective 'experience' (Loeckx and Van den Broeck 2006: 285).

This autonomy is relative. Space is related to the society of today and tomorrow, to citizens and groups, owners, investors and managers, who will want to (and effectively will) stake their own claims on the space, whether justified or not, and who will base these on their own interests and values. That is why 'space' is sometimes considered a neutral asset, a backdrop or a battleground even. In such a case, people tend to overlook its characteristics and potential quality and merely focus on square metrage. The mission of planners and designers is to include a space's own spatial autonomy, spatial quality and sustainability in the societal debate. In more recent UN publications (UN-Habitat 2009) and programmes the importance of 'space and place' and their intrinsic characteristics in relation to the 'habitat' of people as well as the possible contribution of spatial planning in creating a qualitative environment is more and more emphasised.

The question remains as to how we can represent this space, as we see it, experience it and wish to change it. Design is looked upon as a medium to read (analyse), interpret and define spaces and places, to represent possible futures and necessary transformations and innovations and promote them, to explore different understandings of, and shared terms for, spatial quality. Design, seen as a research method, starts from the concrete characteristics of a particular space and place. It has the potential to reveal a different kind of knowledge about space and place, in addition to thematic, sectoral and technical knowledge, and has the power to integrate different dimensions of space and place in images expressing visions and concepts. Design proposals can frame different opinions, opportunities, interests and values. Partially under the influence of communicative and participatory planning methods, design approaches have moved on to include more users and stakeholders in the creative negotiation and decision-making process and hence can endow strategic projects with enriched, qualitative and inclusive substance by using its creative and eye-opening capacity. In Chapters 6 and 7, theories and pratices are developed to show how spatial design can be used to develop knowledge and to 'integrate' spatial components and actors in order to 'qualify' space in a co-productive way.

SPATIAL DESIGN: A CORE ACTIVITY IN SPATIAL PLANNING

Within our concept of strategic spatial planning as a four-track approach (Figure 5.1) (Van den Broeck 1987, 2004, 2010; Albrechts 2004; Albrechts and Van den Broeck 2004; Albrechts *et al.* 1999) or as a 'multi-planar' process (Hillier 2007, 2008), 'designing' as an activity and 'the design' as a product can fulfil different roles and take on different forms.

The first track is a thinking and working trajectory, a thought process, possibly 'a trajectory or plane of immanence or consistency' according to Hillier (2008: 47), which is aimed at developing and designing a vision for the long term; it pertains to potential futures. It is an open-ended trajectory, with a divergent character; it can evoke fundamental conflicts because of the value-bound nature of the subject matter and thus can lead to (social) checkmates. It is a trajectory that is often pushed aside by politicians, and even by people who are daily confronted with reality but who prefer to act and respond immediately, precisely because of its aforementioned characteristics and its potentially structural character. And yet

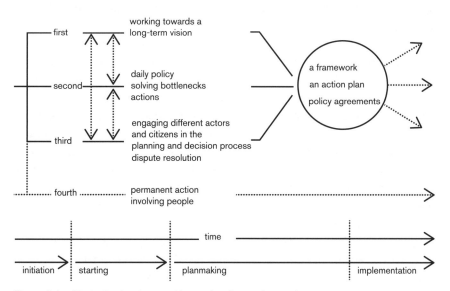

Figure 5.1   Strategic planning: working on four interacting tracks.

this trajectory can lead to a framework providing citizens with a view and a per-spective on a potential future and which can also motivate and encourage them. Many times there is no clear or uniform result, no real road to choose. Often it is merely a learning process; at times it can be a clearly marked road. The design process can take on different forms here. If it involves becoming familiar with or analysing a place, the process can be very detailed and mainly oriented towards material reality. If a learning process is involved, or the representation of potential futures and the encouragement of debate and divergent thinking, schematic rep-resentations can be used or metaphors, stories, photos, utopias, etc.

The second track, possibly a 'plane of transcendence or organisation' (Hillier 2008: 47), attempts to provide an answer to daily reality, to political, societal and human needs, to action and response. It deals with problems, 'puts out fires' and 'scores' well politically and often 'justifies' the involvement of planners. It thinks and acts in terms of very concrete and feasible goals, aims at short-term results and counts on currently available knowledge, possibilities and budgets; it is a trajectory that uses mostly fast research methods and (generally) avoids difficul-ties and fundamental points for discussion; it accepts and uses existing relations of power. At the same time, it is also a trajectory that we can use – and therein lies the difference with the 'art of muddling through or incrementalism' (Lindblom 1959) – to encourage citizens to think by initiating actions that can trigger further processes; it does this by stringing together small changes, small steps, which seduce people into looking beyond the here and now, and which will elicit fun-damental arguments, albeit of a limited dimension. This can lead to strategic and structural actions about which there is a consensus and which thus contribute to developing a long-term vision.

Designing in line with this trajectory – why not call this urban design – uses the premise of material reality as its starting point and aims to bring about a concrete change of the spatial fabric in a highly concrete situation. This 'place focus' of design and its potential for strategic projects is explored further in Chapter 7. In this form of design, it is also recommended that representative techniques are used that allow us to gain an insight into the space's characteristics and qualities as the strategic project evolves. It is also worth searching for more visual methods of discussing information, concepts and desirable quality, especially those dimen-sions of space and spatial quality that are more difficult to make transparent and open to all involved actors (see Chapter 6).

The third thinking and working trajectory tries to engage actors actively in the planning, design and decision-making process. Like the second subprocess, it is a converging and more closed process that unfolds within an organised societal framework, an existing planning, juridical and policy framework. It has to lead to agreements about concrete programmes, actions and strategic projects within budgetary possibilities and margins; it sets out to achieve this by negotiation with actors in a number of arenas. It is delimited by the political context, and thus by time, by interests and by relations of power. In practice, and as a result of the context, the (substantial) involvement of actors and the reaching of agreements can be considerably limited because various types of logic are confronted with one another. The design method and representations are highly policy oriented in this case, that is, the products have to facilitate negotiation, and take into account calculation of cost, budgeting and agreements. Chapter 6 analyses how design improves communication, and hence also negotiation, and considers sense-oriented dimensions of spatial quality in strategic projects, whereas Chapter 7 looks at how place focus enables design to integrate different actors and interests within strategic projects.

And, finally, there is also a working and thinking trajectory that sets out to actively involve the general public in fundamental issues, in policy and in actions. It is a trajectory that enables citizens, particularly non-conventional actors, to 'take part', to play an active and essential role in the process. It is aimed at creating progressive insight into difficult matters, at strengthening social, political and intellectual capacity and capital (Friedmann 1992; Innes 1996), and at creating both new social fabrics and those that create (new) ties between various layers and classes of the population, between policy and citizens, thus fostering a new type of citizenship (Mazza 2007). It is a trajectory that self-evidently implies social innovation (see Part I of this book); it ties in with the first trajectory and is complementary to the third as regards character: open-ended, unpredictable, unrelated to time, necessarily permanent and of a divergent nature. Within this framework, designing has to be seen mainly in its communicative sense. How can spatial knowledge and insight be obtained and grow, how can quality be recognised, how can change concepts become the subject of discussion, etc.? Where does the local dynamic and power lie? Which methods of representation are suited to achieving this?

A 'strategic plan' (see Figure 5.1) is considered as the result of such a process at a certain 'political' moment, containing the policy for an area, a vision, goals and objectives, an action plan, and agreements between actors. The integration of the four tracks, each with its own rationality, remains a complex process and its success depends on many factors: the planning environment and context and the willingness, professionalism, inspiration and creativity of the actors. It should be clear that the combination of 'positive' circumstances, creating a chance for a 'transformative and innovative moment', will not be there at all times. In this sense the four-track model is an 'ideal' one but at the same time the only possibility for real and structural socio-spatial transformation. Within this 'philosophy' spatial projects and actions will be 'strategic' only if they are at the same time the result of a learning and search process with an open character and a process aiming at the transformation of socio-spatial reality. 'Open' means that such transformative processes should not focus upon a result defined in advance, but that this result should be developed and grow through confrontation of possibilities, values, visions, ambitions and interests. Such processes need a 'process architecture and structure' that combine a collective learning process with concrete socio-spatial transformation through spatial interventions (Van den Broeck *et al.* 2010). Obviously the relation between process and project is a tricky one. Positioning projects in such a wider context, the only way to make them 'strategic', is not easy, for instance because of yearly budgets or some actors (not only politicians) push-ing for immediate realisations and the speeding up of procedures and decisions. 'Space' for learning, discussion, acquiring knowledge (also local knowledge), involving actors, etc. is often very restricted.

Spatial design as defined here can, within limits, help to overcome this ten-sion (see Chapter 7). However, a considerable amount of research is required to gain an understanding of the nature of 'spatial design' and in particular to develop methods that allow its different roles to be fulfilled in an optimal manner and to relate them to one another. The content of the designs can be quite dif-ferent, as is obvious from the various roles and forms. The design methods and techniques used today are aimed too exclusively at the representation of physical end products and not sufficiently at the different forms of representation required within a planning process. One hypothesis could be that spatial design is the conglomerate of integrating activities and products that allows us to represent and imagine different types of knowledge and insights into the characteristics of a space and a place, its potential, the potential sustainable futures (becom-ings) and their effects. This should be done in ways suited to communication, consultation and negotiation with all of the actors during the various development phases and at the various thinking levels of a planning process. In the following chapters, some aspects of this hypothesis will be developed in more detail, that is, integrating the capacity of designing with the design itself, and the manner in which spatial quality can be operationalised through design. The two following chapters focus mainly on the design process within the second and third tracks. Up until now there has been little research available concerning the role of design in the 'visioning and capacity building' processes, the first and the fourth tracks, despite there being a lot of practice and experience.

REFERENCES

Albrechts, L. (2004) 'Strategic (spatial) planning re-examined', *Environment and Planning B, Planning and Design*, 31: 743–758.

Albrechts, L. and Van den Broeck, J. (2004) 'From discourse to facts: the case of the ROM Project in Ghent, Belgium', *Town Planning Review*, 75 (2): 127–150.

Albrechts, L., Leroy, P., Van den Broeck, J., Van Tatenhove, J. and Verachtert, K. (1999) *Geïntereerd Gebiedsgericht Beleid, een methodiek*, Leuven/Nijmegen: K.U.Leuven and K.U.Nijmegen.

De Meulder, B., Loeckx, A. and Shannon, K. (2004) 'A project of projects', in A. Loeckx, K. Shannon, R. Tuts and H. Verschure (eds) *Urban Trialogues: Visions_Projects_ Co-productions*, Nairobi/Leuven: UN-Habitat and K.U.Leuven.

Döring, J. and Thielmann, T. (eds) (2008) *Spatial Turn. Das Raumparadigma in den Kultur- und Sozialwisschenschaften*, Bielefeld: Transcript.

Friedmann, J. (1992) *Empowerment: The Politics of Alternative Development*, Oxford: Blackwell.

Healey, P. (2008) 'Making choices that matter. The practical art of situated strategic judge-ment in spatial strategy-making', in J. Van den Broeck, F. Moulaert and S. Oosterlynck (eds) *Empowering the Planning Fields, Ethics, Creativity and Action*, Leuven: ACCO.

Hillier, J. (2007) *Stretching beyond the Horizon: A Multiplanar Theory of Spatial Planning and Governance*, Aldershot: Ashgate.

Hillier, J. (2008) 'Interplanary practice towards a Deleuzian-inspired methodology for crea-tive experimentation in strategic spatial planning', in J. Van den Broeck, F. Moulaert and S. Oosterlynck (eds) *Empowering the Planning Fields, Ethics, Creativity and Action*, Leuven: ACCO.

Innes, J. (1996) 'Planning through consensus building; a new view of the comprehensive planning ideal', *Journal of the American Planning Association*, 62 (4): 460–472.

Lefebvre, H. (1974) *The Production of Space*, Oxford: Blackwell.

Lindblom, C. (1959) 'The science of muddling through', *Public Administration Review* 19: 79–88.

Loeckx, A. and Shannon, K. (2004) 'Qualifying urban space', in A. Loeckx, K. Shannon, R. Tuts and H. Verschure (eds) *Urban Trialogues: Visions_ Projects_ Co-productions*, Nairobi/Leuven: UN-Habitat and K.U.Leuven.

Loeckx, A. and Van den Broeck, J. (2006) 'Tien stellingnames over stadsprojecten', in L. Boudry, A. Loecxk and J. Van den Broeck (eds) *Inzet/Opzet/Voorzet. Stadsprojecten in Vlaanderen*, Antwerp/Appeldoorn: Garant.

Löw, M. (2001) *Raumsoziologie*, Frankfurt am Main: Suhrkamp.

Madanipour, A. (2007) 'Ambiguities of urban design', in M. Carmona and S. Tiedell (eds) *Urban Design Reader*, Oxford: Architectural Press.

Mazza, L. (2007) 'Redesigning citizenship'. Keynote speech at the 43st ISOCARP Inter-national Congress 'Urban Trialogues: Co-productive Ways to Relate Visioning and Strategic Urban Projects', Antwerp, September 2007.

Soja, E. (1989) *Post-Modern Geographies: The Re-assertion of Space in Critical Social Theory*, London: Verso.

UN-Habitat (2009), *Planning Sustainable Cities. Global Report on Human Settlements*, London: Earthscan Publishers.

Van den Broeck, J. (1987) 'Structuurplanning in de praktijk, werken op drie sporen', *Ruimtelijke Planning*, 19: 53–120.

Van den Broeck, J. (2004) 'Strategic structure planning', in A. Loeckx, K. Shannon, R. Tuts and H. Verschure (eds) *Urban Trialogues: Visions_Projects_Co-productions*, Nairobi/Leuven: UN-Habitat and K.U.Leuven.

Van den Broeck, J. (2010) 'What kind of spatial planning do we need? An approach based upon visioning, action and co-production', in K. R. Kunzmann, W. A. Schmid and M. Koll-Schretzenmayr (eds) *China and Europe, the Implications of the Rise of China for European Space*, London: Routledge.

Van den Broeck, J., Albrechts, L. and Segers, R. (2010) *Strategische Ruimtelijke Projecten, Maatschappelijk en ruimtelijk vernieuwend*, Brussels: Politeia.

CHAPTER 6

DEVELOPING SHARED TERMS FOR SPATIAL QUALITY THROUGH DESIGN

Marleen Goethals and Jan Schreurs

Prior to a specific design process: developing shareable basic terms

Strategic spatial projects emerge through a complex interplay between different actors, each of whom has his or her own interests and perspectives (Loeckx 2007: 116). Experience acquired in professional practice has shown that actors find it difficult to look beyond their own interests, to empathise with each other's perception of the situation or with the yearnings of users (Kaplan *et al*. 1998: 27). This results in drawn-out processes, which sometimes do not lead to implementation at all, or in situations in which the quality of implementation is viewed differently by different parties.

Although it can be expected that everyone involved is striving to achieve spatial quality, it is difficult to define this concept or, when there is disagreement, to work out which option offers the best spatial quality. Spatial quality is of interest to everyone (Carmona and Sieh 2004; Lynch 1984; Reijndorp *et al*. 1998). However, it cannot be simply imposed by 'governmental regulation'. The actors must engage in dialogue to reach agreement on what kind of spatial quality they should be striving to achieve. To do this, the actors must understand each other. They must find 'shared terms' in which the planning assignment and the assessment of its quality will be expressed (Hajer *et al*. 2006). When actors use agreed shared terms, spatial quality becomes more transparent and the debates about it more effective. The defined shared terms are project specific and the process of formulating them has to be repeated by new actors for each new project. Nevertheless, consciously or otherwise, they are based on a number of general, reproducible quality categories.

We therefore performed a literature search for a set of general terms defined prior to specific project circumstances that are used to describe spatial quality. We consulted the theory of urban planning design set out by Kevin Lynch in *Good City Form* (Lynch 1984) and environment behaviour research, for example research into user preferences for the structuring of green open spaces (Kaplan *et al.* 1998) or design recommendations based on post-occupancy evaluations (Cooper Marcus and Francis 1998). These general quality terms must not only stand above specific contextual aspects, but must also be more open than formal design solutions. For example, 'provide wayfinding' is more general and comes prior to 'use a grid', which will be the best solution only within particular contexts and gives designers less opportunities to adapt to the context (Schreurs 2005: 11). It is therefore better to deal with spatial qualities by conceptualising them within 'dimensions of performance' that can be expected of the space and not as design patterns, codes or guidelines as advocated in some popular urban design handbooks (e.g. Urban Design Associates 2003).

Dimensions of performance make the needs of users visible and do not restrict 'designers' options'. 'Performance programs . . . make explicit what conditions a design decision is intended to meet – its performance – allowing designers to decide on particular responses' (Zeisel 2006: 52). Insight into the way a space is expected to perform makes it possible even for non-experts to influence the design within a process. 'They are put in the position not of individual clients being asked to express personal desires and tastes but of knowledgeable participants whose ability to tailor the research to a particular situation is valuable to design' (Zeisel 2006: 59). Dimensions of performance are also not restricted to a particular scale. In every project, at every scale, in every spatial and social context and in every intended programme, they can be expressed, refined and mutually harmonised afresh by the stakeholders.

Spatial quality is not intrinsically bound to the physical characteristics of the space. People's wishes, needs or appreciations play an important role in defining spatial quality. Environments do not 'have' quality in themselves, but 'acquire' quality through the appreciation that people have or express for them (Jacobs 2000: 25; Schreurs 2005: 9). These appreciations may differ between individuals and are coloured by culture, upbringing, social class, education, etc. (Kaplan *et al.* 1998: 25). The value-based character of quality means that its expression may also change in accordance with changes in society and in people's needs (Jacobs 2000: 25).

From the above it is clear that transparency when discussing spatial quality is an important precondition for an effective debate and wide-ranging agreement on strategic projects. Concepts that can express spatial quality well, exist prior to the specific circumstances of a project and can be shared by all actors can make this dialogue more accessible. This chapter will therefore be devoted to them. First, value-based dimensions of performance that people expect from a space will be presented on the basis of Lynch's *Good City Form* and of environment behaviour research, paying particular attention to the dimension of 'experiential value', which is more difficult to communicate. In the second part we will use three exemplary strategic urban projects as examples to investigate how designers justify this kind of experiential value and put it into practice in the context of specific strategic projects. Finally, the last part will shed light on the vital role of the design process in creating project-specific shared terms to describe experiential value.

FIVE DIMENSIONS OF PERFORMANCE

To enable a group of people to evaluate the quality of their environment, in *Good City Form* Lynch (1984) proposes a set of dimensions of performance that an environment should be able to deliver. This set is built on a very wide empirical basis. Lynch analysed descriptions of spaces, aims of real urban projects and 'urban utopia', interviews with spatial planning students, and the motivations of urban developers in the distant past and contemporary planners, designers, lawyers, architects and others. From these he drew up a long list of appreciations of space, which he then reduced to five 'dimensions of performance'.

Depending on the aims being pursued, the actors will express and weight these five dimensions differently. Lynch (1984: 115) compares a human settlement with a 'learning ecology'. Ideally this 'learning ecology' should strive to achieve 'the continuity of a dynamic and stable interdependence between similar types, different types and the inorganic setting' as well as 'progressive change'. This 'progressive change' is value based. According to Lynch, a society that wishes to assure the continued existence of the human race and its culture (and all other living species) (continuity), wishes to reinforce the feeling of connection to a time and place (connectedness) and wants to promote individual development (Lynch 1984: 115) automatically ends up with his five dimensions of performance when evaluating its environment. Since the values proposed by Lynch correspond to those a society in sustainable development should be striving towards, the following 'dimensions of performance' seem to be suitable as a theoretical basis for a shared understanding of spatial quality:

- Vitality – the extent to which the manifestation of the settlement supports the health and survival of the human race and the whole ecosystem.
- Sense – the extent to which the manifestation of the settlement positively influences the perception thereof.
- Fit – the extent to which spatial and temporal patterns correspond to the usual behaviour of users.
- Access – the extent to which a settlement offers the inhabitants access to activities (housing, work and services) and resources (food, water, energy), facilitates contacts between them and makes possible access to other places (centres, symbolic places, natural environments) and to information.

- Control – the extent to which people can use the space to manage their personal exchanges with their social context (e.g. guaranteeing privacy in homes), and the extent to which the creation, restoration, alteration and management of the space and its activities are controlled by the users of that space.

Traffic flow research, safety audits, market research and feasibility studies, research into ecological requirements, statistical needs research, for example the need for green spaces, employment, training programmes and leisure amenities – there are many different sector research techniques available to support the 'access', 'vitality' and 'fit' dimensions. They also promote the 'control' dimension because they make the environment more manageable. These studies can adequately overcome the barrier between user client, paying client and designer – the barrier that comes into being if the designer is no longer able to discuss needs directly with the client, because the users are unknown or cannot be directly involved.

Because of their relatively objectifiable nature, the 'access', 'vitality' and 'fit' dimensions seem to be at an advantage when assessing spatial quality. They are easier to express in the form of 'hard' requirements, and it is easier to make them transparent and open for debate between the actors. This seems to be much more difficult with the 'sense' aspects, which relate to perceptions of space. Here it seems that the actors have to rely on their own personal experience or on the expertise of designers.

DIMENSION OF PERFORMANCE: 'SENSE'

The enumeration of the dimensions of performance convincingly expresses the fact that Lynch certainly sees spatial quality as being much wider than simply sensory or aesthetic factors linked to a physical manifestation. Even when discussing dimensions of performance explicitly related to perception, he emphasises not so much the 'attributes of the thing' but the 'interaction between person and place. Perception is a creative act, not a passive reception' (Lynch 1984: 131).

Since Lynch focuses on the active contribution that people make when it comes to perception, empirical research could also be conceived for these aspects, which makes it possible to lower the barriers between user client, paying client and designer. The interaction between place and user can be explored through research during the programming stage (e.g. research involving users drawing preferred walking routes on the map of a square that is to be redesigned), through design recommendations based on post-occupancy evaluations (Cooper Marcus and Francis 1998) or through insights from environment behaviour research

(Kaplan *et al.* 1998). The expert perspective of designers on space can also be studied. Analysis of the arguments used by eloquent designers in exemplary projects may clarify the so-called 'tacit attributes' – design decisions that are understood intuitively by designers but not by their audience – thereby turning user clients and paying clients into 'knowledgeable participants' (Zeisel 2006: 59). This type of research can expand the knowledge that can be obtained from personal experience or the designer's expertise and clarify the 'sense' dimension of performance in project definitions.

Lynch attaches great importance to the perception and understanding of environments, which can give rise to absolute enjoyment and emotional experience, confer rich and inexhaustible significance and contribute towards people's mental development. Through cognitive processes the perception of space also influences the way society works. The ability to recognise things, to estimate the use of time, to find one's way, to read the signs, makes the environment understandable and usable. The sensory perception of an environment therefore also influences the other dimensions of its performance ('vitality', 'fit' and 'access'). An environment with experiential value functions better, and vice versa. The scientifically determined need to experience *variation*, *complexity* and *extent* provides relief and invites people to explore (Kaplan *et al.* 1998; Cooper Marcus and Francis 1998). In this sense these experiential needs are very important for Lynch's 'vitality' and 'access'. Also, the experience of a *comfortable* microclimate, with adequate sunshine and protection against wind and weather, is both a primary sensory experience (Cooper Marcus and Francis 1998) and a precondition for optimal functioning ('fit') and physical health ('vitality') (Lynch 1984). Because, on the one hand, 'sense' is such an important dimension of performance, but, on the other, is not easy to make transparent and open to debate between the actors, in the rest of this chapter we will restrict ourselves to 'sense' in our search for shared terms for spatial quality.

Subdimensions of 'sense'

Because the way an environment is understood and valued is strongly defined by upbringing, culture and social class, the significance of a place may be different for each person. The biological basis of our perceptive ability and shared cultural norms, however, mean that there are a few fundamental constants in the way different people experience the same place (Lynch 1984). These constants, – the subdimensions of Identity, Formal Structure, Congruence, Transparency, Legibility and Significance – can therefore operate as shared basic terms for the experiential quality of a project. Using these subdimensions Lynch describes three types of experience. The first group, Identity and Formal Structure, is about people's shared need to situate themselves in both space and time. The second group, Congruence, Transparency and Legibility, addresses the shared need to understand the purpose of the space, how the world operates and what residents, traders, the government, etc. are saying to us through the manifestation of the space. The third group, Significance, describes the shared need to express values through the manifestation of the space, or to derive values from it.

Identity is the extent to which a place can be distinguished from other places. Distinguishing places is the fundamental precondition for goal-oriented action. People, however, also ascribe a specific character to certain places: lively, unique, special, etc. The sensory perception of light, colour, shape of a place or the sensation and smell of the wind can give people pleasure. This direct pleasure from perception also leads people to use such 'sensible places' as a hook on which to hang their memories, feelings or values. By emphasising and exploiting its natural, historical, architectural and morphological characteristics, the identity of a place can be strengthened (Lynch 1984).

Formal Structure is the extent to which the physical manifestation of a small settlement helps people to imagine its structure. In the case of a larger settlement it is the extent to which the manifestation of the space helps people to orientate themselves. There are many points of reference available for this: 'the recognition of a characteristic form or activity in area or centers, sequential linkages, directional relations, time and distance, landmarks, path or edge continuities, gradients, panoramas, and many others' (Lynch 1984: 135). If foreigners are able to orientate themselves easily within a city this means less time wastage and annoyance. The accessibility of the city is increased if the formal structure, or the ordering of the various components, is understandable. Good accessibility further increases a city's opportunities for economic and cultural development.

This dimension of performance is relevant to every type of human environment. Whereas in a traditional city the architectural volumes make the urban order understandable, in the peripheral open areas of the city, the landscape, 'a thin horizontal vegetal plane', is understood as a 'primary element of urban order' (Koolhaas, quoted in Waldheim 2006: 42). Through 'landscape urbanism' a 'fluid exchange between (natural) environment and (engineered) infrastructural systems' becomes possible, even in urban centres (Waldheim 2006: 43). The tendency to view the contemporary city through the lens of the landscape is based on a growing concern about the environment (Waldheim 2006). Nevertheless, the basic components of an understandable environment in both traditional and open cities are essentially the same, namely to create 'coherence' and 'distinctiveness' (Kaplan *et al.* 1998: 13).

It is worth investing some effort in understanding an environment: 'There are pleasures . . . in puzzles, ambiguities, and mysteries' (Lynch 1984: 143). This is confirmed by research on environmental preferences. In addition to their need for an understandable environment, people also demonstrate the need for environments whose complexity invites them to explore (Kaplan *et al.* 1998: 13).

Congruence refers to the extent to which the physical manifestation of the space matches the use of that space, or the extent to which the abstract form of a place corresponds to the abstract form of its functions. For example, is a wide road in the settlement also a heavily used main thoroughfare? Or is a large square genuinely associated with large groups of people? Lynch's statement that 'congruence is the perceptual ground of a meaningful environment' (Lynch 1984: 138) explains what the term could mean in the context of a project in which the physical manifestation has not yet been designed. Congruence is then the extent to which the (visual) perception of the space makes it possible to suspect or recognise its purpose or function.

Transparency/Immediacy refers to the extent to which production, technical, social and natural processes can be directly perceived within a settlement. As well as the purely practical aspect of seeing where specific functions take place, the need for a transparent environment is related to a characteristic that is common to many people, namely that they are interested in understanding life in a settlement ('sense of life'). People can take pleasure from observing elementary processes such as people moving around and working; children being educated and growing up; birth and death; human affection; the changing of the seasons; the draining of an area; evidence of maintenance and care. Lynch also sees educational qualities in this aspect of transparency of an environment. People, and particularly young people, can learn how society functions by perceiving these technical, productive, natural and social processes (Lynch 1984: 139).

Legibility is the extent to which the inhabitants of a settlement can communicate effectively with each other using symbolic physical elements such as flags, front gardens, crosses, signs, gates, rustic fences, graffiti, etc. These signs inform us about the status, group affiliation, political tendencies and cultural background of the residents. The way the space is structured may suppress, tolerate or stimulate this 'spatial talk' (Lynch 1984: 139).

Lynch refers to *Significance* as the extent to which for its users a space serves as a symbol of values, life processes, historic events, the social structure or the nature of the universe. The appearance of a settlement can make a person more aware of his community, his history, the cycle of life and the universe of time and space and enrich his life. These symbols are culture specific (Lynch 1984: 142).

FROM SHARED BASIC TERMS TO PROJECT-SPECIFIC TERMS: THREE CASES

Lynch's dimensions of performance are primarily intended for use in evaluating existing environments. They can, however, also be deployed in a design process. In the second part of this chapter, three exemplary urban projects will be used to analyse the arguments relating to experiential value used by designers and stakeholders. Although Lynch's terminology is not used literally – these designs are discussed in a very direct language – it will become clear that the experiential value of these projects is fully covered by Lynch's subdimensions of 'sense' and related concepts from Kaplan and Cooper. Conversely, the cases we present will also clarify these theoretical concepts.

The cases are Ville-Port in Saint-Nazaire, France, the master plan for the public space 'Gentse Torenrij' (Ghent Towers), Belgium, and the structural plan for the redevelopment of the station area in Roeselare, also in Belgium. They were chosen because of the powerful arguments put forward by the designers and other actors involved, particularly in relation to the aspects covered by 'sense' as a dimension of performance. The first case has been implemented and is extensively documented in publications. The other two have not yet been implemented at the time of writing but the design process or a phase of it has been completed. The information is based on first-hand accounts of the design processes, in which one of the authors was involved in her capacity as a professional designer and coach.

SAINT-NAZAIRE

For the Ville-Port project in Saint-Nazaire (planning and implementation 1997–2000), Manuel de Solà developed a planning strategy for the redevelopment of a run-down industrial area between the town centre and the 'Bassin de Saint-Nazaire' (Figure 6.1). This area was the heart of the town before World War II. It was home to the east–west oriented main road towards the quay used by transatlantic steamboats to South America. The building of a huge German submarine base on the quayside cut off Saint-Nazaire from its vital artery, the River Loire. The reconstruction after the town was destroyed by the Allies was no longer focused on the docks, but was structured around a new north–south axis between the station and the town hall. In the year 2000 the new urban district of Ville-Port recreated the link between Saint-Nazaire and the Loire (Figure 6.2). Publications about the project gave a convincing justification for the decisions made in the design process and expectations about how users would experience the space were made explicit. The project is structured around three ideas, according to the

Figure 6.1 The run-down industrial estate at the submarine base of Saint-Nazaire and the mouth of the Loire before reconversion. Source: Manuel de Solà-Morales and Dominique Macel in Confino and Seigneur (1999a: 21).

designer: 'The topographical option, the theme of memory and respect; and the ambiguity of certain spaces' (de Solà, quoted in Confino and Seigneur 1999b: 30).

These three ideas relate to the perception of 'Identity'. This is clear and straightforward with regard to the topographical option and the theme of memory. The Loire Valley and the docks can be perceived in many different ways in Saint-Nazaire. Gaps in the bunker allow the light to be seen reflected in the water of the dock, the promenade on the roof offers views over the mouth of the Loire, the harbour and the town, and the geological relief of the valley is emphasised through a series of descending squares. Inside the bunker, a covered public space brings walkers right up to the edge of the dock. From the town, people get a view of the impressive monumental bunker, which henceforth will form part of the identity of Saint-Nazaire.

The new urban district, however, also differentiates the 'Identity': 'My project does not claim to merge this district into the existing town, but to lend it a personality' (Solà, quoted in Confino and Seigneur 1999a: 23). The generic harbour

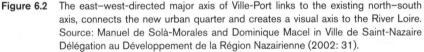

Figure 6.2   The east–west-directed major axis of Ville-Port links to the existing north–south
axis, connects the new urban quarter and creates a visual axis to the River Loire.
Source: Manuel de Solà-Morales and Dominique Macel in Ville de Saint-Nazaire
Délégation au Développement de la Région Nazairienne (2002: 31).

atmosphere benefits from the addition of various features: 'the leisure amenities,
the supermarket, the car parks, the open spaces etc. – all things which are not
found in the town centre' (de Solà, quoted in Confino and Seigneur 1999a: 23).
Within the base, a tourist attraction has been created that evokes the history of
the packet boat and Saint-Nazaire. A supermarket and a cinema complex, two
types of building that would traditionally have been located in the periphery, add
to the multi-functional facilities offered within the town centre and also confer a
benefit normally found only in the periphery, namely a large car park right in front
(Figure 6.3). The 'Identity' of the new urban district is characterised by ambiguity: harbour, periphery, but also centre (Confino and Seigneur 1999b: 30). The
addition of recognisable town centre activities and urban types of public space
and building gives this harbour area 'Congruence' with its special urban purpose
(Figure 6.4).

'A memorable physical setting reinforces a special event' (Lynch 1984: 133). In the new public spaces, major events are held that highlight the identity of Saint-Nazaire as a harbour town: major sailing competitions, festivities surrounding the launching of new cruise liners, art and music events. The activity and manifestation of a place can work together to define its character. 'The new public spaces have become ideal places to host all kinds of shows and major events linked to the "Identity" of the town, offering the base as a unique backdrop and the harbour

Figure 6.3   A car park and a supermarket, which one would normally expect to find on the periphery, define the ambiguous character of Ville-Port: harbour, periphery and centre in one. Source: Manuel de Solà-Morales in Confino and Seigneur (1999a: 23).

Figure 6.4   Urban types of public space and buildings create the scene for the new monument of Saint-Nazaire: the submarine base. Source: Manuel de Solà-Morales in Confino and Seigneur (1999a: 23).

creating a powerful contextual "Identity"' (Ville de Saint-Nazaire Délégation au Développement de la Région Nazairienne 2002: 37).

By addressing the 'Formal Structure', the project makes it possible to imagine the structure of the town in a different way. A new east–west-oriented pedestrian axis opens up the new urban district to the harbour and links to the existing north–south axis. The new *axe majeur* (major axis) follows the route of the former Avenue Principale that ran to the dock where the packet boats moored. Because of its physical manifestation (continuous public space, wide and long views of the monument) it can be considered of equal importance to the main north–south axis, and consequently becomes part of the town's primary access infrastructure. Just as the north–south axis makes visible the location of the station and the town hall, the *axe majeur* allows long-distance views (from the Maison du Peuple) to a new, important destination, the submarine base, and the docks and the Loire behind it.

This 'Formal Structure' is topographical in nature and transcends architectural preferences:

> The aim is to open up this town, from the Maison du Peuple to the Loire, and thus to transform its orientation by converting a longitudinal space into a transverse space. All the proposed changes tend to the same end: to excavate the four lobes of the base in order to create transparency right to the water, the superposition of the ramp and the accompanying facilities, the residential buildings etc.
>
> (de Solà, quoted in Confino and Seigneur 1999a: 21)

In the 'Formal Structure' the monumental submarine base serves as a beacon, as 'a reference element around which things happen' (Batteux, quoted in Confino and Seigneur 1999a: 26). 'It is staged within the neighbourhood and now once again has a façade towards the town: the back of the base has now become the main entrance to the harbour with its new activities' (Ville de Saint-Nazaire 2002: 33).

The actors realise that to make this order understandable, 'Transparency' and visual relationships are essential. Re-using a monumental building for new functions is not enough: it must also be made visible as a beacon within the town. The natural slope of the valley down to the Loire does not suffice: a 'direct visual relationship' between the town and the water and with the harbour activity is essential. 'The base has transformed the perception of the quiet slope down to the water. Making it transparent and providing access to its roof therefore conditions the urbanisation of this place' (de Solà, quoted in Confino and Seigneur 1999a: 22). This was done step by step. Making the roof of the base accessible with its breathtaking views of the harbour and the Loire, together with the placing of benches and a balustrade, were among the first interventions. 'Providing access to the roof makes it possible to convert this war machine into an attractive place, which is aesthetic thanks to the complexity and beauty of its structure' (de Solà, quoted in Confino and Seigneur 1999a: 23). This intervention gave residents and also visitors the opportunity to understand the renewal process taking place in Saint-Nazaire. By building the roof promenade, de Solà created the necessary touch of 'clarity and emotion' (Devillers, quoted in Confino and Seigneur 1999b: 29).

The term 'Transparency' used by Lynch, however, is broader than its architectural meaning. It also means making natural and social processes visible. This is achieved in Ville-Port by allowing the public space to offer views of activities at multiple different levels. The promenade on the roof of the submarine base offers an oblique view of the ceaseless, never-sleeping docks and shipbuilding activity with its shift-working timetable. The differences between the levels in the public space increase the likelihood that there will be 'visual linkages' between walkers on the sloping street and visitors parking in the lowest square, or with children playing in the middle square (Figure 6.5).

> These interlaced views merge the wealth and vitality of the urban space, the old Italian squares and the Parisian boulevards. Reciprocal glances and multiple viewpoints bring the space to life, which is vital because its dimensions and its very purpose render it harder and more peripheral.
>
> (de Solà, quoted in Confino and Seigneur 1999b: 29)

The way in which public spaces are arranged takes into account established user preferences. *Variation, complexity, extent and comfort* seek to persuade people to enter the bunker: 'kiosks prevent the space from being experienced as

Figure 6.5 The topography of the squares emphasises the valley relief and increases the chance of visual links between people walking on the sloping street and visitors in the car park. Source: Manuel de Solà-Morales in Confino and Seigneur (1999a: 25).

too huge and empty, while protecting against draughts' (de Solà, quoted in Confino and Seigneur 1999a: 23). The design details of a balustrade and benches on the roof promenade acquire urban relevance, capitalising on the visual asset of this place, the vast view over the Loire and the harbour (Cooper Marcus and Francis 1998):

> This parapet magnificently frames the horizon because it is unpolished, hazy, and it interacts with the grey of the concrete, the sky and the water. It has been designed to be very thin, but it continues through the landscape of the base. How can this be represented in an urban planning project? It is on such a different scale, and yet these things have such a strong significance and can completely change the way a landscape is read.
>
> (Devillers, quoted in Confino and Seigneur 1999a: 24)

The sloping road and the gaps in the submarine base add complexity to the clear 'axe majeur'. They invite the visitor in, without revealing everything at once. The interior of the submarine base is surprising: 'The base should become a mosque, a bazaar criss-crossed by little alleyways. It should lose its severity as a closed block and become a kind of secular cathedral that will be a pleasure to walk across' (de Solà, quoted in Ville de Saint-Nazaire 2002: 33) (Figure 6.6). In the words of Lynch: 'We want definable elements rather than defined ones, complex connections, regions remaining to be explored and some freedom to camouflage' (Lynch 1984: 143).

Figure 6.6   The public space in the interior of the submarine base surprises the visitor and adds complexity to the simple clarity of the main axis. Source: Manuel de Solà-Morales in Confino and Seigneur (1999a: 25).

Although de Solà did not refer to the aspect of 'Legibility' as a design theme, it is clear from a visit to the site that the public space that has been created and the buildings lend themselves well to communication, not so much by residents – there were no signs of people making their mark on the new blocks of flats – but for both commercial and official communication – the usual company signboards, well known from peripheral commercial centres, and the municipal flagpoles, which immediately make it clear that there is 'something' to experience here during the day. At night the 'artistic' lighting of the public space proclaims the same message.

The considerations of those involved in the Ville-Port project in Saint-Nazaire show that 'Significance' or conferring symbolic meaning was a fundamental driver of the project. In around 1980, when a deep crisis in the shipbuilding sector threatened to rob Saint-Nazaire, a town that was not attractive to tourists or as a residential centre, of its significance as an industrial town, the civic authorities looked for development strategies and visions of the future that would enhance the ability of the town to attract new investors. Although Saint-Nazaire is geographically a maritime town, the submarine base and abandoned harbour area prevented the town from having direct contact with the sea.

> What is the point of Saint-Nazaire if it is not to be a harbour? . . . We had to recognise this fundamental vocation, despite the submarine base and its impact on harbour activities, despite this wound in the town. . . . This may seem madness, but it was necessary to turn the town and people's heads back towards the sea.
>
> (Batteux, quoted in Pénot and Radu 1999: 6)

The new Ville-Port now acts as a mediator between the town, the harbour and the mouth of the Loire.

The desire to bring the town back into contact with the harbour and the water raised the issue of whether or not to demolish the bunker. The arguments that were used in favour of keeping the bunker show that the mayor ascribed major *symbolic* significance to the bunker and the new urban manifestation of Saint-Nazaire.

> The heart of Saint-Nazaire is here, on this transatlantic quayside, which gave the town its meaning. Because the base was built there, the reconstruction has turned the town on its axis by 90 degrees; to destroy the base would be to eliminate this new meaning . . . urban development is not a reversible phenomenon; ruined cities can be reborn but without recovering their former state, and what has been done cannot be completely undone. . . . Our cathedral is the harbour and the base.
>
> (Batteux, quoted in Confino and Seigneur 1999a: 26)

ROESELARE (ROULERS)

In Roeselare, the station square, the bus station and the railway station lack the
convenience and the character to be recognised as town centre functions. A utili-
tarian railway viaduct and chaotic traffic movements in the vicinity of the station
form a mental and physical obstruction between the town centre and the suburban district of 'Krottegem' (literally 'Slum Town'), which is seen as unattractive.
The project to redevelop the station area is intended to simplify and smooth out
the traffic flow, give the station square the profile of a central town square and
improve the convenience of the railway and bus stations. In addition, there is a
strategic objective: to upgrade Krottegem through better integration of the neighbourhood in the town. The 'Roeselare Central' project created by the Belgian
railways design agency, the town and the public transport companies was sub-
mitted to the Flemish urban policy authority for a grant in 2007. The urban policy
jury criticised the proposal and offered the town a concept subsidy programme. In
the course of such a programme the town can improve the quality of the project.
The design agency, uapS, is using this intensive and interactive design process
to rework the 'structure sketch' outline for the redevelopment of the station area
in Roeselare, paying special attention to developing arguments for a richer experiential quality.

    To this end the project is seen in the wider context of the urban landscape.
The station square, together with the canal head, the 'Ronde kom' (a former flax
ret basin, now an urban pond) and the 'Grote Bassin' (great basin), belong to
a series of open spaces with landscape potential (Figure 6.7). Their large scale
contrasts with the surrounding small-scale urban fabric. Most of these open
spaces are surrounded by buildings, which are more prominent and taller than
the usual building block fabric. This statement provides insight into the 'Identity'
of Roeselare and is a decisive feature of the new project. It is a justification for
maintaining the large-scale image of the station square (De Meulder and Goethals 2008; Goethals 2009).

    The station area forms part of an elongated railway and canal landscape
with green embankments, railway tracks, goods yards and silos. The new public spaces within the station area are conceived as part of this green picture:
a wider embankment to the south (which further highlights the natural railway
landscape), trees in the station square and a park/campus on the northern goods
yard. Two tower blocks accompany the silos of the canal head to form part of
the Roeselare skyline (Figure 6.8). At the same time they benefit from the view
over the landscape described earlier. Thanks to a new programme (dwellings in
a parkland setting created from a former goods yard and dwellings and shops on
the square, a renewed and convenient public transport hub) and greater cohesion of the public space, this landscape is no longer a fracture through the town,

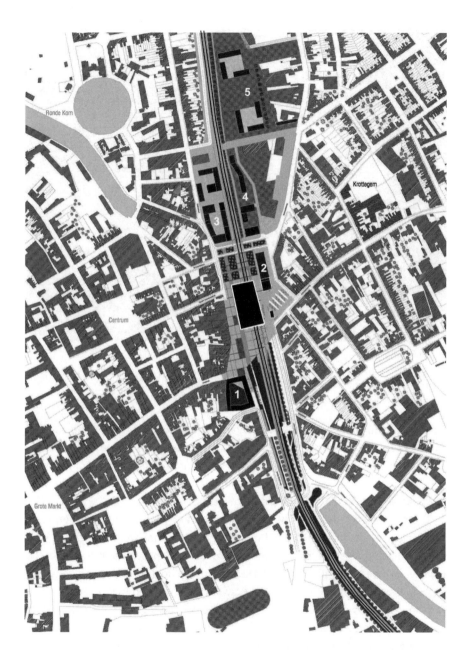

Figure 6.7 The area around the station is being integrated into the railway and canal landscape of green embankments, railway tracks, goods yards and silos. The expansive station square, together with the canal head and the round basin, form a series of open spaces with landscape potential. Source: uapS (2008).

Figure 6.8   Two massive tower blocks on the station square provide context for the canal head silos in the skyline of Roeselare. Source: uapS (2008).

but it has become a recognisable destination that creates order on the scale of 'Greater Roeselare' and a breath of fresh air (extent) for the surrounding smaller-scale fabric of building blocks. The large-scale landscape layer becomes more coherent. The town's capacity for orientation is improved, the 'Formal Structure' of Roeselare is clarified, and its 'Identity' is reinforced.

The new design reduces the number of access routes to the station area, which also results in an improved 'Formal Structure' on two different levels of scale. On an urban scale this intervention creates a simplified traffic layout for the town as a whole. The rather technical solution of the double dogbone roundabout for road traffic from the first structural drawing is remodelled to create an avenue with an elongated square as its central reservation, so that over its entire length the station square can function as a 'hyphen' between Krottegem and the centre (Figure 6.9). Just as in Saint-Nazaire, the actors understand the importance of visual relationships. Transparent links from the shopping street to the new shopping centre in the station complex and to the bus station benefit the functioning of the various activities within the station area.

If the station square is to be experienced as a central urban square, there is a need to work on 'Congruence'. This oversized square is more reminiscent of an

Figure 6.9   An urban avenue, with an elongated square as the central reservation, leads from Krottegem to the new station square. Source: uapS (2008).

urban periphery than a central town square. This is due to the profusion of car parks, the advertising signboards, the residual vegetation, the traffic jams, the bicycles parked at random and a small supermarket. All that is left for pedestrians is a patchwork of repeatedly altered residual spaces. By creating interplay between a number of different design elements, the designers have sought to alter the perception of this space fundamentally. Because of the typological choice for this building programme, this open space within the town becomes recognisable as a central town square. In the north there will be two rows of large building blocks with green inner courtyards. With their commercial ground-floor levels they clearly and recognisably mark out the limits of an urban square. By emphasising parts of the space – a hard-landscaped square, a grassy square and a square for buses – the extensive square generates a *variety* of atmospheres and uses without destroying the large-scale experience of the square as a whole.

GHENT

With the redevelopment of the adjacent Korenmarkt and Braunplein central city squares in 1998, the Ghent city administration intended to reinforce both the retail function and tourism. Braunplein, an undefined, featureless parking area, dominated by newly exposed historic buildings, was to become a fully fledged urban square. The winning design for Braunplein of Robbrecht & Daem and Van Hee provided for a small park, the 'Green', in this city centre area, which had been completely hard surfaced until now. A referendum among the population showed that they lacked green space in the city centre; in this area focused on shopping and tourism, there was a desire for 'Transparency' of natural processes. The merit of the designers was that they found a compatible form for a green space in this place with a strong historical overlay: a sunken church garden, significant as a reference to the former churchyard, generating 'Identity' for the renewed centre.

In 2007 the city administration, the city council and the public transport company agreed to stop providing public transport stops at Korenmarkt, but to site them in Cataloniëstraat instead (Figure 6.10). This would create more space on

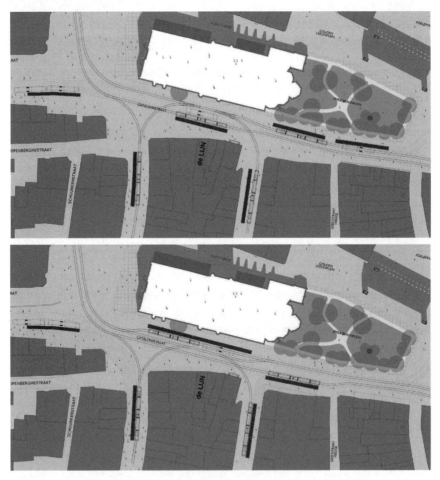

Figure 6.10 Above: Configuration of public transport stops as initially desired by the city council, administration and public transport company. Below: Configuration of public transport stops after negotiation by design. Source: Robbrecht et al. (2007).

Korenmarkt for pavement cafes and events. Within this framework the designers developed a master plan for redeveloping the squares and adjacent streets. However, the proposed configuration of bus/tram stops would have made it less safe for cyclists and for pedestrians crossing Cataloniëstraat. The configuration was confusing and would have interrupted the views of the famous towers. There was barely any space left for pavement cafes in Cataloniëstraat and the tram and bus stops would cause noise and odour pollution in the sunken 'Green'. To resolve these drawbacks, the designers worked on alternative sites for the configuration of stops. In the end a good compromise was reached, which was set out and justified in the master plan (Figure 6.10). Once again the arguments brought forward during the workshops and the final master plan made use of assumptions about how the new public space would affect the behaviour and experience of users.

A number of interventions were intended to make the 'Identity' of this historic place more obviously perceptible. By erecting a new City Hall on Braunplein the designers were seeking to correct the relationship between the overly expansive, featureless space and the surrounding façades. That would restore the more small-scale character it had had before the historic monuments were exposed. The smaller historic squares that had been amalgamated to form a larger area would then once again emerge.

Two tall contemporary columns on Korenmarkt are intended to make visitors aware of the north–south axis of the square, thus making clear the 'Formal Structure' of Ghent city centre (Figure 6.11). The columns were designed to emphasise that the majestic east–west axis of the famous spires on Korenmarkt is crossed by a second important north–south development axis running through the city. These contemporary structures also reinforce the 'identity' by referring to the history of the place, namely the presence of a large and small Korenmarkt, and to the local tradition of erecting obelisks in city squares (Robbrecht et al. 2007).

The public space around the towers consists of a cluster of squares. The idea of giving these squares a distinctive character when redeveloping them (green or hard surfaces, intimate or busy) was a response to the needs of visitors to orientate themselves and to people's preferences for public spaces with variation in textures, colours and atmospheres and differences in level (Robbrecht et al. 2007). With a wide low wall around the 'Green' the designers were seeking to offer the 'comfort' needed for enjoyment. This natural stone plinth would serve simultaneously as a bench, a step and a protection against the bustle of the city. Nevertheless, this design feature was not sufficient to create the 'other, intimate world' that was intended. Creating distance between the 'Green' and the disruptive bus and tram stops was therefore the main aim of the negotiation design of the master plan. The same applied to the creation of a direct visual link from the north–south shopping axis.

Figure 6.11 Two contemporary pillars make clear that the majestic east–west axis of the famous series of towers is being crossed at Korenmarkt square by a north–south growth axis in the city. Source: Robbrecht *et al.* (2007).

DESIGN PROCESS: INDISPENSABLE FOR SPECIFYING AND SHARING BASIC TERMS

In the three cases we can recognise the basic terms for experiential quality that have been conceived as dimensions of performance. Each of them has been expressed in a very specific way, which is different in each case. Clarity about the way the stakeholders want to define these terms in the context of specific strategic projects has emerged through a design process. In the last part of this chapter we will look at the way in which project-specific shared terms for spatial quality, and more specifically for experiential value, come into being and the vital role that design processes play in this. We will do this on the basis of a literature survey and the observation of design processes, more specifically the cases of Roeselare and Ghent.[1]

Using Lynch's dimensions of performance, it is possible to manage the process of defining the quality of a specific project and to ensure that all perspectives required for a sustainable and socially innovative developing community are considered. When formulating specific projects, a specific impetus to create the desired spatial quality usually already exists: the personal wishes of actors, but also existing views on its incorporation in a wider urban whole (e.g. structural drawings/plans) and lists of planning requirements at larger or smaller scales (lack of green space, need for training centres, strengthening the local economy, traffic problems and public transport, adding to the housing stock, public space and facilities on offer, etc.). This information shapes the contours of 'Vitality', 'Fit' and 'Access'.

The situation is different when it comes to the 'Sense' dimension of performance. 'Sensorial and atmospheric issues' usually appear in the process only once a designer starts to work (Schreurs 2007: 330). For many actors the content of the abstract concept is unclear at the beginning of a process. Parameters such as this are difficult to express simply in words. Design is indispensable in order to give a project-specific meaning to the basic terms. Not only does this direct attention towards the 'sensorial and atmospheric issues', but also insights into the possibilities inherent in the current and future physical setting of the project may bring to light contradictions and enhance or alter the presupposed needs: all dimensions of spatial quality can be influenced by research by design.

IMAGING, PRESENTING, TESTING AND THE CONCEPTUAL SHIFT

In 'inquiry by design' the sociologist John Zeisel, who focused on environment behaviour research, argues in favour of the indispensable role that designers play in defining spatial quality. Zeisel is primarily thinking about the social and psychological needs of users, in other words needs that largely coincide with Lynch's 'Sense' dimension of performance. According to Zeisel, imaging, the graphic mode of thought and expression inherent in design, is fundamental in these processes. 'Designers use "image information" heuristically as an empirical source for basic cognitive design decisions' (Zeisel 2006: 25). To answer questions such as 'What do teenagers define as their neighbourhoods in suburban areas?' or 'What do people consider to be a central square?' they use personal experiences and mental images of squares, urban districts, residential neighbourhoods that they know and love. 'Image information conveys a feeling or a mood of some environment' (Zeisel 2006: 19, 25, 49).

Designers make their ideas visible so that they and others can evaluate and develop them further. By making sketches, plans, models or photographs they express their mental images to the outside world so that they are open to debate.

Evaluations, confrontations, reflections are all types of test that will follow the presentation. 'After presenting a design idea in any form, designers step back and examine their products with a critical eye, sometimes in groups, sometimes alone' (Zeisel 2006: 26). Many different criteria can be imagined for this testing process:

Design testing means comparing tentative presentations against an array of information like the designer's and the clients' implicit images, explicit information about constraints or objectives, degrees of internal design consistency, and performance criteria – economic, technical, sociological, and neurological. . . . Critically analyzing tentative design responses and adding new information can progressively improve designs, testing is essential to design as inquiry.

(Zeisel 2006: 26)

This gives rise to a cycle of three basic activities, 'imaging, presenting and testing', which is repeated over and over again.

One interesting feature of Zeisel's point of view is that he sees the contribution and influence of other actors involved in the project as an essential component of the design process. The constructive attitude among those actors that is necessary for this is, however, highly dependent on how well the designers – and other actors – are able to substantiate their requirements and design decisions. 'Making tacit attributes of design explicit through testing helps designers re-image and re-present their designs with greater precision' (Schon 1974, in Zeisel 2006: 27). As was stated in the first part of this chapter, only an effective line of argument for design decisions, based on the dimensions of performance expected by users, can make the actors involved 'knowledgeable participants' (Zeisel 2006: 59).

By testing and providing 'test information', concepts of what the final product will be may change, both in the minds of designers and for the other actors. Zeisel refers to this process of alteration and adaptation of concepts as 'conceptual shift'. Using this new information and altered insights, the designers (and the actors) embark on the next cycle of 're-imaging, presenting and testing'. To achieve this, 'backtracking to adjust earlier decisions' is necessary. 'Backtracking is an integral part of design. The spiral metaphor indicates this activity' (Zeisel 2006: 30) (Figure 6.12).

Through testing, contradictions will come to light. In the iterative design cycle these are replaced by syntheses. Actors and designers adjust their opinions. Thanks to conceptual shifts and the integration of conflicting demands in the design, the stakeholders will successfully share project-specific terms. Design concepts visualise the shared terms that are specific to a particular project.

This design activity – exploring the potential of the site, (re-)formulating the vision for the spatial development, finding out the demands in terms of spatial quality shared by those involved including the experiential value – is referred to in the literature using terms such as 'design research', 'negotiated design', 'research by design' and 'negotiating by design'.

We see research by design as a process of collective deliberation, in which the participants (citizens, experts, administrators) try to understand each other and the

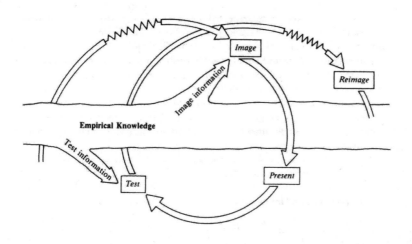

Figure 6.12 Design development spiral. Source: Zeisel (2006).

problem situation more fully by getting to know each other and persuading each other. Ideally a learning community should emerge that can solve problems collectively. Effective planning then means more than rationally persuading people; it also has to do with building up a common narrative and a shared history.

(Hajer *et al.* 2006: 23)

In what follows, it will be shown through observation of the design processes in the projects described above in Roeselare and Ghent that the combination of the visualisation of possible manifestations of the project and verbal description of their expected performances may open up new possibilities to the actors during the process of determining quality, and can help them to gain a better insight into their interests and at the same time to think in a co-productive way (Loeckx *et al.* 2009: 262).

In both design processes the designers and the other actors, mainly representatives of various government bodies such as traffic authorities, heritage authorities, economics, youth services, festivities and architectural policy, and public transport companies, were good at formulating criticisms and presenting arguments for alternatives. This becomes clear from the analysis of their arguments earlier in this chapter. They also took on the ideas of the other actors that had proven their worth. They stimulated dialogue on every new design variant. They produced images on which the actors could indicate specific problems, so that both the designers and the other actors kept pace with each other in acquiring new insights. When it came to formulating experiential qualities, the designers were by far the dominant force, but they did succeed in having the importance of these qualities recognised by the other stakeholders so that they ended up forming part of the shared quality terms.

ROESELARE

The design process for Roeselare Central took place in three phases, each of which resulted in a new design variant after progress had been made in the way quality was defined. During workshops the designers showed analyses of the urban landscape, proposals for traffic flows, concepts for the station square, variants in the form of models according to the agreed number of development rights, etc. The actors involved actively participated in forming these ideas. They encouraged new lines of thought and presented arguments to explain why other options were less advisable.

After a first phase that involved four successive cycles of imaging, presenting and testing, the designers exhibited design variant 1. This was no longer a commercial ribbon but a wide square promoting exchanges between Krottegem and Roeselare centre. A complicated traffic structure with a double dogbone roundabout and a tunnel, which according to the 'image information' from the designers failed to fit in with the intended metamorphosis from a station square to a central town square, had vanished. To avoid dividing up the large square too much, the footprint of the existing station was retained. Commercial development, which the first structural plan expected to occur in the station extension, was accommodated in the new buildings surrounding the square.

Invited by the mayor, who chaired the working group, the design agency from the railway company (which owns the vast majority of the land involved in this project and for which the integration of shops in station complexes is a lucrative development) evaluated design variant 1 in the form of a 'counter project', design variant 2. The presentation made it clear that the railway company design agency wished to see commercial development incorporated in the station building, since its experience with earlier projects had shown that retail outlets integrated in a single cluster with a station enjoy significant success. The other ideas from the new structural drawing, the large square, the scrapping of the tunnel and double dogbone roundabout, the typology of the residential and office development, the idea of making the railway landscape more coherent, etc., were accepted. This shows that these actors had undergone a conceptual shift. In particular, their acceptance that the scale of the urban landscape is a decisive element of the design is remarkable, since this quality transcends the interests that are directly involved – public transport, shops and even enhancing the status of Krottegem.

Nevertheless, design variant 2 was criticised: the distance between the new shopping complex and the existing shopping street was too great. The mayor therefore asked the designers of the first design variant to develop a design variant in the third phase that would integrate the positive aspects of design variants 1 and 2. After these cycles of imaging, presenting and testing it emerged from the arguments supporting the third design variant that they had also undergone a 'conceptual shift'. They had revised their earlier design decision not to provide any shopping expansion in the station building (backtracking). They moved the station back to the shopping street and increased the area of the station, albeit only in the long axis so that the large square was retained, articulated as a sequence of subsquares. The concept of the continuous commercial ribbon was reconciled with the concept of the large square between Krottegem and the town centre. The design process resulted in a 'both–and narrative'.

GHENT

Since the location chosen for public transport stops impaired the atmosphere of the 'Green' on Braunplein, the designers used three cycles of imaging, presenting and testing to develop alternative proposals for the stops. Although this was not to the liking of the city administration and the public transport company, the latter provided increasingly accurate information (test information) in each presentation on the configuration of the stops, because their representatives were able to indicate and clarify specific errors in the plans (making tacit attributes explicit). The main purpose of this clarification was that buses or trams stationary at their stops must not impede a tram or bus with different stops.

During the presentation of the second variant the city administration asked to suspend the process of looking for alternatives. The designers did, however, continue their attempts to optimise the chosen variant. This resulted in a third design variant with a good public transport flow combined with a quiet atmosphere in the 'Green', an easily understandable configuration of stops and improved safety for cyclists and pedestrians. It was only after this solution had been found, making the design acceptable to them, that the designers made the conceptual shift that was imposed upon them at the beginning of the design process. The others, for their part, recognised that the new design variant had been enriched by including experiential qualities that had previously appeared unachievable.

ORGANISATION OF THE DESIGN PROCESS

In complex projects such as strategic urban projects the cycle of imaging, presenting and testing needs to be organised. It is important to facilitate testing, information exchange and conceptual shifts in order to arrive at well-considered, shared, project-specific terms. In both the processes that were observed, a good consultation structure provided for multiple bilateral and plenary workshops for the actors. To this end additional design expertise was added to that of the actors who took part in the previous stages of the project.

The imaging–presenting–testing cycles that bring about the conceptual shifts among the actors and which are required to achieve the desired consensus are directed by designers. The role of a consensus builder, however, is equally crucial. The consensus builder polls each actor for his/her evaluation after each cycle, formulates a conclusion and summarises new tasks and project aims. In Roeselare this was the mayor, who as chairman of the working group and steering group ensured that the process of enrichment did not succumb to practical difficulties such as impingement on timetables of current tender contracts and subsidy processes. Since there was the prospect of a subsidy from the government of Flanders, the actors involved in the preliminary process were more willing to listen. In Ghent this role had been delegated less clearly, but the consensus-building tasks were carried out both by the head of the city administration and by the design team whose authority is widely recognised.

In Ghent the design variant on which consensus was reached was immediately followed by implementation plans. In Roeselare, however, the implementation process is more complicated and drawn out. However successful the process has been, it does not yet offer a guarantee of a successful completion in which all of the objectives that have been set out are actually implemented. To prevent agreed qualities from being eroded during subsequent phases of the project it is necessary to maintain the information that has been acquired and to understand the dimensions of performance which underlie design decisions. It is therefore recommended that the actors should continue to be involved in subsequent phases of the project, for example in the form of a quality committee on which the parties involved in the research through design are represented. Keeping the results of research by design within the process is equally important (Schreurs 2007), for example by appending them as an explanatory memorandum to legal documents. Further detailed work on constituent projects that is carried out by newly involved actors and designers may give rise to new processes of collective quality determination.

CONCLUSION

Lynch's list of five 'dimensions of performance' (Lynch 1984), supplemented by concepts from environment behaviour research, integrates and gives structure to all the different approaches to the quality of space that a sustainably developing society should seek to achieve. It can also furnish a basis for the much-needed shared understanding of spatial quality within a specific project. By defining quality on the basis of dimensions of performance, the needs and requirements of users become visible and 'designers' options' are not restricted. These dimensions of performance are formulated in each individual project in both specific and concrete terms, although we can still recognise the general basic terms used by Lynch.

Although spatial quality is wider than experiential quality, it is the dimensions of performance associated with the latter that are most difficult to formulate. Without design work and the associated imaginative capacity these concepts will not become available to support the dialogue between actors. Designers must be able to argue effectively, using words and images, which dimensions of experiential quality they consider important and why. The aim is to make explicit as many 'tacit attributes' as possible. As a result of this they are opened up for the other parties who are then involved in the design process on an equal footing. They can now intervene and respond, resulting in successive design cycles being started until agreement is reached. These cycles require the participants to undergo conceptual shifts in which they revise their opinions and expand their understanding. These shifts are essential for all parties concerned, both the designers and the other stakeholders. To ensure that this takes place effectively, the design process needs a suitable organisational form, in which the development of a consensus will be assured. Good design processes deliver high levels of experiential quality, transcending the more obvious interests of those involved. Conflicting interests are not watered down to a grey result, but are integrated within a both–and narrative.

NOTE

1   Marleen Goethals has been able to observe the design processes from close quarters, in Roeselare as Flemish urban policy adviser and in Ghent as a member of the design team.

BIBLIOGRAPHY

Carmona, M. (2001) 'Sustainable urban design – a possible agenda', in A. Layard et al. (ed.) Planning for a Sustainable Future, London: Spon Press.

Carmona, M. and Sieh, L. (2004) Measuring Quality in Planning. Managing the Performance Process, London: Spon Press.

Confino, F. and Seigneur, F. (1999a) 'Confiance, créativité et réalisme pour un projet précurseur', Projet Urbain, 17: 20–28.

Confino, F. and Seigneur, F. (1999b) 'Manuel de Solà: un peu de clarté et d'émotion', Projet Urbain, 17: 29–30.

Cooper Marcus, C. and Francis, C. (1998) *People Places: Design Guidelines for Urban Open Space*, 2nd edn, New York: John Wiley & Sons.

De Meulder, B. and Goethals, M. (2008) *Conceptsubsidie Stadsvernieuwingsproject 'Roeselare Centraal': Projectdefinitie Ontwerpend Onderzoek*, Brussels: Ministerie van de Vlaamse Gemeenschap Agentschap voor Binnenlands Bestuur Team Stedenbeleid.

Euro Immo Star (2006) 'Herinrichting stationsomgeving Roeselare', Report of the designated master plan, Roeselare.

Goethals, M. (2009) 'Debate by design: rethinking the station square', in A. Loeckx (ed.) *Framing Urban Renewal in Flanders*, Amsterdam: SUN.

Hajer, M., Sijmons, D. and Feddes, F. (2006) 'Inleiding: De politiek van het ontwerp', in M. Hajer and D. Sijmons (eds) *Een plan dat werkt. Ontwerp en politiek in de regionale planvorming*, Rotterdam: NAi Uitgevers.

Jacobs, M. H. (2000) *Kwaliteit leefomgeving, Kennisontwikkeling*, Wageningen: Alterra, Research Instituut voor de Groene Ruimte.

Kaplan, R., Kaplan, S. and Ryan, R. (1998) *With People in Mind. Design and Management of Everyday Nature*, Washington, DC: Island Press.

Loeckx, A. (2007) 'Urban policy and projects in flanders, reviewing the project mode', in J. Van den Broeck (ed.) *Isocarp World Congress Special Bulletin*, Antwerp: ISOCARP.

Loeckx, A., De Meulder, B., Boudry, L., Martens, M., Borret, K., De Wever, H., De Bruyn, J. and Patteeuw, V. (2009) 'Ten considerations regarding urban projects and concept grants', in A. Loeckx (ed.) *Framing Urban Renewal in Flanders*, Amsterdam: SUN.

Lynch, K. (1984) *Good City Form*, Cambridge, MA: MIT Press.

Ministerie van de Vlaamse Gemeenschap Agentschap voor Binnenlands Bestuur Team Stedenbeleid (2007) *Conceptsubsidie Stadsvernieuwingsproject 'Roeselare Centraal': Beoordelingsfiche*, Brussels: Ministerie van de Vlaamse Gemeenschap Agentschap voor Binnenlands Bestuur Team Stedenbeleid.

Pénot, G. and Radu, V. (1999) 'Le sens de la ville', *Projet Urbain*, 17: 4–10.

Reijndorp, A., Truijens, B., Nio, I., Visser, H. and Kompier, V. (1998) *De kern van het ruimtelijk beleid. Een onderzoek naar het begrip ruimtelijke kwaliteit*, The Hague: Wetenschappelijke Raad voor het Regeringsbeleid.

Robbrecht, P. en Daem, H., Van Hee, M. J., Technum (2007) 'Masterplan Torenrij Gent', Report of the designated master plan, Ghent.

Schreurs, J. (2005) 'Denkkader voor ruimtelijke kwaliteit. Over de inzetbaarheid van indicatoren', in M. *Geldof, K. Laenen, J. Schreurs, K. Stuyven, M. Van Loon, F. Vanhaverbeke, T. Vannuffelen, and P. Vermeulen* (eds) *Ruimtelijke kwaliteit aan de kust. Indicatoren voor de ruimtelijke kwaliteit van de publieke ruimte en de architectuur aan de kust*, Brussels: Vlaamse Gemeenschap.

Schreurs, J. (2007) Communicating quality: Words and images'. Paper for Quality Conference at the Welsh School of Architecture, Cardiff, 4–6 July 2007.

Stad Roeselare and Pillaert, D. (2007) *Aanvraagformulier voor ondersteuning van stadsvernieuwingsprojecten 3de Oproep*, Roeselare: Stad Roeselare.

Technum (2006) 'Korenmarkt – Cataloniëstraat nota aanvullende locatiestudie, mogelijke scenario's en voorontwerpen', location study report, Ghent.

uapS (2008) Masterplan for Roeselare Centraal, Roeselare.

Urban Design Associates (2003) *The Urban Design Handbook. Techniques and Working Methods*, New York: W. W. Norton.

Ville de Saint-Nazaire Délégation au Développement de la Région Nazairienne (2002) 'Marché de définition de Ville-Port Petit-Maroc', Project definition for design competition, Saint-Nazaire.

Waldheim, C. (2006) 'Landscape as urbanism', in C. Waldheim (ed.) *The Landscape Urbanism Reader*, New York: Princeton Architectural Press.

Zeisel, J. (2006) *Inquiry by Design*, New York: W. W. Norton.

CHAPTER 7

TRANSCENDING BOUNDARIES

DESIGN AS A MEDIUM FOR INTEGRATION IN THE 'RURBAN' LANDSCAPE

ELKE VANEMPTEN

INTRODUCTION

For a long time the area on the boundary between the urban and the rural was 'planning's last frontier' (Jed Griffiths in Gallent *et al*. 2004), but from the beginning of the 1990s spatial planners and designers increasingly focused more attention on what will be called here the 'rurban' condition. This hybrid spatial condition developed from tendencies such as suburbanization, relocation of industry to the outskirts of the city and the construction of extensive mobility networks. Nowadays, peripheral development is widely discussed in the literature, reflecting a growing consciousness about the various challenges posed by this 'rurbanity' (Hidding 2006; van den Brink *et al*. 2006; Hoggart 2005; Gallent *et al*. 2006). One of the main points of discussion revolves around the issue of 'integration', more particularly the integration of different land uses and functions in rurban spaces. Van den Brink and colleagues (2006: 147), for instance, indicate that the traditional rural–urban opposition has been replaced by a metropolitan landscape that reflects 'the integration of built-up and non-built-up distinctively urban and rural land uses'. In these rurban metropolitan landscapes, scarcity of space and attempts to reinforce the economic basis of agriculture led to the creation of a broader perspective on the combination of land uses and functions such as nature, landscape and agriculture (Hidding 2006: 241). However, this closer integration of multiple land uses and functions implies that a whole range of actors (farmers, entrepreneurs, local residents, urban recreants, policy-makers, etc.) with different visions and interests are involved in different ways in the transformation of the rurban landscape. To achieve coherent outcomes, therefore, especially within the frame of strategic projects, it seems essential to create partnerships between these actors (Gallent *et al*. 2006). Since planning and design are collective activities aimed at (re)developing space in a sustainable and qualitative way by establishing interrelations between the different activities and networks in an area (Healey 2004), managing the complexity of change (Gallent *et al*. 2006), and dealing with 'the presence of one or more actors pursuing various divergent and often clashing objectives that follow different rationales' (Sartorio 2005: 27), the problem of integration of different land uses and actors in rurban areas is of real concern. For Albrechts (2006), the concept of integration is a fundamental principle of planning and urbanism. However, despite its centrality, it has been explored to only a limited degree in spatial planning and design theory (De Boe *et al.* 1999; Healey 2006; Kidd 2007).

This chapter examines the meaning and significance of integration in a condition of rurbanity from a planning perspective, with a focus on spatial design as the basis of many planning activities.[1] First I develop a definition of integration in strategic projects, using Albrechts' work in particular and the place focus suggested by Healey. Then I move on to explore methods of place-based integration, using the proposition that design is well positioned as a medium for integration because it uses space as its 'raw material'. Following Massey, space is considered here as 'open, multiple and relational, unfinished and always becoming' (Massey 2005: 59, 61) and hence harbouring an important potential for integration. Design, I then go on to argue, is particularly well adapted to the exploration of the multiplicities and relationalities inherent in space and to the interaction with a multitude of actors (Sternberg 2000; Lang 1994, 2005). Design can build upon these features to generate the substance of a project, starting from what is present in socio-spatial reality (cf. Mandanipour 1997). I then assess this argument about the integrative potential of design through two contrasting case studies that aim to establish a peri-urban park: Parkbos in Belgium and Parc de la Deûle in France. Finally, I conclude that an intelligent design strategy can indeed play a role in bringing about meaningful integration and offer a possibility/method for a more action-oriented strategic planning, which could improve spatial quality and thus liveability.

DESIGNING RURBAN REALITY: THE QUEST FOR INTEGRATION

The diffuse condition resulting from the geographical expansion of the traditional, compact and clearly delimited city has been examined at great length. A broad range of concepts have been proposed to capture this scattered condition: the *città diffusa* of Francesco Indovina (1990), the *middle landscape* of Peter Rowe (1992), the *sprawl* concept used by, amongst others, Robert Bruegmann (2005), the *vernacular landscape* of John Brinckerhoff Jackson (1984), the *Zwischenstadt* of Thomas Sieverts (2003), the *rurban* area (Bauer and Roux 1976),[2] the *nevelstad* (Borret 2002), and so on. Although these concepts emerged from different national and regional contexts, they all address a similar condition of spatial fragmentation on a regional scale, a variety of urban and rural functions and land uses in close proximity to each other, and all within a highly dynamic and rapidly changing environment. Furthermore, they symbolize the loss of validity of spatial boundaries between city and countryside, and institutional boundaries between sectors and policy fields. These similarities suggest the ubiquity of the rurban condition and, more importantly, its potential; it stimulates us to transcend institutional and spatial boundaries, to act as a real-life laboratory for integration through the use of contemporary planning and design methods. The goal of this chapter is not to describe this rurban condition extensively but to focus on the challenges and opportunities it poses. Sieverts (2003), for instance, claims that designing the open areas in urbanized environments is one of the most important tasks for spatial planning, as these will become the stabilizing frame of the *Zwischenstadt* in the future (e.g. Emscher Park). The emergence of a post-industrial/post-urban landscape that reaches out far beyond the boundaries of the compact nineteenth-century city, and which encompasses a wholly different socio-spatial context, does indeed require specifically adapted development concepts, styles and paradigms. The (re)development, design and management of these *Zwischenstadt/* rurban landscapes therefore constitute a relatively new task for planning and design, one that puts integration at the centre (Jirku 2007; Gallent *et al.* 2006).

INTEGRATION IN SPATIAL PLANNING AND DESIGN

Albrechts *et al.* (1999: 71) consider integration as central to strategic spatial planning and define it as the pursuit of solutions in which different land uses and functions are integrated in such a way that each can gain from the development of the others and so produce some kind of 'added value', for example improved spatial quality or social innovation. Just as Albrechts and colleagues define a 'functional type' of integration, the majority of the spatial planning and design literature also treats specific aspects of integration, mainly institutional integration (Counsell *et al.* 2006; Healey 2006; Allmendinger 2003) or spatial integration (Brandt and Vejre 2004; De Boe *et al.* 1999). Brandt and Vejre (2004: 21), for instance, describe multi-functionality as the integration of different functions in the same unit of land at the same. Healey elaborates on the integrative role of the planning system addressed by both Albrechts (2006) and Kidd (2007: 161). Integration is defined as a relational activity that implies some kind of synergistic linkage and interconnection. Furthermore, Healey draws attention to the potential of place focus in integration by arguing that 'the advocacy of the role of the planning system in "joining up" diverse governance initiatives rests on the idea that "territory", "place" and "spatial organisation" have some particular value as a focus of attention in the "search for integration"' (Healey 2006: 64). According to her, planning has a key role to play in integration given its capacity to 'integrate disparate policies and strategies around a place focus' (Healey 2006: 65; see also Gallent *et al.* 2006; van den Brink *et al.* 2006).

Pursuing Healey's argument, it is essential to include a place focus in defining the meaning of integration in planning and design. For instance, actors from different backgrounds and with different interests and motivations confront each other within the framework of a strategic spatial project because they all have potentially conflicting spatial claims concerning the same place, and hence inevitably have to negotiate and collaborate. Amin (2004) refers to this inevitability as 'the politics of propinquity'. His general observation on space applies to rurban areas in particular: 'different microworlds find themselves on the same proximate turf . . . the pull on turf in different directions and different interests needs to be actively managed and negotiated, because there is no other turf' (Amin 2004: 39). In other words, space juxtaposes different 'microworlds' (uses of space, functions, activities, etc.) and, hence, especially where there is limited availability of high-quality space, forces different actors to enter into dialogue and negotiation in order to integrate these microworlds and their activities in a sufficiently productive way. When redeveloping space within the framework of a project, the land involved is clearly demarcated and its different microworlds can be unfolded and identified. In ideal circumstances, each microworld is represented by an actor with particular interests. The juxtaposition of microworlds in a project-based approach provides a good and sufficient reason for the integration of the different spatial claims formulated by the various actors involved. Since negotiations will concern the demarcated land together with its microworlds and actors, a strategic project creates a spatial framework, a place focus if you like, for integrating different spatial claims, representing different land uses and functions, and different actors.

In conclusion, integration concerns the establishment of interconnections at a certain spatial scale between different spatial claims, the associated land uses and functions and the actors representing these in order to create some kind of added value. In this way, depending on what is being integrated, different types of integration, such as spatial, functional and social, can arise. There are many and various ways to achieve integration, but the use of a place focus to enhance the integrative nature of strategic projects seems most appropriate from a spatial planning and design perspective. Having defined integration in planning, I move on to consider design as a particularly appropriate method to bring about the integration of different land uses and functions starting from the specific qualities of particular places. Integration as a fundamental characteristic of planning will then be linked with design as a creative, multi-dimensional medium to form a basis for many spatial planning activities.

THE RURBAN AREA AS A FIELD FOR PLANNING
ACTION:[3] DESIGN AS A MEDIUM FOR INTEGRATION

In recent years, a considerable literature on urbanism has appeared, which broad-
ens the scope of design as an essential medium in establishing people–place
relationships, for incorporating landscape values, and for generating consensus in strategic spatial projects (Mandanipour 1997, 2006; De Meulder 2000;
Carmona et al. 2002; De Rynck et al. 2003). I will argue here that spatial design
is particularly adapted to function as a medium for integration in the context of
strategic spatial projects because of the way it uses space as a raw material to
develop the substance of the project. Design can be described as a creative,
analytical and problem-solving activity that interprets, expresses and legitimizes
socio-economic processes that affect the development of a space (based on
Mandanipour 1997; Loukaitou-Sideris and Banerjee 1998; Llewelyn-Davies et
al. 2007; Carmona and Tiesdell 2007). It aims to establish relationships and connections between the physical, 'tangible' dimension of space (form, structure,
morphology) and the social, aesthetic 'intangible' dimension (use, perception
and experience), weighing and balancing objectives and constraints. The result
should be a vision for an area, expressed through sketches and texts, which binds
the individual components together and can act as a basis for discussion and
communication for the combined action of the different actors. Since the body of
knowledge and ideas of design are shared with other fields (urban planning, landscape architecture, environmental psychology, urban studies, etc.), Lang (1994)
considers it to be an integrative discipline. In a strategic project, design as a multi-
disciplinary activity of shaping and managing [r]urban environments (Mandanipour
1997) generates substance; it tries to safeguard a certain level and form of spatial
quality by combining the required spatial functions, and aims to unite the interests
at play in the project environment. Design in particular can respond to and work
with the relational and multiple dimensions of space, as highlighted by relational
geographers and planners (Massey 2005: 59, 61). In so doing, design draws
together the many strands of place-making and works creatively through the multiple dimensions and potentialities present in space (Lang 1994; Llewelyn-Davies
et al. 2007; Larice and Macdonald 2006). It is claimed that qualitative design
generally builds upon the constraints and opportunities it finds in space itself in
order to create a synthesis of multiple microworlds that interact with each other
in the context of a strategic spatial project (De Meulder 2009). Urban design,
and landscape design even more so,[4] are assumed to take the potential of the
site (such as valuable ecologies, views, organizational systems, material palettes)
as a starting point (Czerniak 2006: 107). Using typo-morphological analysis and
methods such as design charrettes, design can work with the particularities of a

place as well as its socio-institutional context, and build upon this to generate the substance of a project (Lang 1994; Carmona *et al.* 2003), linking technical, social and creative aspects (Mandanipour 1997; Jirku 2007) and enhancing the spatial quality of a place. In other words, the spatial characteristics of the project's site provide the raw material for design as a tool to shape space. They provide clues for integration, which the designer can mobilize. Design has the ability to mobilize the relational potential of space and hence it can be a medium for integration. Since modern landscape theories increasingly consider landscapes, which are one particular aspect of space, as holistic-relational entities within which 'natural and human processes merge and where economic, social and ecological objectives can be balanced in the pursuit of sustainable development' (Selman 2006: 1, but also Graham and Healey 1999; Massey 2004; Antrop 2007), I will look at landscape as a source for the integrative abilities of design.

J. B. Jackson, one of the most influential writers on landscape, looks at it as a space or a system of man-made spaces on the surface of the earth, 'a portion of land which the eye can comprehend at a glance' (Jackson 1984: 3). Landscape is 'space-as-a-surface' (Massey 2005: 119). Although landscape is limited in size to what the 'eye' perceives, it encompasses many more layers than the eye detects (such as socio-cultural, time, scale layers). Landscape is therefore much more than just a visual perception. According to Terkenli (2001), landscape is composed of highly interrelated and interactive aspects such as 'form', 'meaning' and 'function'.[5] Because of this multi-faceted meaning, tripartite nature and multi-layered structure, landscape allows for an approach from different angles and in several ways, so providing a basis for integration. Since landscape contains social, cultural, economical and ecological entities, activities and layers, it can provide a framework within which the relations between these dimensions materialize. In other words, landscape (or for that matter space) has 'integrative relational potentialities' (Van den Broeck 2004: 175).

INTEGRATION AND DESIGN: TWO CASE STUDIES

As argued previously, the integration of different spatial claims, voiced by different actors, and the associated land uses and functions has become a pressing challenge for planning. I argued that within the frame of strategic spatial projects, design is a promising medium through which to establish place-focused forms of integration because of the ways in which it builds creatively on the multi-dimensional, relational and multiple potentialities of space in general and landscape in particular. I will now test this by means of two cases: Parkbos in Ghent (Belgium) and Parc de la Deûle near Lille (France). The case studies are based on a detailed analysis of a series of plans and designs, related policy documents, reports of meetings and newspaper articles. These data are complemented by in-depth interviews with many of those involved, particularly designers. The two strategic projects under analysis both occur in rurban areas and hence integration issues figure centrally. In the Deûle case, the regional spatial planning strategy, water policy (initially) and a metropolitan urban liveability strategy (later) had to be integrated into a strategic project for park development (Laconte *et al.* 1982). In the Parkbos case, the public policy wish for an urban forest collided with existing land uses (such as agriculture and castle parks), so requiring functional integration amongst others. Both strategic projects responded to the need for leisure and recreation of urbanites and proposed a green network around the city to meet that need. In both cases the spatial claims of farmers in the strategic project area were particularly challenging from an integration point of view. Both strategic projects were experimental in reafforesting the region and in shifting the focus of spatial designers and planners from the urban centres towards the periphery and the larger (landscape and regional) scale. They try to establish a renewed dialogue between city and periphery, between man and nature, and between production and consumption. Design played a key role in this dialogue, although the two strategic projects mobilized it in different ways, for different purposes and with different results. In what follows, I will assess the integrative potential of design in strategic projects. In the Parkbos strategic project, I will argue that design could not deliver on its integrative potential because it was forced to work within the constraints of a sectoral set-up, because traditional thinking persisted, because there was a lack of funding, time and support for a detailed translation of the conceptual design, and because of maladjusted use and timing of planning instruments, of which one result among others was a sector-based allocation of land. Then I will show in an analysis of the Parc de la Deûle strategic project that the extent to which design can deliver on its integrative potential depends on conditions such as the moment in the process, the type of design or the degree of freedom allowed in the initial assignment.

PARKBOS: EQUILIBRATING BETWEEN INTEGRATED THINKING AND SECTORAL BARGAINING

PRELIMINARY PHASE: SEEDS OF INTEGRATION

Although the strategic project on the Parkbos site ('Park Wood') was only formalized around 1997, the roots of the project go back to the early 1980s. In 1983, the political responsibility for forest matters was transferred from federal to regional level. This, combined with the old political demand for afforestation (see Van Herzele 2006),[6] led to the idea of creating additional woodland, and eventually to the project for the Parkbos. A more tangible project idea, that is, the realization of urban forests,[7] emerged when the forest-related policy became entangled with the development of a new Flemish spatial policy in the 1990s. During the development of the Flanders Spatial Structure Plan (*Ruimtelijk Structuurplan Vlaanderen*), the forest policy line was integrated into spatial policy. The Spatial Structure Plan proposed urban forests as a solution for such urban problems as liveability, particularly with regard to the lack of open space catering for recreational needs, and thus hoped to counter urban flight and slow down suburbanization.

In this preliminary phase, the integration of two policy lines was instigated with the aim of meeting the needs of both the spatial planning and the forestry sectors, and of creating a win–win situation by connecting them in one policy concept. This is an example of 'institutional' integration (although not established through design) in which the linkage results in the reinforcement of both policy lines and offers an important element of added value. In this case, integration increased the chances for implementation.

A localization study was conducted in 1997 to search for a suitable place to build this urban forest (Van Elegem *et al.* 1997). It identified several 'green poles' in the area around Ghent, but chose the Kastelensite as the first pole to be developed (Figure 7.1), for both physical–spatial and institutional reasons (e.g. the possibility of constructing a science park at this location; see Voets 2008).

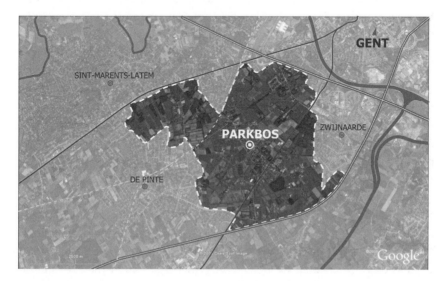

Figure 7.1   Location of Parkbos to the south of the city of Ghent. Source: Google Earth, modified by author.

This peri-urban site on the outskirts of the city already encompassed widely diverse land uses such as agriculture, castle parks, housing, different transport infrastructures and small-scale economic activities. The selection of the Kastelen-site increased the need for improved integration (functional and spatial) of all these activities. The urban forest concept, which originated as an abstract, top-down idea in policy circles, had to be adjusted to the specific spatial, social and economic conditions of the selected site. This, together with the torrent of spatial claims, land uses and activities, and the necessary cooperation between many different government and other (mainly public) actors, ultimately gave rise in 2001 to the commissioning of a design-based research study for the park-forest site (Studiegroep Omgeving *et al.* 2001a; David *et al.* 2005; Leinfelder 2007). The design brief stipulated integration as a goal, expressed in terms of multi-functional land use and the necessary weighing of different spatial claims (Studiegroep Omgeving *et al.* 2001b). As a first result, the aim of the project was broadened from afforestation to the creation of a landscape park of 1,200 ha with 300 ha of additional woodland.

THE DESIGN AND ITS INCENTIVES FOR INTEGRATION

The planning agency appointed to create an urban design for the landscape park first developed a 'structure sketch' (*structuurschets*) in close cooperation with such administrations as the Flemish Land Agency, the spatial planning and the land department, and the cooperative Bossanova, composed of the initiators of the project (the province of East Flanders, the Flemish forest administration and the Flemish Forestry Association). This conceptual design showed a desirable development of the area, positioning the various claims one against another by imagining forestation 'from the edge' with three poles of woods and a network of other woods-like connections in between (alleyways between trees, rows of trees, and shelter belts, i.e small strips with herbaceous plants, bushes and small trees, etc.). One of the aims, for instance, was to integrate the existing landscape structure as far as possible with the farming and other activities into a landscaped park. Concepts such as 'edge forests' (*randbossen*) and 'field forests' (*veld-bossen*) were proposed in order to reach that goal.

The design concept laid out in the structure sketch is rooted in different con-cerns and interests that have often travelled a long way before being integrated into the Parkbos idea. This integration process was the result of the interplay between visions emanating from different policy sectors and of a negotiation process between different involved actors (Wackenier 2005). The role of design can be characterized mainly as building further upon an already established pro-gramme and visualizing a common view that expressed the consensus between the different actors involved at that time (but which did not represent all actors affected by the project, as will become clear later). Furthermore, the integration issues in the Parkbos project were the result of the discourse on multi-functional forests and of the actual site, which contained many valuable historical, cultural and economic elements. The task of planning came down to making this multi-functionality workable and to making it happen. An integrating function was ascribed to the landscape aspect on which the concretization of the integration was based (Studiegroep Omgeving 2002). For instance, as a result of the dominance of landscape elements, the structure sketch focused on the functioning of the area as a park (Leinfelder 2007: 339). The idea of a compact urban forest was abandoned during this phase under pressure from local actors (farmers and the city of Ghent) and area-specific characteristics. The city of Ghent, for example, focused attention on the integration of the forest project into the existing landscape (spatial integration) and made cooperation subject to consideration of existing valuable landscape elements (see Van Herzele 2006).[8] As a result, this more landscape-based approach became the new standard and the idea of creating a forest changed from a compact whole to a division into several smaller areas of woodland (Van Herzele 2006).

TRANSLATING THE DESIGN CONCEPT INTO LEGAL CATEGORIES: INTEGRATION OR FRAGMENTATION?

The design, however, provoked discussion among the local population. The farmers were unhappy at the idea of seeing their land turned into forests and demanded legal certainty that their farming activities could continue on the areas remaining after the construction of the woodland poles. Environmental organizations and many residents also protested against the plans to build a science park in the area, which would result in less forestation and a new and allegedly unnecessary business area. As explained in more detail below, the spatial claims became subject to sectoral bargaining as a result of the protests, political pressure to offer legal certainty and the use of an inappropriate planning tool, and the conceptual design was translated into a spatial implementation plan (henceforth RUP) that provided for a monofunctional classification and gave priority to one land-use category, namely agriculture (Leinfelder 2007). As a result, the forest development itself was changed. During the design process, the concept of forest transformed from compact whole to fragmented segments interconnected by edge forests and field forests. The RUP, however, returned partially to the compact whole, and the amount of woodland was reduced (Figure 7.2). Additionally, the space for water and nature was significantly reduced, while horticulture gained considerable expansion possibilities[9] (David et al. 2005; Cappon 2006).

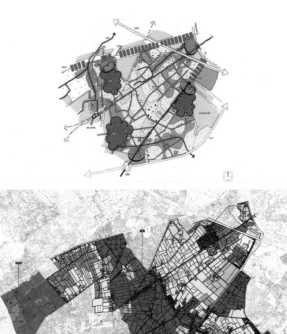

Figure 7.2   Top: Structure sketch – conceptual design. Source: Studiegroep OMGEVING, Econnection and Buck Consultants International (2001b), map 2 'gewenste ruimtelijke structuur' gewestelijk RUP bosontwikkeling-bedrijvigheid. Bottom: Spatial development plan (RUP) Parkbos. Dark grey: woodland, white: agricultural land. Source: Departement Ruimtelijke Ordening, Woonbeleid en Onroerend Erfgoed, Afdeling Ruimtelijke Planning, Vlaanderen (2006), verordenend grafisch plan 13.

Although the initial assignment prescribed integration[10] and the conceptual design also initiated certain forms of integration, an analysis of the (provisional) results suggests that this integrative dimension has not been maintained. For instance, are the different functions 'benefitting from each other's development'? (cf. Albrechts *et al.* 1999). On a macro scale, the Parkbos seems to be integrated in terms of space, functions and visions. A large number of potentially conflicting functions, such as woodland, agriculture, landscape, castle parks and science park, are combined within the project. However, despite the presence of these functions within the boundaries of the Parkbos, they do not interact or provide any benefit on a micro scale. Since areas with multiple land use cannot be assigned to one particular policy sector, the translation of the conceptual design into the RUP led to monofunctionality (Leinfelder 2007). In the RUP, the different functions are separated by means of a five metres wide 'green buffer'. The integration of different land uses is established neither from a visual perspective (separated by a buffer) nor from a political one (no support for the science park among inhabitants) nor a spatial one (no field or edge forests, but one large area). According to Leinfelder (2007), the main reasons for this loss of the integrative dimension are the inability of the traditional technique of functional zoning to deal with multiple space use, neglect in institutionalizing the role of the Parkbos as a public open space, and lack of guarantees that the reconstruction of the open space would happen in a spatially qualitative manner taking into account existing contextual elements. Leinfelder highlights traditional zoning of functions and activities; this illustrates how actors fall back on existing rigid planning instruments and methods (such as concentric development or zoning strategies), which are not tailored to the specificity of the rurban condition. Furthermore, at this stage of the process, the RUP's exclusive focus on development, while a detailed design had not yet been produced, contributed to the loss of the integrative dimension. Legal certainty and translation of designs into documents with juridical value is at some point necessary in order to get the project implemented, but it should always be accompanied by a creative element, an overall (inclusive landscape) design process, and the involvement of all crucial actors from the beginning.

Despite the fact that there were many obstacles to integration in the park-forest project, some interesting clues can be found here on how design deals with integration issues, for example in the detailed design for the science park (Figure 7.3). The designers built upon site-specific characteristics and landscape elements and elaborated them to establish integration in the desired form by establishing typological, morphological, visual and functional relationships and connections. The embedding of the site as a portion of woodland, the extension of the landscape structure of the surrounding *bulkenlandschap* (a characteristic terrain of protected undulating, tree-fringed patches of land) and the construction of the necessary buildings in as compact a manner as possible are examples of measures that give active expression on the scale of this subproject to functional and spatial integration considered necessary in the initial assignment. The key question here is the extent to which these measures actually contribute to the combined interaction with the whole landscape, which the actors want to achieve. Although the science park is conceived as a fragment of woodland and tries to link to the existing and proposed network of paths, in reality it operates autonomously and builds mainly on an internal logic. Since the goal of this landscape park is primarily to offer recreational possibilities and scenic and ecological values, it

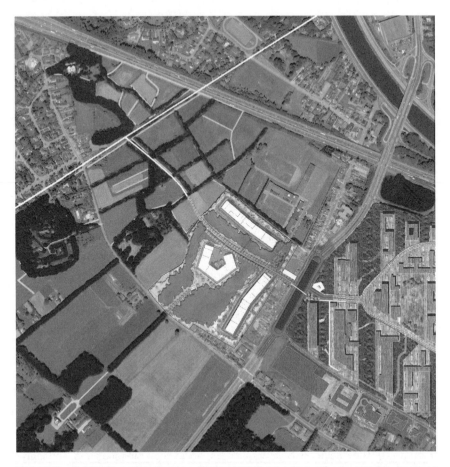

Figure 7.3   Landscape plan with strengthening of *bulkenlandschap* (a characteristic terrain of protected undulating, tree-fringed patches of land) that connects the science park to its environment. Source: OMGEVING and Idea Consult (2007: 63, Figure 47).

does not gain from the presence of the science park. On the contrary, a valuable site for afforestation or nature enhancement is lost, and during the evenings and weekends it will become a rather deserted place. Despite the fact that landscape was used as the frame to integrate distinct functions, the design did not succeed in creating added value for all functions involved. Obviously, not all designs are able to invent win–win situations under all conditions. How and when design is mobilized in a strategic project matters a great deal, as I will argue in the second case study. In the Parc de la Deûle project, the integrative capacities of design depended on governance conditions such as the availability of political support on the right (regional) scale, and on a greater coherence between the design vision and the evolution of the process.

THE LANDSCAPE AS GLUE: THE PARC DE LA DEÛLE AND ITS 'INTEGRATING' DESIGN

The Parc de la Deûle strategic project[11] shows the role of an intelligent design strategy in both bringing about and further enhancing institutional, functional and spatial integration. Furthermore, it emphasizes the importance of governance in creating the optimal conditions for design to be able to integrate different actors and their spatial claims in a strategic project. The project to create a peri-urban park of regional importance around the Deûle river in the metropolitan area of Lille-Roubaix-Tourcoing originated in the 1960s and 1970s within the frame of OREAM Nord, a regional study agency[12] (Figure 7.4). OREAM's main ambitions were to protect the water resources of the Lille agglomeration area while responding to the needs of the former mining area and to the recreational needs of its inhabitants (Estienne 2006). For a number of reasons, such as land development needing approval at the national rather than the regional level, the ambitious scale and design of the project, and the lack of support for a proposal that would occupy important agricultural areas, not much happened with the original design (Estienne 2005; Laconte *et al.* 1982). In the 1990s, the project got off to a new start. The new impulse stemmed from the strategy of metropolization encompassing Lille and its surrounding municipalities, in which regional development was linked to the need for urban regeneration (Paris 2002). The lack of green space was by then perceived not only as a social handicap, but also as an economic one, undermining the international attractiveness of the metropolitan area (Denhin 2003). As a result, for reasons of urban greening and the maintenance of agricultural activities, and with the political support of the Lille metropolitan community institutions (*Communauté Urbaine de Lille*), the Deûle project was absorbed into the formal plan during the revision of the strategic plan for the Lille metropolitan area (*schéma directeur de Lille Métropole*). Although the metropolization strategy brought the *public* actors together and established the necessary political basis for the development of the Deûlepark, concrete substance had yet to be given to the park. Therefore, a design competition was organized by the *syndicat mixte du Parc de la Dêule*. In 1995, the agency JNC International, in cooperation with landscape architect Jacques Simon, won the competition with an innovative design strategy that imagined a park in the interstices of the landscape, blending urban and rural, farmer and citizen.

A 'PARC EN RÉSEAU' AS DESIGN CONCEPT: INTEGRATING URBAN AND RURAL, SPATIALLY, FUNCTIONALLY AND SOCIALLY

Just as in the 1960s design, the JNC/Simon design had several recreational and ecological goals. More importantly for the argument here, it wanted to do

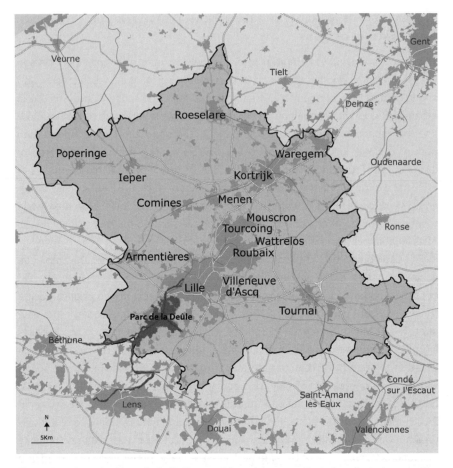

Figure 7.4   Location Parc de la Deûle: spatial, social, economic and ecological connection
between Lille and Lens. Source: Syndicat Mixte du Schéma directeur de Lille
Métropole, ADULM (Agence de Développement et d'Urbanisme de Lille Métropole)/
COPIT – 2000 (modified by author).

something about the lack of identity caused by the fragmentation of the territory,
to reunite the urban and rural, and to create an accessible, coherent landscape in
an attempt to augment the area's liveability. The design strategy, building on the
1960s experience, cleverly combined the needs of the urban society (such as
recreation) with those of the rural concerning the legitimacy of the agrarian activity
in the vicinity of the expanding urban tissue. In the designerly quest for common
objectives and synergies, assets to revitalize the rurban area were created and the
added value for both sides made explicit. The integration of urban and rural functions, societies and spatialities was further realized by making use of the design
concept of a 'parc en réseau' or network park (Figure 7.5). This concept was

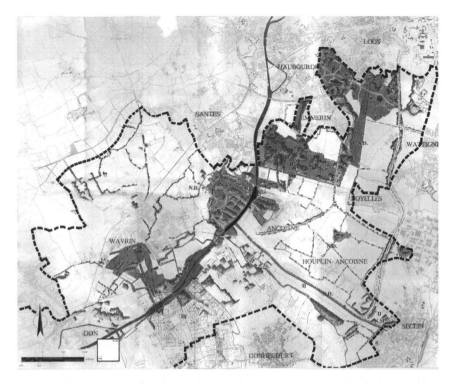

Figure 7.5   Master plan Parc de la Deûle, with indication of the perimeter by 2015. Source:
Jacques Simon and JNC International (1995).

based upon the idea of an archipelago in which the islands symbolize publicly
owned pieces of land,[13] interconnected by a network of paths and existing agricultural areas (Simon and JNC International 1995: 37). This path system aimed
to (re)connect the communities with each other on both the spatial and social
level, and integrated the surrounding, mainly agrarian, areas into the park without
the need to purchase them. Furthermore, the design strategy made use of available sites that were either public property or had no economic value (because of
pollution or a high nature value). On these sites, regional recreational areas are
(being) developed. By installing a park in the interstices of the landscape, a basis
for interactions between urbanites and the rural population was established. The
Deûlepark becomes a 'tentacular space' that appropriates the fringes and cohab-
its with the mosaic of 'rurban' functions (Hubert 2006: 75).

   Using this approach, the designers managed to develop a concept that found
support in policy circles as well as among farmers and urban recreants. In addition to the involvement of representatives of the agricultural community (*chambre
d'agriculture*), representatives of all of the different cultures in the area served

as a source of inspiration feeding the design.[14] The flexibility of the network park concept further enhanced the support base; for instance, it allowed piece by piece development, depending on the financial possibilities and the availability of the land. To maintain coherence during this elongated implementation phase, a design charter was established. This charter, which was formally accepted by the *syndicat mixte*, acts as a framework for future developments and captures the general principles and spatial criteria of the design. It led to more manageable development because it does not require the development of the whole of the park at once. At the same time, it secured the continuation of the general principles in future developments.

Although design can deliver integration by using contextual opportunities, because of its capacity to explore the multiple dimensions of space, it also obtains this capacity from building upon the spatial structures and potentials embedded in the landscape itself. The network park concept originated from and makes use of the intrinsic potential of the landscape. The designers looked beyond an industrial past that left a derelict, contaminated and fragmented space, and turned a feature usually perceived as negative (fragmentation) into a positive one. In this operation, landscape itself was the glue that connected the rurban tissue (cf. Sieverts 2003). Landscape was reconsidered as forming a vector of identity, the 'cement' of the coherence of the peri-urban tissue (Simon and JNC International 2006: 4). As Hubert (2006) indicates, the majority of the structuring axes of the design are inspired by the 'territorial forces'. Spatial features, such as the hydraulic network with the channels 'la Deûle' and 'Séclin', the basins and meanders, the morphology of the landscape, and the history of the area, made up the basis of the design. The general design concept of a 'network park' followed directly from these preconditions set by the specificity of the place itself. The creation of coherence and identity is an important aspect that can be realised in this way. It is established by interconnecting the different fragments in a path network, which also creates a network of ecological corridors (Simon and JNC International 1995: 43), and by enhancing the landscape's character through the creation of a common vocabulary (Figure 7.6). Throughout the park the same small landscape elements (such as pollard willows and similar rows of trees), materiality, structure, textures, colours and signs can be found, stimulating the recognizability and the building of an identity (Simon and JNC International 2006: 9). As such the landscape elements became a medium to work with, and a new whole arose. In this design, the landscape elements are the glue that connects the different spatial fragments, the different land uses, the urban and rural connotations, the farmer and the citizen.

Figure 7.6   Transformation induced by the project. Note the appearance of a visually permeable boundary between the park space and the agriculture space. Source: Yves Hubert for JNC International (top) and Christian Louvet for Espace Naturel Lille Métropole (bottom).

CREATING THE CIRCUMSTANCES FOR AN INTEGRATING DESIGN:
COMPARING PARK DE LA DEÛLE AND PARKBOS

If both strategic projects are compared from the perspective of integration through design-based methods, it is clear that the Deûle project design succeeds better in delivering integration than the Parkbos project. I want to argue here that an explanation for these different results is to be found in the preconditions set and the type of design chosen, and in the attitude and approach of the designer and commissioner.

First, the point of departure, the specifications of the assignment and the amount of freedom it allowed affected the integrating capacities of the design. In both strategic projects, the task for the designers was to develop some sort of peri-urban park. The difference between them was that in Ghent the concept for this park was already determined, whereas in Lille the network park concept resulted from the analysis of the actual spatial, as well as socio-economic, conditions of the site by designers. In Ghent, the designers had to work with the predetermined concept of an urban forest encompassing a sectoral compromise between the forestry and the spatial planning sectors, which was made before the actual site where it was to be realized was known. Design efforts were targeted at finding ways to implement the concept on the site, while taking into account valuable spatial particularities (e.g. the castle parks) as much as possible. Additionally, although both stemmed from public policy initiatives aimed at improving liveability, the roots of the Deûle project encompassed more manifest and visible problems such as water supply, pollution and a deteriorated landscape. The preconditions for design were thus different in each case. This alone, however, cannot explain the difference in integrating capacity. Furthermore, the strong sectoral as well as juridical approach hindered the possibilities for integration in Ghent. The design was limited to a conceptual level and went directly from this to fixation in legal plans (RUP). Also, because of the fact that landscape design is not generally accepted in Belgium, leading to, among other factors, a lack of finance, the Parkbos project possessed no such design. This shows that the mindset and attitude of the commissioner are important as well as the commissioning preconditions, the type of design and its level of detailing. It implies, furthermore, that the point at which design is introduced into the process can influence its possibilities for creating spatial quality and social innovation through integration. For instance, design can also be used to analyse spatial and social circumstances and to determine different development possibilities (see Chapter 4 in this volume). However, in the end, the solution depends on the quality of the design itself, not all design being equally creative and inventive.

Second, the openness and modesty of the design itself matters. For instance, the Deûle design, learning from a previous, failed strategic project for the same site, did not try to control and change the whole area, as in the previous design. Following Jirku (2007: 54, 62), to design a large landscape park, while ignoring existing appearances and uses of the landscape such as agriculture, or by trying to capture within it an all-encompassing romantic vision, is to ignore economic facts. Instead, the design needs to focus on the structure of the area, the design of pathways, public areas and the form and distribution of land for agriculture. The development and organization of the agricultural parcels needs to be carried out by the farmer and not by the designer (cf. Mandanipour 1997). In other words, the design needs some kind of modesty while still providing general and firm directions of development. The Deûle case shows that a design strategy that does not fix everything but allows for future adaptation also makes integration easier. The design of the Deûlepark remained open-ended by implementing the idea of an incrementally growing park, and this clearly made a major difference in terms of the support base, the long-term perspective of such landscape-focused strategic projects, and establishing integration. The design strategy for the Deûlepark turned out to be intelligent in that it took into account different actors, and utilized spatial particularities, two elements that are indispensable for a design trying to generate win–win situations.

And, finally, the process and governance characteristics of the strategic project also influence the integrating ability of design. For instance, in the Parkbos project the process was fairly closed and top-down, whereas in the Deûlepark the process was more open, enabling the designers to involve locals, and so resulting in a broader support base. In this project, design was mobilized to create a coalition between the different actors, public or private, who supported the spatial transformation envisaged in the strategic project.[15]

CONCLUSION

The development, organization and maintenance of open areas on the boundary between urban and rural are increasingly the subjects of attention today. More and more landscape-based strategic projects have emerged in these 'rurban' areas, challenged by the need to transcend boundaries and integrate different spatial claims, land uses and functions. Combining the challenges for planning suggested by Sieverts (designing open spaces in urbanised environments) and Healey (integrating disparate agendas, activities and actors) with Amin's 'politics of propinquity' (different microworlds on the same turf), I argued that a place-based focus is an appropriate starting point for spatial planning and design to work towards spatial, functional, social and institutional integration in rurban conditions. I showed that qualitative design, as a substance-generating and key part of a strategic project, has the ability to promote integration because it is multi-dimensional and because it uses space as its raw material. It can use the relational dimension of space and landscape to assemble the various facets of place-making and create a substance that takes account of, and is embedded in, the multiple dimensions of space. Given that design can start from the specific socio-cultural and geographical characteristics of a site, it is particularly well positioned to deliver the kind of tailor-made forms of integration that strategic projects demand. Opting for an integrative rather than sectoral focus design thus works to enhance the strategic dimension of planning processes in strategic spatial projects. In the Lille project, the concept of the network park originated from clever usage of the existing morphology. As such, the design succeeded in weaving together rural areas, post-industrial spaces and urban fragments as well as farmer, recreant, cyclist and local resident by allowing for multiple usage. At the same time, it gave the impetus for an augmented spatial quality, and thereby liveability, by establishing a strong landscape identity through the introduction of a common vocabulary throughout the site. Furthermore, design solutions can help carry through strategic projects from the planning phase to the implementation phase, but, as the very different outcomes in the Parkbos and Deûlepark cases show, this requires careful reflection on how, when and which design is mobilized in strategic projects. In the case of the Parkbos, design was mobilized as a problem-solving medium. Its purpose encompassed extending the concept of an urban forest to one of a landscaped park, and bringing about the necessary integration of different spatial claims, the actors who voice them, and the land uses and functions linked to those claims. It showed that establishing integration is not always an easy or obvious task. Traditional, sector-based thinking, maladjusted use and timing of planning instruments, and a lack of innovative solutions for the rurban development condition form obstacles to an integration approach.

This research shows that design is a good method for place development and, by taking into account existing spatial structures as well as the manifold spatial claims, improves the action orientation of strategic planning. It plays a central role in the four-track approach set out in the introduction to this part. It does so not only by designing alternative futures (first track) and, using its place-based focus, pointing to feasible actions to get to these alternative futures (second track), but also by involving all relevant actors (third track). More research is needed, however, to specify the conditions under which design can play its integrative role in strategic projects. One challenge for the mobilization of design methods in strategic projects that needs further research is the way in which general design principles can be maintained throughout the project, particularly in the implementation phase. The use of a design charter, as in the Deûlepark strategic project, suggests one possible solution to this challenge. Furthermore, the design techniques and strategies used, and the type of design linked with the role and position of design within the project, are other examples of such conditions. For instance design's position as a political tool, as a social act expressing certain values, is a topic that deserves further attention.

NOTES

1 Urban design is increasingly considered to be not just a part of the discipline of planning, but also to operate at its intersection with urbanism and landscape design (Llewelyn-Davies 2000; Larice and Macdonald 2006; Mandanipour 1997).

2 The 'rurban areas' in this chapter indicate areas where the traditional distinction between rural and urban tissues and societies is no longer applicable and where the separation of both has lost its significance for spatial planning (cf. Gallent *et al.* 2006). Bauer and Roux, who first coined the French term 'rurbanization', from which 'rurban' is derived, used it to refer to processes of urban sprawl (Bauer and Roux 1976 in Hoggart 2005).

3 Title partially based on Sieverts (2003).

4 Sieverts argues that 'landscape planning, town planning and urban design must form a conceptual and creative unity in approaching the *Zwischenstadt'* (or the rurban area) (Sieverts 2003: 115). The scale, composition and structure of the rurban area give reason for new design practices such as landscape urbanism (Reed 2006: 283), enabling design to transcend the opposition of town and country (Shane 2006: 65). Many strategic projects in the rurban area combine and complement both urban and landscape design strategies, which will be clear from the Deûle project discussed later.

5 She sees, for example, a cultural landscape as 'a visible expression of the humanized environment perceived mainly through sensory, and particularly visual, as well as cognitive processes; a medium and an outcome of human action and perception' (Terkenli 2001: 200) and concludes that form stands for the visual, whereas meaning stands for the cognitive and function for the biophysical processes and invested/articulated human experiences.

6 Shortly after World War II afforestation was already an issue in Flanders. This originated from the discontent with the unbalanced division of policy attention for woodlands, which at that time mainly targeted the Walloon region in the south of Belgium, which already contained a substantial volume of woodland (Van Herzele 2006).

7 The development of a policy line about multi-functional forests in the vicinity of cities gave way to the appearance of an urban forest concept that, according to Van Herzele (2006), is a rather intellectual concept which is not embedded in any socio-cultural tradition.

8 In a formal statement in March 1999 the city of Ghent declared its support. Van Herzele remarked that no consideration was given to 'how the forest project will be integrated into the present cultural landscape with its valuable landscape elements' (Van Herzele 2006: 688).

9 At first, the planning agency stipulated that horticulture development was not desirable in the area.

10 This was expressed in terms of multi-functional land use and the balancing of the different spatial claims.

11 The Parc de la Deûle received the Council of Europe 2009 Landscape Award. This award honours exemplary practical initiatives on the domain of landscape quality objectives, related to the European Landscape Convention.

12 Organisations d'Etudes et d'Aménagement des Aires Métropolitaines du Nord. The core activity of this regional agency was the study and development of the area of Nord-Pas-de-Calais in northern France.

13 The location of the publicly owned properties was of specific interest for the design in this case. It determined the phasing of the implementation of the project as well as the general frame to develop the park by connecting these fringes that were already public property, an act which minimized the need to acquire private land by the *syndicat mixte* and contributed as such to the implementation possibilities of the project.

14 At several moments during the design process, different types of actors were actively involved in developing a support base for the project. For the design of the 'Parc Mosaïc', a part of the Deûle project near Houplin-Ançoisne, associations and residents from different communities present in the metropolitan area served as direct resources for the thematic gardens (Denhin 2006). Their involvement contributed to the social support base for the park and enhanced the awareness of the strategic park project. Additionally, in March 2006, a *Conseil consultative métropolitain des usagers*, a committee grouping the different existing local committees and associations, was inaugurated (Simon and JNC International 2006).

15 The farmers were, for instance, involved in the development of the design as crucial and important actors. Because of clever strategies enabling the continuation and broadening of agricultural activity, farmers became allies. One such strategy was the application of the principle of differentiated maintenance, which adapts maintenance to the functioning of each place, the usage and the ecological objectives (Simon and JNC International 2006: 8). For instance, the greenery is conceived in such a way that farmers can use machinery that is already in their possession (Denhin 2003).

REFERENCES

Albrechts, L. (2006) 'Shifts in strategic spatial planning? Some evidence from Europe and Australia', *Environment and Planning A*, 38: 1149–1170.

Albrechts, L., Van den Broeck, J., Verachtert, K., Leroy, P. and Van Tatenhove, J. (1999) *Geïntegreerd gebiedsgericht beleid: een methodiek.* Brussels: K.U.Leuven and K.U.Nijmegen.

Allmendinger, P. (2003) 'Re-scaling, integration and competition: future challenges for development planning', *International Planning Studies*, 8: 323–328.

Amin, A. (2004) 'Regions unbound: Towards a new politics of place', *Geografiska Annaler Series B: Human Geography*, 86: 33–44.

Antrop, M. (2007) *Perspectieven op het landschap. Achtergronden om landschappen te lezen en te begrijpen*, Ghent: Academia Press.

Bauer, G. and Roux, J.-M. (1976) *La rurbanisation ou la ville éparpillée*, Paris: Seuil.

Borret, K. (2002) 'Nevelstad-spotting: Analyses vanuit concreet-ruimtelijke invalshoek', *Ruimte en Planning*, 22: 244.

Brandt, J. and Vejre, H. (2004) 'Multifunctional landscapes – motives, concepts and perspectives', in J. Brandt and H. Vejre (eds) *Multifunctional Landscapes*, Vol. 1, *Theory, Values and History*, Southampton: WIT Press.

Bruegmann, R. (2005) *Sprawl: A Compact History*, London: University of Chicago Press.

Cappon, R. (2006) 'Concepten voor open ruimte verbindingen. Verkennend onderzoek naar alternatieve en meer flexibele instrumenten'. Unpublished thesis, Universiteit Gent, Faculteit Toegepaste Wetenschappen.

Carmona, M. and Tiesdell, S. (eds) (2007) *Urban Design Reader*, Oxford: Architectural Press.

Carmona, M., De Magalhães, C. and Edwards, M. (2002) 'Stakeholder views on value and urban design', *Journal of Urban Design*, 7: 145–169.

Carmona, M., Heath, T., Oc, T. and Tiesdell, S. (2003) *Public Places – Urban Spaces: The Dimensions of Urban Design*, Oxford: Architectural Press.

Counsell, D., Allmendinger, P., Haughton, G. and Vigar, G. (2006) ' "Integrated" spatial planning – is it living up to expectations?', *Town and Country Planning*, 75 (9): 243–246.

Czerniak, J. (2006) 'Looking back at landscape urbanism: Speculations on site', in C. Waldheim (ed.) *The Landscape Urbanism Reader*, New York: Princeton Architectural Press.

David, P., Vanhaeren, R., Vloebergh, G. in co-operation with.Demulder, F. (2005) 'Planningshistoriek van het parkbosproject', in G. Allaert and H. Leinfelder (eds) *Parkbos Gent. Over visievorming en beleidsnetwerking*, Ghent: Academia Press.

De Boe, P., Grasland, C. and Healy, A. (1999) *Study Programme on European Spatial Planning Strand 1.4: Spatial Integration*, Stockholm: Nordregio.

De Meulder, B. (2000) 'Stadsontwerp in Vlaanderen, nu ook verkrijgbaar als stationsromanneke', in K. Van Synghel (ed.) *Jaarboek Architectuur Vlaanderen 1998–1999*, Brussels: Ministerie van de Vlaamse Gemeenschap.

De Meulder, B. (2009) 'design@urban.project.eu Ontwerpen voor en aan de Europese stad, 1980–2008', in A. Loeckx (ed.) *Stadsvernieuwingsprojecten in Vlaanderen. Ontwerpend onderzoek en capacity building*, Amsterdam: SUN.

Denhin, P. (2003) 'Utiliser l'espace naturel comme moteur d'un nouveau développement économique: l'expérience de Lille Métropole (France)', *Actes,* conference proceedings of III Symposium international sur espaces naturels périurbains, Fedenatur.

Denhin, P. (2006) 'Lille Metropolitan Natural Area: "Public participation, last stage of communication. Turning consumers into agents" ', *Bilan de la réunion technique,* conference proceedings of La communication efficace dans les espaces naturels périurbains, Fedenatur.

Departement Ruimtelijke Ordening, Woonbeleid en Onroerend Erfgoed, Afdeling Ruimtelijke Planning Vlaanderen (2006) *Spatial Development Plan (RUP) Parkbos*, Brussels: RWO.

De Rynck, F., Boudry, L., Cabus, P., Corijn, E., Kesteloot, C. and Loeckx, A. (2003) *De eeuw van de stad: over stadsrepublieken en rastersteden*, Ministerie van de Vlaamse Gemeenschap, Project stedenbeleid, Brussels: Ministerie van de Vlaamse Gemeenschap.

Estienne, I. (2005) 'L'aménagement paysager des territoires: Lieu de rencontre entre chercheurs et acteurs', in Lille School of Architecture and Landscape (ed.) *Conference Proceedings of Colloque EURAU 2005: 2nd European Symposium on Research in Architecture, Urban and Landscape Design: Considering Space on a Large Scale.* Lille: Lille National School of Architecture and Landscape (published on CD-ROM).

Estienne, I. (2006) 'La redécouverte de l'eau dans les stratégies d'aménagement à grande échelle de la métropole lilloise', *Cahiers Thématiques*, 6: 250–263.

Gallent, N., Shoard, M., Andersson, J., Oades, R. and Tudor, C. (2004) 'Inspiring England's urban fringes: multi-functionality and planning', *Local Environment: The International Journal of Justice and Sustainability*, 9: 217–233.

Gallent, N., Andersson, J. and Bianconi, M. (2006) *Planning on the Edge. The Context for Planning at the Rural–Urban Fringe*, New York: Routledge.

Graham, S. and Healey, P. (1999) 'Relational concepts of space and place: Issues for planning theory and practice', *European Planning Studies*, 7: 623–646.

Healey, P. (2004) 'The treatment of space and place in the new strategic spatial planning in Europe', *International Journal of Urban and Regional Research*, 28: 45–67.

Healey, P. (2006) 'Territory, integration and spatial planning', in M. Tewdwr-Jones and P. Allmendinger (eds) *Territory, Identity and Spatial Planning: Spatial Governance in a Fragmented Nation*, London: Routledge.

Hidding, M. (2006) *Planning voor stad en land*, 3rd edn, Bussum: Uitgeverij Coutinho.

Hoggart, K. (ed.) (2005) *The City's Hinterland. Dynamism and Divergence in Europe's Peri-Urban Territories*, Aldershot: Ashgate Publishing.

Hubert, Y. (2006) 'Le Parc de la Deûle. Entre villes et campagnes, un parc diffusé dans le territoire', *Les Cahiers de l'Urbanisme*, 58: 72–80.

Indovina, F. (1990) *La cittá diffusa*, Venice: Daest.

Jackson, J. (1984) *Discovering the Vernacular Landscape*, New Haven, CT: Yale University Press.

Jirku, A. (2007) 'Adding third nature to second nature: Design strategies for peripheral landscapes', *Journal of Landscape Architecture* 1: 50–63.

Kidd, S. (2007) 'Towards a framework of integration in spatial planning: an exploration from a health perspective', *Planning Theory & Practice*, 8: 161–181.

Laconte, P., Haimes, Y., North Atlantic Treaty Organization and NATO Advanced Study Institute (1982) *Water Resources and Land-Use Planning: A Systems Approach: Proceedings of the NATO Advanced Study Institute on 'Water Resources and Land-Use Planning'*, The Hague: Martinus Nijhoff Publishers.

Lang, J. (1994) *Urban Design: The American Experience*, New York: Van Nostrand Reinhold.

Lang, J. T. (2005) *Urban Design: A Typology of Procedures and Products*, Oxford: Elsevier/ Architectural Press.

Larice, M. and Macdonald, E. (eds) (2006) *The Urban Design Reader*, London and New York: Routlegde.

Leinfelder, H. (2007) *Open ruimte als publieke ruimte, dominante en alternatieve planningsdiscoursen ten aanzien van landbouw en open ruimte in een (Vlaamse) verstedelijkende context*, Ghent: Academia Press.

Llewelyn-Davies and Alan Baxter and Associates (2007) *Urban Design Compendium 1, Urban Design Principles*, 2nd edn, London: English Partnerships and the Housing Corporation.

Loukaitou-Sideris, A. and Banerjee, T. (1998) *Urban Design Downtown: Poetics and Politics of Form*, Berkeley: University of California Press.

Mandanipour, A. (1997) 'Ambiguities of urban design', in M. Carmona and S. Tiesdell (eds) *Urban Design Reader*, Oxford: Architectural Press.

Mandanipour, A. (2006) 'Roles and challenges of urban design', *Journal of Urban Design*, 11: 173–193.

Massey, D. (2004) 'The political challenge of relational space: Introduction to the Vega Symposium', *Geografiska Annaler Series B: Human Geography*, 86: 3.

Massey, D. (2005) *For Space*, London: Sage.

OMGEVING and Idea Consult (2007) *Wetenschapspark rijvissche. Inrichtingsstudie en haalbaarheidsstudie, eindrapport*, in opdracht van Stad Gent. Ghent: Omgeving and Idea Consult.

Paris, D. (2002) 'Lille, de la métropole à la région urbaine', *Mappemonde*, 66: 1–7.

Reed, C. (2006) 'Public works practice', in C. Waldheim (ed.) *The Landscape Urbanism Reader*, New York: Princeton Architectural Press.

Rowe, P. (1992) *Making a Middle Landscape*, Cambridge, MA: MIT Press.

Sartorio, F. S. (2005) 'Strategic spatial planning. A historical review of approaches, its recent revival, and an overview of the state of the art in Italy', *disP – The Planning Review*, 162: 26–40.

Selman, P. (2006) *Planning at The Landscape Scale*, London: Routledge.

Shane, G. (2006) 'The emergence of landscape urbanism', in C. Waldheim (ed.) *The Landscape Urbanism Reader*, New York: Princeton Architectural Press.

Sieverts, T. (2003) *Cities Without Cities: An Interpretation of the Zwischenstadt*, London: Spon Press.

Simon, J. and JNC International (1995) *Parc de la Deûle. Présentation préalable au rapport final*, Syndicat Mixte du Parc de la Deûle.

Simon, J. and JNC International (2006) *Prix du paysage 2006. Santes ou la 'nature retrouvée', Wavrin ou la nature domestiquée'*, Syndicat Mixte du Parc de la Deûle (Maître d'ouvrage), rapport préparatoire pour le ministère de l'ecologie et du développement durable.

Sternberg, E. (2000) 'An integrative theory of urban design', *Journal of the American Planning Association*, 66: 265–278.

Studiegroep Omgeving, Econnection and Buck Consultants International (2001a) *Voorstudie voor het gewestelijk ruimtelijk uitvoeringsplan voor bosontwikkeling en bedrijvigheid tussen Gent en De Pinte. Deelrapport 1*, Studie in opdracht van AROHM-afdeling Ruimtelijke Planning. Studiegroep Omgeving, Mortsel.

Studiegroep Omgeving, Econnection and Buck Consultants International (2001b) *Voorstudie voor het gewestelijk ruimtelijk uitvoeringsplan voor bosontwikkeling en bedrijvigheid tussen Gent en De Pinte. Ontwerp Eindrapport.*, Studie in opdracht van AROHM-afdeling Ruimtelijke Planning. Studiegroep Omgeving, Mortsel.

Studiegroep Omgeving (2002) *Verslag workshop landschapspark parkbos 14/10/2002*, R408-034.

Terkenli, T. S. (2001) 'Towards a theory of the landscape: the Aegean landscape as a cultural image', *Landscape and Urban Planning*, 57: 197–208.

van den Brink, A., van der Valk, A. and van Dijk, T. (2006) 'Planning and the challenges of the metropolitan landscape: innovation in the Netherlands', *International Planning Studies*, 11: 147–165.

Van den Broeck, J. (2004) 'Strategic structure planning', in A. Loeckx, K. Shannon, R. Tuts and H. Verschure (eds) *Urban Trialogues: Visions_Projects_Co-productions*, Nairobi/Leuven: UN-Habitat and K.U.Leuven.

Van Elegem, B., Embo, T., Kerkhove, G. and Houthaeve, R. (1997) *Studie van de bebossingsmogelijkheden en de afbakening van een regionaal bos en een stadsbos in de regio Gent. Een zoektocht naar het stadsbos.*, Brochure van de Provincie Oost-Vlaanderen, dienst Planning en Natuurbehoud, Gent.

Van Herzele, A. (2006) 'A forest for each city and town: story lines in the policy debate for urban forests in Flanders', *Urban Studies*, 43: 673–696.

Voets, J. (2008) 'Intergovernmental relations in multi-level arrangements: Collaborative public management in Flanders'. Unpublished PhD thesis, Faculty of Social Sciences, Catholic University of Leuven.

Wackenier, L. (2005) 'Van stadsbosidee naar parkbosconcept', in G. Allaert and H. Leinfelder (eds) *Parkbos Gent. Over visievorming en beleidsnetwerking*, Ghent: Academia Press.

COMMENTARY ON PART II

SOME REFLECTIONS ON PROJECTS AND DESIGN

Paola Viganò and Bernardo Secchi

The two chapters provide an interesting reading of urban and territorial projects at different stages of implementation and construction that have encountered very different social and political conditions. In Chapter 6 the authors refer to the concept of performance and the need to construct a common judgement around the project starting from performance categories. In Chapter 7 the role of the landscape project as mediator between places, subjects and actors is central. In both cases one can observe project experiences that contribute decisively, although with different degrees of success, to engendering broader transformations in space and time and which are therefore strategic.

SOME REFLECTIONS ON THE PROJECT AS A PRODUCER OF KNOWLEDGE

Paola Viganò

PRINCIPLES AND VALUES

In the performative approach referred to in Chapter 6, 'developing shared terms for spatial quality through design' emerges continually in the debate; each time a formalistic interpretation of the design needs to be overcome and each time the practical use of the spaces together with how they are perceived, rather than their purely formal elements, are placed in relationship to each other. This approach highlights the importance of holistic human relations with the urban space; the experience of space and the confrontation of different experiences and perceptions of space enrich the idea of a socially constructed knowledge, which intersects with the design contribution as part of this process.

Careful observation of the physical characteristics of space show to what extent the body and its movements are affected by everyday living, indeed the degree to which relations with things and natural phenomena determine spatial comfort: from an attentive to a sensory way of relating to the city, to readability, to urban sequences.

The crisis of modern space has led to a questioning of the performance level on which the modern city project has been built, deposited in laws and regulations that have oriented and imposed the very transformation itself. Today any return to a performative approach, even when based on Lynch's contribution, must start from a reflection on the changes in performance levels, which, though accepted in the past, have become partially obsolete and need to be re-discussed. In particular, it is the relationship between the main principles and the local values that has changed, is changing continuously and demands a complex understanding, often beset by ambiguity.

Here lies one of the main research questions relating to one of the four tracks of the multi-track planning approach advocated by this book. On the one hand, Lynch's self-same approach is based on a supposed homogeneity of reactions and behaviours; on the other, values are preferences shared intersubjectively (Habermas 1992) and generate social configurations in which affinities and differences are established in provisory, non-generalisable bodies of rules. The categories used in the reading of the projects are no exception: sense in its subdimensions of identity, legibility and significance, among others, provides culturally and site-related categories that impose a certain prudence in their use.

The reading of the different case studies enables at least a partial bridging of the gap between principles and values that could hamper the construction of a shared judgement on the quality of the project and on the quality of the space that is the outcome of the same. At the same time, it is clear that the 'value rationality' related to the first track of the multi-track planning approach proposed in this book, and which focuses on designing alternative futures, also remains fundamental both to the other tracks that consider the short-term issues of the here and now and to the encounter with the ideological and strategic components of design. What is being questioned here is the role that the project might take on, the capacity of the project to produce knowledge and its position in the political and social arena.

WHY AND HOW TO READ A PROJECT?

The iterative process, the process of exchange, integration via pluralised discussions, enriches the project and reinforces its capacity to combine and match collective images (Secchi and Viganò 2009). Reconstructing these matters and developing a critical knowledge of these processes is no easy thing. It is a question of going through documents, texts and representations, which are often highly sophisticated, almost always incomplete or fragmentary. In reconstructing the evolution of the project one has to ensure that the fractures, the stopping and turning points, the lack of a single line of thought emerge in the process. Attention to these aspects may help to render explicit the implicit attributes that the practice of reading attempts to make visible.

The analyses carried out, particularly highly detailed in the case of the Flemish projects, are good examples of this. It is useful to say that they were possible thanks to the direct participation of the authors in the process, though their roles were different but crucial in both cases. This is not a marginal consideration; indeed we lack critical analyses of urban design processes able to go beyond the superficial, mainly because of their temporal horizons (often long and fragmented) and the complex multi-layered nature of crossed relations among actors. Conceptually the urban project is a black box that asks for innovative forms of criticism. The attempt proposed here, for example, places the observer directly into the arena, which is at one and the same time a spatial, social, political and institutional one, and in which a non-neutral eye (and this might be considered a weak point) is at the same time a reflexive one. This reinforces the possibility that the process that is played out is not fully transparent.

The project, in its different forms, plays a crucial role within the collective process of constructing physical–spatial transformation, but one which is reduced to the sole capacity of storytelling, a technique re-proposed in recent years in many urban and planning projects. On the contrary, the insertion of the project within a collective discussion brings about new, original, non-generalised and specific knowledge. We need to dwell on this point, because it throws a different light on the hypothesis put forward in Chapter 6 of using performative categories to read projects rather than just situations. We can hypothesise that design reading is one way to access a body of knowledge embedded in the design activity, partly as a result of collective construction, partly as a result of the design activity itself.

PROJECT AS KNOWLEDGE PRODUCER

In this sense the two authors of Chapter 6 propose viewing projects as deposits of interpretations, descriptions and ideas about the city, about a place, and this can be read as an attempt to make explicit the contribution to knowledge formation contained in them. If this is correct, design is more than a neutral mediator among different actors; it has a critical role to play among actors, subjects and places. It is not the analogy between inquiry and the design activity that I am stressing; I look upon the research product of the design activity through the hypothesis that design *is* inquiry. Through the product of design operations we can understand the formation of a specific and original body of knowledge (Viganò 2010).

Through conceptual operations, which provide a space and a time of abstraction that enables the formulation of a way of thinking about contemporary territories, design enlightens the understanding of our contemporary condition. The project confers individuality on each and every place through its descriptive ability; it enables the situation to be recognised. Design builds relationships, uses all anomalies, discontinuities, differences. Projects, even from an etymological point of view, always provide a vision of the future; design participates in the process of constructing the future as a sequence of rational and shared choices.

The design process is not only inserted into contexts, but also is context in itself and produces situations within which knowledge is exchanged and modified. Abstract knowledge does not exist as such; rather, and from a pragmatist perspective, one should speak of experience within which knowledge can assume a meaning.

The reading of urban strategic projects can reinforce this hypothesis and at the same time highlight both the originality of and the need for research that involves design and its social role.

SOME REFLECTIONS ON DESIGN AS A MEDIUM FOR INTEGRATION IN THE 'RURBAN' LANDSCAPE

BERNARDO SECCHI

Chapter 7, referring to two case studies, Parkbos at Ghent and Parc de la Deûle in the metropolitan area of Lille, poses questions as to the role of the landscape project as mediator between places, subjects and actors. The two case studies recount extensive but different and partially opposing stories. The former tells the story of a substantial failure; the latter of a success.

The reasons for these two different results can be put down to the ways in which the two projects originated, the process of their construction, their sectoral character, striving towards a rapid judicial definition of the results in the one case and, at the opposite end of the spectrum, the open but projectually clearer and defined character of the other. Hence, apparent success and failure can be put down to 'methodological' questions in the general sense, perhaps more concretely to two different conceptions of planning and two different eras in town planning. Judging it from a rather simplified, reductive manner, the Parkbos project harks back to and still falls within an idea of town planning defined as the different land uses codified within strict regulations, whereas that of the Park de la Deûle is forward looking, starting from a careful reading of the territory as the deposit of actions and visions of a multiplicity of actors who have to be mobilised first and foremost in order to create a shared project resulting from common agreement.

Indeed, the notes that follow do not express a judgement of the two projects, other than that already expressed by the facts, but rather develop some considerations on the way the two cases are examined in Chapter 7. In order not to be misunderstood, I start by saying that it is studies which raise problems that can be defined as interesting, not those that lead to a sort of apathetic quietism in the researcher. From this point of view Elke Vanempten's work is highly stimulating, because it raises two important questions.

The chapter can be divided into two parts: an introduction, somewhat academic, in which some important analytical categories are introduced, but without sufficiently clear definition, the main ones being peri-urbanity, rururbanity and integration, which are then referred to in another series of categories that defines them differently; and a second part in which the two case studies are examined, the first as an attempt to find a balance between an integrated conception and sectoral negotiations, the second concerned with the use of a landscape project as the glue between two different actors.

Categories such as peri-urbanity and integration cannot be treated as terms that indifferently refer to different situations. They are not abstract enough as terms to allow such a broad span of interpretations. Accumulating literature on the subject without observing that many of the works cited refer to different situations is not much use, albeit often done.

Since the end of the 1960s the phenomenon of urban dispersion has been making headway in Europe, especially in some regions such as Flanders, where it has been known for much longer, and has now taken on unusual proportions. Despite the fact that all urbanists of preceding years have tried to understand the growth of the city, right from the start the fact of urban dispersion raised strong criticism and above all a proliferation of names and locutions created to describe it. Elke Vanempten cites some of them, but the list could be a lot longer. This proliferation hides two aspects: on the one hand the inclination of every scholar to invent proper labels, and on the other, and much more importantly, the different categorisations of the situations also reflect some of the real differences in dispersion phenomenon. The *Zwischenstadt* is indeed different to the 'diffused city' or to the American suburban sprawl.

The 'diffused city', for example, was in no way the result of an outward spillage of the population from the centre, but was the outcome of a totally separate territorial development of the selfsame dispersed city, in which inhabitants, for the most part, assumed reciprocal consumer and relational habits very similar to those of city dwellers. This was in contrast to the dispersion around Milan or in the Salento region, and different again to that in Flanders and the metropolitan area of Lille. The situations in the Ghent area and in the Deûle basin are also different from each other: in terms of history; morphological characteristics; demographic and employment structure; activities carried out; social structure; and institutional relations. We do not have the authority to speak of peri-urbanity or sprawl in all these situations, but all the same we must define what we mean by integration as accurately as possible. Often this term seems to imply a certain *mixité* of the land uses involved, of activities and social practices. However, in areas differing from each other in terms of history, morphological characteristics, demographic and employment structure, activities carried out, structural and institutional relations, the term takes on further and different meanings.

The second problem as regards the idea of the urban plan to which both case studies refer is the question that is at the centre of the theme 'design as a medium for integration in the "rurban" landscape'. Traditional urbanism, striving to define land use and the regulations that would render it stable in time as a result of negotiations leading to the construction of the plan itself, adopted the idea of a project that first and foremost entrusted itself to a sort of evidence of a collective interest – in the specific case of Parkbos, the interest of maintaining a vast surface as woodland. First and foremost it entrusted itself to a sort of evidence of collective interest; in the specific case of Parkbos, to the interest of maintaining a vast area as woodland. This often entailed extensive negotiation to convince the different actors, and finally entailed the embedding of the procedures involved in regulations which ensured that the selfsame results might recur over time, thus giving a certain stability. Before the start of any negotiations the purpose of the project coincided with the creation of a programme defined by and with the actors to be involved. Despite the great difficulties that always surround the definition of 'public truth', I consider personally that this idea was not unreasonable in the 1930s and postwar, that is, in the last period of modernity and the period of maximum expansion of the European city.

However, from the 1970s onwards the situation changed: social behaviour altered with the powerful emergence of the independence of the individual; in many European regions the structure of the economy changed with the emergence of widespread small entrepreneurship in all sectors; institutions changed with the decentralisation of many competencies and the questioning of strongly hierarchical institutional structures. In this situation of 'new modernity' the urban plan also changed, being compelled to seek its own legitimacy in a broader consensus rather than with constant reference to a 'public truth' that mirrors a collective interest. For this reason considerably more intelligence and imagination has to be dedicated to any reading of the different territorial dimensions: starting from the physical, visible dimensions, from the deposits left by the 'palimpsest' of the territory by past generations, not only their techniques and their imagery, but also their material interests, and the different natural and artificial landscapes; continuing by exploring different scenarios as the basis of a hypothesis for constructing a possible future; and finally by subjecting pertinent strategies and projects to a process of verification or falsification. This seems to be what has been achieved in the case of the Park de la Deûle.

REFERENCES

Habermas, J. (1992) *Faktizität und Geltung*, Frankfurt am Main: Suhrkamp Verlag.
Secchi, B. and Viganò P. (2009) *Antwerp. Territory of a New Modernity*, Amsterdam: SUN.
Viganò P. (2010) *Il progetto come produttore di conoscenza*, Rome: Officina.

PART III

SOCIAL AND SPATIAL SUSTAINABILITY IN STRATEGIC PROJECTS

CHAPTER 8

WHY SUSTAINABILITY IS SO FRAGILELY 'SOCIAL'...

Constanza Parra and Frank Moulaert

Despite the great efforts of sociologists, planners, social geographers, politi-cal ecologists, etc. to solidify the social pillar in the Holy Trinity of sustainable development, the social keeps occupying a lower status. The first section of this introduction explains why this is. The next section zooms in on strategic planning, showing its natural links with social sustainability, while revealing why these sel-dom strategically materialize. The third and final section makes a plea in favour of a more integrated approach to social sustainability, which could also empower stra-tegic planning approaches and projects. To this end, the sustainability approach is linked to the social innovation approach, in which, although phrased differently, social sustainability is the central principle of collective action. Therefore, it is argued, social innovation is the best way to guarantee social sustainability in stra-tegic planning.

SUSTAINABILITY – SOCIAL SUSTAINABILITY – AND WHY IT IS UNSUSTAINABLE AS CONCEIVED TODAY

In Chapter 9 (p. 183) Stijn Oosterlynck, Trui Maes and Han Verschure brush up the notion of sustainability. Throughout the history of the concept, it appears that the social pillar had to fight for its status and became significant only over the last decade of the sustainability debate (Figure 8.1).

First expressed in the first wave of environmentalism and materialized in the Brundtland Report, today there exists a certain consensus regarding the three core principles that define the notion of sustainable development: economic via-bility, social equity and ecological sustainability. Following the classical definition given by the Brundtland Report of sustainable development as 'a kind of develop-ment that meets the needs of the present without compromising the ability of future generations to meet their own needs' (World Commission on Environment and Development 1987: 9), it has been argued that matching development goals and human needs entails equilibrated articulation between the economic, social

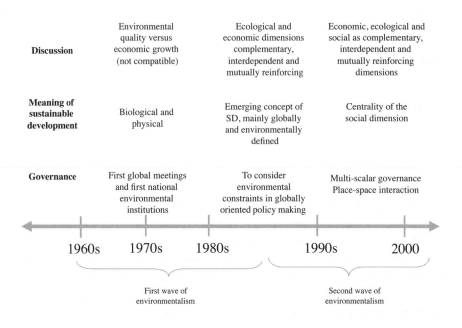

Figure 8.1   The building up of the concept of sustainable development (Parra 2010: 6).

and ecological systems, which, despite their own individual logics, shape and are shaped by their continuous mutual interrelation and embeddedness.

The *social* sustainability dimension has traditionally been related to values such as equity, solidarity, fairness and social justice among human beings, which should be guaranteed from intergenerational and intragenerational viewpoints. To reach sustainability, therefore, ideological premises point out the need to enhance those democratic values promoting social cohesion, social mobility, civil society participation and enhancement of cultural identities, among others. In other words, this social dimension refers to a particular type of governance capable of dealing with two key interrelated aims: (1) harmony between human beings and nature through a respect for ecological limits; (2) harmony between human beings with reference to cohesion, solidarity and democracy in order to guarantee equity.

Indeed, the centrality attributed to the social dimension was already emphasized in the Brundtland Report (World Commission on Environment and Development 1987), which pointed out that sustainable development needs a social system capable of finding solutions to tensions stemming from a non-equilibrated kind of development. Nevertheless, current dominant theoretical positions regarding sustainable development are hesitant about the centrality of the social dimension.

Even where human needs and societal arrangements occupied a fundamental place in seminal sustainability definitions, during recent decades there has been a predominance of work feeding either the weak or the strong sustainability perspectives, respectively privileging economic or ecological methodological disciplinary logics. As the literature shows, the persistent debate opposing weak (Common and Perrings 1992) and strong (Holling 1973; Latouche 2003) approaches hardly ever hints at human beings and social relationships, thus placing the social at a disadvantage compared with the economic and ecological sustainability dimensions. We believe that the confrontation between these two approaches to important societal sustainability challenges delivers rather inert responses that fail to integrate the social sustainability pillar, blurring its meaning and role, and thus voiding sustainable development of its human and social distinctiveness. Following Leroy (2003), this situation could in part also be explained by the quasi-non-existence of the environmental variable in classic and modern economic sociology. In fact, the inclusion of the environmental variable into socio-institutional analysis is rather new and therefore its research agenda remains under construction (Berger 1995).

The reasons explaining the relegation of the social sustainability pillar can be remitted to a history of conceptual evolution that precedes the publication of the Brundtland Report by far. They might be found in both the environmental ethical roots of the concept and the scientific disciplines that first became involved in the conceptualization of the sustainability problematic.

The natural environment and the utilization of natural resources have been the subject of attention for almost all societal groups. For instance, in early societies this preoccupation appears in the connections between religious and magical rituals, performed to guarantee nature cycles in harmony with the needs of human life. In modern times, the industrial revolution revealed how human action was abusing nature. This evidence drove utopians and romantics to emphasize the virtue of nature as a spiritually rejuvenating alternative to industrial society (Wheeler 2004). The ecological ethical basis of sustainability has also been connected to the search for more 'sustainable' forestry practices during the eighteenth century (Vivien and Zuindeau 2001), as well as to the birth of precursory conservationist and protectionist ideals leading to the foundation of the world's first nature parks.

During the twentieth century the environmental question was addressed from a different point of view. The effects of fast economic growth and the Fordist industrialization model, denying the socio-environmental side of human life, did not go unnoticed. But growing ecological degradation triggered a novel environmentalist awareness that found an echo at different levels of society. Both scientists and environmentalists called attention to the finite and limited character of natural resources and thus voiced an alert about a development model that was severely threatening the earth's biophysical carrying capacity (Carson 1962; Ehrlich 1968; Sachs 1972; Meadows *et al.* 1972). The 1970s were also marked by a series of international meetings chaired by the United Nations as well as by the foundation of the first European and national institutions dealing with environmental issues. The particularity of what has been called the first wave of environmentalism starting in the late 1960s is its critique of a development model founded upon growth rates considered incompatible with or antagonistic to an environmentally healthy planet.

Beginning in the 1980s, the debate opposing growth and environmental quality was reformulated in terms of the emerging sustainable development paradigm (Pearce 1993). Leaning on an early definition given by the International Union for the Conservation of Nature (IUCN) World Conservation Strategy (IUCN *et al.* 1980), the concept of sustainable development inherited a strong ecological imprint. However, and different from the previous period, the new sustainability paradigm perceived environmental quality and development no longer as conflicting, but rather as complementary, interdependent and mutually reinforcing (Elliot 1994). Unlike Meadows and colleagues (1972), the Brundtland Report (World Commission on Environment and Development 1987) did not focus on alarming public opinion concerning environmental issues, nor on criticizing the notion of development itself. Instead, it opted to revise the concepts of development and growth, taking into consideration their environmental and social dimensions. Sustainable development was thus coined as a call for an alternative development paradigm capable of building favourable bridges between development and environmental constraints and potentials.

However, the question of how sustainable development should be ensured continued to be presented as a 'global' issue. In their time, both the activation of the ecological alarm (1970s) and later the institutional birth and political positioning of sustainable development resulted from governance dynamics orchestrated on the global scale. This is perhaps one of the reasons why the 'social' remained in the background for such a long time. In fact, the classical definition of the social sustainability pillar in terms of equity, justice and fairness among human beings fits a model of sustainability with a spatial perspective oriented towards the global and emphasizing the need to reduce inequalities between the north and the south. Therefore, the potential role of the other spatial levels remained unclear until sustainability materialized as a territorial challenge, notably through the implementation of the Local Agenda 21 programme and the application of sustainability to different public policy fields, which started to occur only towards the end of the 1990s.

With the territorialization of sustainable development, the social dimension necessarily recovers its centrality as the societal connecting thread building complementarities between the different dimensions of sustainability. This argument does not reduce the relevance of the other two pillars of sustainable development, but rather advocates the need to understand their articulation as indivisible from society in terms of social relationships and governance. Such a view offers an additional plea in favour of the social sustainability pillar through a focus on 'place' and 'scale', and more precisely based upon the governance distinctiveness of each embedded territory

However, despite these positive insights into reconsidering the notion of sustainable development as a dialectical concept articulating its three pillars, in practice democratic governance is often introduced as a fourth pillar of sustainability (Chautard *et al.* 2003)[1] in the form of a steering procedure overarching the three 'traditional' pillars, while social sustainability, as the third pillar, is then slimmed down to 'equity' or a social justice agenda. The positive side of this restrictive definition is that justice becomes visible on the development agenda and that governance is displayed as concerned with all three priorities. But the negative side is that the link between the process dimension of social sustainability (especially the pursuit of socially cohesive societies through transformation of social relations) and the pursuit of social justice through redistribution becomes superficial or is even broken.[2]

THE AMBIGUOUS STATUS OF SOCIAL SUSTAINABILITY IN STRATEGIC PLANNING

As explained by the authors of Chapter 9 (p. 183), social sustainability is not a priority in strategic planning. Under the impulse of the European Spatial Development Programme, and especially the Aalborg Charter, a call was made in favour of effective land use and spatial development planning. The Aalborg Charter was confirmed in the Aalborg Commitments, in which over 600 local authorities committed themselves to giving a more prominent role to urban planning and design 'in addressing environmental, social, economic, health and cultural issues for the benefit of all' (see Aalborg Commitments at www.sustainable-cities.eu/, accessed 23 March 2010). Other fora, reports, commitments, etc. followed suit. In reality, little practice can be found in sustainable strategic planning in general and even less when it comes to social sustainability in particular. Quite often the strategic importance of sustainability is obscured or is translated into a spatial quality repertoire in which sustainability criteria are taken together with 'other' spatial quality features (Rapoport 1970). As Chapter 9 (p. 183) points out, either the social sustainability dimension comes in through the planning process door, in which case relationships with the public are enhanced and new joint modes of governance and operation of projects are put in place, or it slips in as one or a few of the features of 'healthy spaces', for example by referring to social and typological diversity, proximity of services, etc. Still, in general, when it comes to operationalizing sustainability for strategic spatial projects, the social dimension seems completely overruled by the ecological questions, with only some concern for participation and equity left under the social label. Tom Coppens (Chapter 10 of this volume, p. 199) addresses a particular aspect of social sustainability in strategic planning (projects), namely the analysis and governance of land-use conflicts. He applies a four-stage model for the analysis of conflict dynamics in strategic projects to the strategic spatial planning project for the Gent Sint-Pieters station area in Flanders. He explores the conflict dynamics within each stage and examines how they emerge, escalate, de-escalate or lead to solutions. In so doing, he stresses the 'shifting interaction between issues, parties and [their] relationships' (p. 208).

Literature and cases other than those cited in Chapters 9 (p. 183) and 10 (p. 199) partly tend to confirm these observations and partly seek to give them a more optimistic reading. Chan and Lee (2008), for example, argue in respect of urban development projects that 'social sustainability refers to maintenance and improvement of well-being of current and future generations. A project is said to be socially sustainable when it creates a harmonious living environment, reduces social inequality and cleavages, and improves quality of life in general' (p. 245). This seems to us the most complete picture of social sustainability, in the sense of equity, that can be found in the spatial design and planning literature. Once again, however, as in several of the sources cited above, the link with participation, co-design and community governance is made indirectly – as the latter are considered to be separate from social sustainability instead of part of its core dimensions. In fact, in this very publication (Chan and Lee 2008: 247), the link between social sustainability and participation is made through 'involvement of inhabitants in urban design of their communities, the finalized design proposal is very likely to meet their needs and desires. At the same time, the citizens may feel that they are part of the community and their senses of belongings are also enhanced', which is considered as part of 'the ability of the fulfillment of psychological needs of the inhabitants'. Of course, to justify governance involvement on its own to meet psychological needs is unsatisfactory; socio-political rationales matter as well. Still, psychological needs are important in justifying the place of governance in sustainability; they suggest that participation and governance, although part of the social pillar of sustainable development, cannot be considered solely as part of an integrated sustainable development agenda but also as part of the socio-psychology of users of space seeking well-being through clearly affirming their belonging to particular territorially defined communities. However, by defending social sustainability as a community well-being issue, we again end up in the dilemma by which sustainability is too easily portrayed as a programme, a list of criteria, of which social well-being (including the right to participation) is but one, and quite often the least important. What is needed instead is a process approach to sustainability that would turn governance into the core of the socially sustainable development process, and the three-pillar sustainability agenda into a regularly revised and re-evaluated outcome of that process.

FORESIGHTS FOR SOCIALLY SUSTAINABLE STRATEGIC PLANNING

In the two previous sections, we explained the position of social sustainability within the sustainable development approach in general and in relation to strategic spatial planning in particular. In this final section we seek to do two things. First, we want to make the sustainable development concept dynamic by putting the governance process at its heart. This means that the sustainability of social relations and collective action becomes the core driver of social sustainability rather than social equity. This will involve better integration of socio-political governance at its interconnected spatial scales into the sustainability approach. But it also means that we will need to consider the three-dimensional sustainability agenda as the outcome of the social process, in which power relations and conflict play a role, and in which political choices favouring social innovation in governance must be made. Second, we want to examine what this dynamizing of the sustainability concept means for strategic spatial planning and strategic spatial projects. We argue that this dynamism is coherently achieved through the social innovation approach.

(SOCIAL) SUSTAINABILITY AS A GOVERNANCE PROCESS

The potential offered by *social sustainability* lies in the precise meaning of the 'social' or what might be called the 'social sphere' in the context of sustainable development. Broadly speaking, the social refers to the manner in which human beings live together and collectively organize societies. At its heart, the social touches on human beliefs, feelings, thought, tastes, preferences, social relations and collective action. It also refers to the role of institutions and forms under which private and collective life is organized in different territories.

In the sustainability perspective we defend here, the social is materialized in terms of governance as a socio-political process. A frequent idea defended by authors addressing governance is the recognition that contemporary societies are governed by a multiplicity of interdependent actors and socio-institutional arrangements. This means that formal agencies alone do not influence the pattern of territorial life (Goodwin and Painter 1996), but also the range of institutional and individual actors from outside the political arena – or civil society as it is often generically referred to (Kooiman 2003).

This socio-political dynamization of social sustainability reveals the complexities of the multi-partner and multi-scalar nature of sustainable development and its governance. Elaborating on the concepts of place and scale as living entities, sustainable development appears to be contingent on the governance distinctiveness of interconnected territories, places and spatial scales. The question here is grasping the capacity of the social life of embedded territories to promote more sustainable interactions between societies and the territories they inhabit (Parra 2010).

With all this in mind, we highlight three critical features of territorial sustainability: the dynamic nature of its governance, the articulation among spatial scales and the pivotal role of the local level as a niche of social innovation. These all foster the production of more sustainable socio-environmental relationships.

From the global to the local, institutions and actors involved in sustainable development (governance) are numerous and diverse. In addition, their interactions at various spatial levels produce new socio-institutionally nested scenarios. These socio-institutional movements reveal the dynamic nature of the governance of sustainable development, meaning that its roles and initiatives evolve over time and according to territorial specificities. There is no single way forward in pursuit of sustainable development (Layard 2001), but rather a limitless governance potential to collectively decide on, produce and encourage societal arrangements and agreements on agendas, actions and projects of which society can take advantage in order to trace more sustainable territorial paths.

Within this multi-scalar reality the *local governance level* (Buckingham and Theobald 2003; Selman 1996) has been recognized as fundamental in the collective negotiation and bargaining that should lead towards more sustainability. In this respect, Chapter 28 of Agenda 21 (United Nations Conference on the Environment and Development 1992) emphasizes the relevance of the local governance level for sustainable development, stressing the central role of local authorities, and the importance of bridging partnerships involving the local state and local civil society. In contrast to top-down planning and 'environmental management' traditions, the retrieving of social sustainability is an invitation guaranteeing equity and justice by means of fostering democracy and governance, which together constitute the essence of sustainable development (Buckingham-Hatfield and Evans 1996).

SOCIAL SUSTAINABILITY, SOCIAL INNOVATION AND STRATEGIC PLANNING

Given the innate difficulty of the sustainable development model in attributing a central and structuring role to social sustainability (especially because of the programmatic instead of dynamic nature of the 'model') and the hard time it has with ethical positioning beyond the environmental, we make a plea here for a return to the concept of social innovation 'to make the necessary repairs' and to make strategic planning more sustainable. In the introduction to Part I (p. 15) Moulaert has already argued that the social innovation approach could give a stronger social coherence to strategic planning in at least two directions: (1) by stressing the ethical issues in strategic planning (projects) and the conflicts they may stir up – although it is understood that value systems and ethical positions are socially reproduced; and (2) once ethical grounds between different stakeholders are shared, socially innovative transformative actions need changes in governance institutions and agency that aim to contribute to sustainability and spatial quality in an equitable and socially just way (see Chapter 2 of this volume, p. 17).

Thus, as shown in the case study of the Schipperskwartier in Antwerp, social innovation is considered as a perspective both 'looking at transformative practice as [ethically based] progressive planning through the application of planning instruments, and also as a socially innovative transformation of institutional frames' (see Chapter 3 this volume, p. 81).

Thus, as the potential of social sustainability within sustainable development and transformative planning needs to be enhanced, we argue that this is best done by starting from the concept of social innovation (Moulaert et al. 2005: 1976), which in any case puts social sustainability in both governance and equity (development agenda) at its core. The implementation of the three dimensions of the concept of social innovation – satisfaction of human needs, changes in social relations and increasing socio-political capability (see Moulaert et al. 2005) – in the light of the sustainability problematic leads to a reading of socio-institutional innovation for territorial sustainability including a collectively produced definition of sustainable paths of development, innovation in the governance for sustainable development and enhancement of environmental rights – as a basis for new environmental citizenship rights. Therefore, socially innovative relations in their indissoluble affinity with nature have the capacity to produce what might be called 'socio-nature embedded scales' feeding both social and environmental rights' enhancement into the governance agenda of different territories. In strategic planning terms this means that consultation and co-production between planners, policy-makers and stakeholders is enhanced throughout the planning process, that the three pillars of sustainability are clearly translated into spatial quality rights from the very beginning, and that the participatory dynamics of the strategic planning process and projects are considered as a fully fledged part of the local democracy process in the territory where the strategic planning process is taking place (cf. Narang and Reutersward 2006). Paraphrasing the above paragraph, social sustainability in strategic planning therefore does indeed mean 'a collectively produced definition of a sustainable development path for the projects at stake and innovation in its governance as multi-scalar place–scale dialectics as well as the enhancement of new social–environmental citizenship rights for all people involved'.

NOTES

1   'Cultural sustainability' has also been used as a fourth pillar.
2   This artificial split between equity and democratic governance parallels slightly the split in traditional planning approaches between agenda setting on the one hand and 'consultation of users' as a minimalistic approach to participation and multi-partner planning on the other.

REFERENCES

Berger, J. (1995) 'The economy and the environment', in N. Smelser and R. Swedberg (eds) *The Handbook of Economic Sociology*, Princeton, NJ: Princeton University Press.

Buckingham-Hatfield, S. and Evans, B. (eds) (1996) *Environmental Planning and Sustainability*, Chichester: John Wiley & Sons.

Buckingham, S. and Theobald, K. (eds) (2003) *Local Environmental Sustainability*, Cambridge: Woodhead Publishing.

Carson, R. (1962) *Silent Spring*, Boston: Houghton Mifflin.

Chan, E. and Lee, G. K. L. (2008) 'Critical factors for improving social sustainability of urban renewal projects', *Social Indicators Research*, 85: 243–256.

Chautard, G., Villalba, B. and Zuindeau, B. (2003) 'Dossier 2: Gouvernance locale et Développement durable', Développement durable et territoires [En ligne], Dossier 2: Gouvernance locale et Développement Durable. Online. Available at http://developpementdurable.revues.org/index1068.html (accessed 23 March 2010).

Common, M. and Perrings, C. (1992) 'Towards an ecological economics of sustainability', *Ecological Economics*, 6: 7–34.

Ehrlich, P. (1968) *The Population Bomb*, New York: Sierra Club-Ballantine.

Elliot, J. (1994) *An Introduction to Sustainable Development: The Developing World*, London: Routledge.

Goodwin, M. and Painter, J. (1996) 'Local governance, the crises of Fordism and the changing geographies of regulation', *Transactions of the Institute of British Geographers*, 21: 635–648.

Holling, C. S. (1973) 'Resilience and stability of ecological systems', *Annual Review of Ecology and Systematics*, 4: 1–23.

International Union for the Conservation of Nature, United Nations Environment Programme and World Wildlife Fund (1980) *World Conservation Strategy: Living Resource Conservation for Sustainable Development*, Gland: International Union for Conservation of Nature and Natural Resources.

Kooiman, J. (2003) *Governing as Governance*, London: Sage.

Latouche, S. (2003) 'Absurdité du productivisme et des gaspillages. Pour une société de décroissance', *Le Monde Diplomatique*, pp. 18–19. Online. Available at: http://www.monde-diplomatique.fr/2003/11/LATOUCHE/10651 (accessed 23 March 2010).

Layard, A. (2001) 'Introduction: Sustainable development – principles and practice', in A. Layard, S. Davoudi and S. Batty (eds) *Planning for a Sustainable Future*, London: Spon Press.

Leroy, P. (2003) 'Un bilan de la sociologie de l'environnement en Europe', in C. Gendron and J.-G. Vaillancourt (eds) *Développement durable et participation publique*, Montréal: Presses de l'Université de Montréal.

Meadows, D., Meadows, D., Randers, J. and Behrens, W. (1972) *The Limits to Growth*, New York: Universe Books.

Moulaert, F., Martinelli, F., Swyngedouw, E. and González, S. (2005) 'Towards alternative model(s) of local innovation', *Urban Studies*, 42 (11): 1969–1990.

Narang, S. and Reutersward, L. (2006) 'Improved governance and sustainable urban development. Strategic planning holds the key', *European Journal of Spatial Development*, April. Online. Available at: http://www.nordregio.se/EJSD/debate060420.pdf (accessed 25 June 2010).

Parra, C. (2010) 'The governance of ecotourism as a socially innovative force for paving the way for more sustainable paths: the Morvan Regional Park case'. Thèse de doctorat en sciences économiques, Université des Sciences et Technologies de Lille.

Pearce, D. (1993) *Economic Values and the Natural World*, London: Earthscan.

Rapoport, A. (1970) 'The study of global quality', *Journal of Aesthetic Education*, 4: 81–95.

Sachs, I. (1972) 'Environnement et projet de civilisation', *Les Temps Modernes*, 316, 736–749.

Selman, P. (1996) *Local Sustainability: Managing and Planning Ecologically Sound Places*, London: Paul Chapman Publishing.

United Nations Conference on the Environment and Development (1992) *Agenda 21: Action Plan for the Next Century*, Rio de Janeiro: UNCED. Online. Available at http://habitat.igc.org/agenda21/index.htm (accessed November 2003).

Vivien, F. D. and Zuindeau, B. (2001) Le développement durable et son espace: antécédents intellectuels pour l'avenir', *Cahiers lillois d'économie et de sociologie* no. 37, no. thématique 'Développement durable et territoires', éditions L'Harmattan, pp. 11–39.

Wheeler, S. (2004) *Planning for Sustainability: Creating Livable, Equitable, and Ecological Communities*, London: Routledge.

World Commission on Environment and Development (1987) *Our Common Future*, Oxford: Oxford University Press.

CHAPTER 9

STRATEGIES FOR SUSTAINABLE SPATIAL DEVELOPMENT

OPERATIONALISING SUSTAINABILITY IN STRATEGIC PROJECTS

STIJN OOSTERLYNCK, TRUI MAES AND HAN VERSCHURE

For decades the environmental dimension and impact of planning have been largely neglected, despite the fact that spatial planning interventions often had a substantial negative impact on the environment. However, since the late 1960s, the 'modernist' planning approach, and the growth-oriented economic development concerns that informed it, increasingly met its environmental limits. There is a growing awareness that the earth's resources are limited (Meadows *et al.* 1974: 40–67) and that we live in a 'finite' world. This awareness has raised a new set of challenges and opportunities for (spatial) planning practice and is reinvigorating its strategic dimension by its stress on the need for long-term thinking and transformative practices (see also Chapter 2). The emerging approaches and answers to these challenges and opportunities are referred to as planning for sustainability. In several countries in the 1990s and the 2000s, often within the existing planning offices of national administrations, sustainable development plans have emerged. *Spatial* planning for sustainability followed suit, albeit rather hesitantly, and remains somewhat exceptional on the national level. Moreover, it was not clear what the contribution of spatial planning could be in relation to sustainable development.

This chapter is concerned with sustainability in strategic spatial planning and especially in strategic projects. It starts from the observation that sustainable spatial development is widely accepted as a concept, but that it is still somewhat elusive and in need of clarification and operationalisation, particularly if it is to be put into practice through strategic spatial projects in specific socio-spatial contexts. Because sustainability as a concept is dynamic and strongly context dependent, it needs the realisation of both visible products (in terms of sustainable spatial development) and processes (in terms of societal understanding of how to achieve sustainable spatial development). In what follows, we first describe how sustainable development became a central issue in spatial planning and design. We then argue that man-made space is not a passive recipient of sustainable development, but an active resource for achieving it. We pursue this argument further by distinguishing three important components of sustainable land use, namely careful land use, multiple land use and reachibility–accessibility–permeability. We define these three components, refer to different strategies for implementing the different components of sustainable land use and analyse tools to assess them in strategic spatial projects, thus arriving at a more operational understanding of sustainable spatial development.

SUSTAINABILITY AND STRATEGIC SPATIAL PLANNING

The concept of sustainable development, famously defined as 'the development that meets the needs of the present without compromising the ability of future generations to meet their own needs' (United Nations World Commission on Environment and Development 1987: 54), emerged from a long series of documents, reports and international meetings, ranging from the 1972 Stockholm Conference on Environment and Development, to the Club of Rome research and its 1972/1974 report *Limits to Growth* (Meadows *et al.* 1974), the Brundtland Report (United Nations World Commission on Environment and Development 1987), Agenda 21 agreed at the Rio Earth Conference (United Nations Conference on Environment and Development 1992), the various reports of the Commission on Sustainable Development (UN CSD) and the Rio +10 conference in Johannesburg in 2002.

The role of spatial planning in sustainable development became more prominent during the 1990s. The first EU Conference on Sustainable Cities and Towns in 1994 discussed the role of local governments in Agenda 21. The Aalborg Charter that resulted from this meeting calls for effective land use and spatial development planning by making use of high-density settlements to organise efficient public transport and energy systems, promoting the mixing of functions and equitable regional interdependency and using strategic environmental assessments to assess all spatial development plans (European Conference on Sustainable Cities and Towns 1994). At the Aalborg +10 conference in 2004, the Aalborg Charter was translated into the Aalborg Commitments. Signed by over 600 local governments, the documents expresses a commitment to the 'strategic role for urban planning and design in addressing environmental, social, economic, health and cultural issues for the benefit of all' (European Sustainable Cities and Towns Campaign 2004: 3). The role of spatial planning in achieving environmentally friendly and sustainable urban growth is also stressed in the reports of various World Urban Fora (Barcelona 2004, Vancouver 2006, Nanjing 2008).

The strategic role of spatial planning and design in addressing environmental challenges is not entirely new, however. Several planning approaches and concepts from the period of pre-modernist or modernist town planning contain elements that indicate attempts to strive for spatial qualities that equilibrate social (specific) environmental and economic concerns (see, for example, the garden cities, neighborhood units, new towns). Some utopian experiments such as Frank Lloyd Wright's Broadacre city, Paolo Soleri's Arcosanti and Yona Friedman's three-dimensional cities are also relevant in this regard.

In recent years a more fundamental debate has emerged in an attempt to match concerns for a so-called green agenda with those for a brown agenda, the green agenda dealing with natural systems (open spaces, water bodies, climate, topography, etc.), the brown agenda dealing with human systems (water use and waste, energy use, transport and mobility, building and physical infrastructure development, reconversion of brownfields, etc.). Environmental impact assessments are the tools being used to screen the environmental impact of programmes and projects, while strategic environmental assessments emerged during the 1990s to make direct links between environmental impacts and policies. In the recent *Global Report on Human Settlements*, eight objectives for sustainable spatial development were identified (UN-Habitat 2009). These objectives include developing renewable energies, distributive power and water systems and sustainable transport, improving eco-efficiency, increasing a sense of place, increasing the green infrastructure (photovoltaic systems) and striving for carbon-neutral cities and for cities 'without slums'. The International Council for Local Environment Initiatives (ICLEI) has supported over 3,000 cities in its efforts to achieve these objectives. Many cities have initiated a local Agenda 21 following the 1992 Rio Earth Conference.

Several international programmes have been set up: the Urban Management Programme (initiated in 1986), Localising Agenda 21 Programme, Sustainable Cities Programme, Safer Cities Programme, Health Cities Programme, City Development Strategy and Global Campaign on Urban Governance (UN-Habitat 2009: 16–17) to name but a few. As long ago as the 1970s, in the wake of the oil crisis, Freiburg (also known as Germany's ecological capital) opted for a sustainable and integrated planning approach in Riesefeld and Vauban with regard to mobility, energy and spatial development (Maes 2009). Sweden has been pioneering sustainable neighbourhood development since the 1990s. The eco-cycle model for the development of Hammarby Sjöstad in Stockholm came about as a result of an integrated planning process including all of the sectors concerned (Maes 2009). The model includes, amongst other features, a holistic infrastructure plan that integrates the basic utilities of energy, water, waste and information and communication technology as a closed local cycle in the urban system. Malmö developed the pilot projects Bo01 Västra Hamnen and Ekostaden Augüstenborg whereby the main stakeholders came to an interdisciplinary contractual agreement to strictly adhere to a set of sustainability ambitions. Inspired by these examples, the construction sector, real estate agencies and government agencies agreed on a number of target standards to produce half of the energy supply on the basis of renewable resources, to reduce energy consumption by 30 per cent between 2000 and 2025 and to reduce waste production in the building process to 10 per cent as a result of recycling and the use of renewable materials.

An increasing number of strategic programmes and projects worldwide have been documented in diverse sources (see, for example, Wheeler and Beatley 2004; Wakely *et al.* 2001; Best Practices Database in Improving the Living Environment containing 3,400 practices from over 140 countries at http://www. bestpractices.org/). Whereas some very interesting lessons can be learned from these strategic programmes and projects and from cities applying them, the following observations can also be made:

- In most cities one observes that the project approach stands out. Innovative projects are initiated, some clearly strategically supporting an overall sustainable citywide development vision (e.g. in Curitiba, Brazil), whereas other cities see projects as token 'sustainability' gestures in an otherwise business as usual scenario (e.g. in the case of Dongtan new town near Shanghai or Masdar City in the United Arab Emirates).
- Locally initiated projects abound in towns and cities around the world (Wakely *et al.* 2001). However, the strategic importance is often neither explicit at the start nor systematically set up to have a wider and/or a fundamental impact on citywide planning practices.
- Several projects do have the improvement of spatial quality as an immediate objective (e.g. improved access to land, urban transport, public facilities, urban parks). Other projects have a more indirect effect on spatial quality as they aim at improving relationships between citizens, at more democratic decision-making planning processes, at establishing new relationships between public and private partners and at experimenting with new participatory modes of operation (see, for example, the participatory budgeting experiments in Brazil).

Notwithstanding these observations, it may well be that the accumulated experiences of such projects gradually do influence spatial planning towards a more fundamental striving towards more spatial quality. However, the focus of most experiences is oriented towards ecological concerns (energy consumption, waste production, pollution, nature protection, etc.), factors that are extremely important and have to be taken into account in strategic spatial projects, whereas other influential factors related to space, spatial planning and design are underdeveloped.

So what does sustainability mean when starting from a spatial point of view aiming at the realisation of spatial quality in strategic projects? Building on the well-known and broadly accepted definition of sustainable development in the Brundtland Report and the Aalborg Commitments, we propose to define sustainable strategic spatial projects as all those that, in terms of content as well as process, contribute to the liveability (in a broad sense) of particular places for all citizens by providing for their real current needs without shifting the negative impact either onto other places or social groups or into the future (see also Albrechts *et al.* 2010). In this chapter, we focus on the specific contribution that space can make to sustainable development. Loeckx and Shannon (2004) warn against seeing space as a passive and neutral recipient for universal ecological processes, reducing its role to land available in limited quantities for human activities. Instead they propose to approach space as a resource for sustainable development and stress the importance of 'the role of "the locus" – the inhabited space – . . . as an inherent component, a critical instance, a modifying agent, within the paradigm of sustainable development' (Loeckx and Shannon 2004: 159). Spatial planning for sustainability is hence concerned not only with finding a space in which human needs are to be satisfied or with maintaining 'healthy' spaces for future generations, but with planning and designing particular places in such a way as to provide specific spatial qualities, such as accessibility, density, ecological, social and typological diversity, proximity of services, to their users (see also relative autonomy of space in Chapter 5). These man-made 'qualifications' of space are not easily renewable and should therefore be dealt with carefully. Marcuse (1998) has been equally critical of an unqualified application of sustainability outside the realm of ecological concerns. He suggests that sustainability should be not so much a goal of spatial development, as a constraint. Marcuse is mainly concerned with the degree to which sustainable spatial development programmes promote social justice and equity, a concern dealt with elsewhere in this book in terms of social innovation (see Part I), but the same could be said about the degree to which they deliver spatial quality as understood by planners and designers. We therefore propose to see sustainability as a necessary part of spatial quality. In the remainder of this chapter, we will be concerned with how space and its organisation through planning and design can contribute to sustainable development.

OPERATIONALISING SUSTAINABILITY FOR STRATEGIC SPATIAL PROJECTS

How can broad and general definitions of sustainable spatial development be turned into a set of *operational* principles that can guide strategic spatial projects in the direction of sustainability? The question of operationalising sustainable spatial development for strategic projects inevitably brings up tensions between the drive for universally (at least within particular political territories) applicable (and officially sanctioned) norms for sustainability, on the one hand, and the need to work in a context-sensitive way, on the other. Modernist planning proposed 'universal norms and standards' to achieve spatial qualities in the built environment (see, for example, the 'existenz minimum' of the modern movement or Doxiadis' minimum spatial requirement of $9\,m^2$ for every human being). In the 1960s and 1970s the use of norms, standards and sets of directive quantitative indicators was very common in urban planning and design. The *grilles d'equipement*, for example, had an important influence on the design and development of French new towns and *grands ensembles*. In the 1970s, however, some urban planners and designers argued that the use of such norms was no guarantee of spatial quality, and they proposed to develop quality criteria instead and, whenever possible and relevant, combine them with some norms generally accepted as 'musts', or with structural conditions (Comité Permanent Loyer et Revenu Familial 1973). Sustainability experts such as Tjallingii (1995) have called for sustainable spatial development strategies that leave enough room to attune them to particular spatial, temporal and social contexts. Sustainable spatial development hence needs to be considered as a dynamic construct whose precise content, as well as the process through which this content is identified, has to be searched for and specified anew in every strategic project. This implies that tools to measure and assess sustainable development need to be used as part of ongoing processes of communication, learning and visioning about how to match needs and resources at the strategic level and assist cities and regions in evolving towards sustainability. In what follows we will pursue our quest for the operationalisation of sustainable spatial development in strategic projects by looking specifically at sustainable land use, identifying and defining its main components, referring to strategies to implement these components and analysing tools to assess sustainability in strategic projects. But first we try to define the notion of 'spatial carrying capacity' as a basic criterion for sustainable land use using the 'ecological carrying capacity' expressed by the well-known 'ecological footprint' as a reference.

SUSTAINABLE LAND USE AND ECOLOGICAL AND SPATIAL CARRYING CAPACITY

Tools and instruments used to implement and assess sustainable spatial development focus mostly on sustainable land use. Central to this, and reflecting the roots of the sustainability concept in environmental concerns, is the notion of 'carrying capacity'. Ecological carrying capacity refers to the maximum number of individuals that a given area can sustain (for food, water, habitat and other needs) without degrading the natural environment for present and future users (Wackernagel and Rees 1996). As human needs are a function of various cultural, political, social and economic processes, ecological carrying capacity can be estimated only in very rough terms. Therefore, current estimations of carrying capacity focus no longer on the maximum population number that a given place can sustain, but on maximum environmental pressures, that is, the maximum amount of emissions that the environment can absorb and of natural resources that can be reproduced. The popularity of the Ehrlich formula – environmental pressure = population × wealth × technology – perhaps best expresses this shift.

Perhaps the most popular operational tool to assess ecological carrying capacity is the 'ecological footprint'. The ecological footprint is a measure (in hectares) of how much land an individual person or a neighbourhood, town or country (or the whole world for that matter) requires in order to sustain its overall level of consumption or lifestyle (Wackernagel and Rees 1996). The ecological footprint takes into account both direct land use for agriculture, cattle raising, wood production, infrastructure, etc. as well as indirect land use. Energy use, for example, is converted into the number of hectares necessary to absorb carbon dioxide emissions. The ecological footprint thus gives an indication of the relationship between the actual environmental pressure and the total amount of resources that the 'biological production system', earth, can produce. As the ecological footprint is insufficient as a tool to measure and assess environmental pressure in absolute terms, its value lies primarily in its educational function of allowing us to compare the consumption and production patterns of different socio-spatial entities (countries, towns, neighbourhoods, etc.) (Albrechts et al. 2010). Moreover, the exclusive emphasis on ecological aspects to the neglect of other quality of space aspects such as aesthetics and vitality, which are often less easy to quantify, leads to a reluctance amongst some spatial planners and designers to apply this tool.

Within the context of strategic spatial projects, the concept of carrying capacity becomes even more complex as the spatial carrying capacity of the site of the strategic project is also dependent on social, psychological, institutional and economic factors. In line with the overall argument in this chapter on the active role of (man-made) space in sustainable development, the four principles of sustainable development, namely the (physical) ecological principle (the embedding of activities in the natural, soil, green and water systems), the economic principle (attuning demand and supply, including in qualitative terms), the social principle (social justice and equity, in particular the creation of benefits for disadvantaged social groups and functions) and the institutional principle (the collective responsibility for the use of land and environmental resources), need to be complemented with a spatial principle. In choosing a particular programme of activities and functions for the strategic project site, the spatial principle requires that these activities and functions are spatially organised through planning and design in such a way that they do not hinder one another (particularly with regard to more and less dynamic activities and hard and soft functions), but, if possible, mutually reinforce or strengthen one another. By thus mobilising the potential of space, sustainable land use becomes a determining factor in the carrying capacity of particular places. All this means that the question as to whether development can be decoupled from a growing use of land and natural resources cannot be answered in a de-contextualised way. The answer will always be place and time specific. It follows that general norms, whether in the form of threshold or target norms, are insufficient to operationalise sustainable land use in strategic spatial projects. The carrying capacity needs to be analysed critically for each specific project area, taking into account some general criteria (see the above four principles) and the specific spatial potential of the area (spatial principle). In fact, the ecological and spatial carrying capacity are necessary criteria to assess spatial quality, but they are not sufficient because they tend to focus on 'negative' factors and characteristics and be operationalised in strict ecological terms. They do not add any value from the perspective of spatial quality. To mobilise human potential to create spatial quality through strategic projects, we define sustainable land use by referring to three different components, starting from the transformative (creative) concept of planning (see Chapter 2) and taking into account the active agency of space in sustainability. Sustainable land use is careful and multiple land use, supported by reachibility–accessibility–permeability (Maes 2009; Albrechts *et al.* 2010). We will now analyse these different components in more detail, paying particular attention to strategies to implement them and tools to analyse them in strategic projects.

CAREFUL LAND USE: DENSITY, MORPHOLOGY AND TISSUE

Careful land use implies an active, well-reasoned, responsible and critical use of land and environmental resources, which is in line with the carrying capacity of the project area. This can be operationalised in four steps. A first step is to *prevent* waste and other negative externalities by careful use of the available space, infrastructure and environmental resources. A second step is to *remedy* waste and other negative externalities by re-use, joint use and reconversion of land and the use of renewable resources. A third step is to *take care of* waste and other negative externalities by soil sanitation, noise insulation and separation of waste water and rainwater. A fourth and last step is to search for an *interesting socio-spatial tissue and morphology* (see performance dimensions of Lynch in Chapter 6) and an *optimal density* in function of liveability (not profitability).

An important spatial quality is the compactness of urban areas, which has long been neglected in spatial planning. Instead, urban expansion and sprawl was seen as a logical consequence of the growth of cities and the associated increase in the need for space. Yet, recently, the relationship between compactness and the efficiency of land use, transportation systems and network infrastructure has come more to the fore. It is argued that compactness and concentration of urban growth in specific places is more efficient, inclusive and sustainable as it lowers the costs of infrastructure provision, consumes less space, provides better access to services and reduces social segregation (see, for example, pp. 158–160 of UN-Habitat 2009). However, both objectives, compactness and concentration, have to be contextualised and their (political) feasibility and relatedness to possible congestion, social disorder or pollution taken into account.

From the point of view of operationalising careful land use in strategic spatial projects an important question is whether or not we should apply general, quantitative norms. Quantitative norms for careful land use are often based on density, for example the number of dwellings per hectare or inhabitants per hectare. However, in an urban context the differences in 'net density' (per hectare of built-up land in an area) are often significantly bigger than the differences in 'gross density' (per hectare of the total surface of an area) because public space, infrastructure and other non-residential functions consume more land in urban than in non-urban areas. On the other hand, collective and road infrastructure attain a lower return in 'rurban' and rural areas than in urban ones. It is therefore of the utmost importance to assess density and careful land use in relation to the specific type of area and the existing situation. Hence, measures of density are often not very relevant for urban areas as they do not say much about the morphology and tissue of the built environment (however, see the floor space index for a density measure that also contains an indication of the morphology of the built environment). The density matrix for Greater London offers an interesting tool that remedies the aforementioned problems (Greater London Authority 2006). It is an index of 'liveable living spaces' and 'number of bedrooms' per hectare, which, together with reachibility–accessibility and degree of urbanity, are assessed by comparing them with the quality of life and satisfaction of the local population.

The relation between density and morphology has been detailed in instruments such as Spacemate, a measurement tool that combines measurements of physical density and morphological patterns (Berghauser Pont and Haupt 2005). Spacemate focuses on the balance and relationship between the available space (surface of area), type of buildings (floor surface) and the open space necessary to make area and buildings reachable. More concretely, Spacemate is a measurement model that combines four variables, namely the floor space index measuring intensity of use (ratio of total floor space to the surface of the site), the ground space index measuring compactness (ratio of total built-up surface to the surface of the site), the open space index measuring the pressure on the open space in the area (ratio of the not built-up surface to the floor space on the site) and the height index measuring potential residential density (average amount of layers of site). By combining these four basic quantitative indices, Spacemate describes and typifies the relevant aspects of the quality of a given area, but leaves enough space for spatial planners and designers to test the degree of sustainability of different spatial designs and plans that try to accommodate particular programmes in particular types of space. Spacemate calculates the 'spatial fingerprint' of a strategic project, taking into account the morphology of the site. Often, a fifth variable is added, namely 'network density', which measures the amount of network in the area. The network density of the project area's spatial tissue is an indication of its porosity (the broadness of its open space and the links between them), the profile of its streets and the distance from one street to the next (Berghauser Pont and Haupt 2005). Another crucial factor for careful land use is the time dynamics of land use (Tummers 2007). Dependent on the activities that take place in a particular area, land use is not static and will register peaks as well as low moments in the intensity of its use (Maes 2009). The Space Syntax measures the coherence of the morphology and tissue of a particular project site and analyses to what extent the existing or planned and designed situation is a sustainable basis for spontaneous development and optimisation (Hillier 1999). The dynamics and potential of the project site are measured as an effect of its location in the larger area and the internal dynamics and coherence as an effect of the spatial organisation of the site (Stegen 2004).

MULTIPLE LAND USE: DYNAMICS AND SOCIETAL SUPPORT

Multiple land use, the second component of sustainable land use, aims for more intensive land use in time as well as in space and promotes the combination of functions and activities in one and the same space, whether simultaneously or consecutively. For multiple land use to be socially sustainable, that is, enjoying sufficient support among the local residents and other users, the different activities and functions need to be attuned, and technical and socio-psychological hindrance needs to be minimised. Multiple land use leads to more lively, dynamic and meaningful places through the interaction of diverse but complementary activities and users. More intensive land use refers to improving the efficiency of the use of ground space and can take several different forms (Maes 2009). A primary strategy to increase the intensity of land use is densification. By building in layers, clustering complementary activities, building in more compact forms and coupling different associated activities and functions (e.g. shared parking facilities, health-care parks) the amount of floor space needed in relation to the total surface of the site can be optimised. One can also anticipate expansion of the programme for a building or site by using modular building concepts, providing a solid structure that can sustain extra building layers in the future or by making sure there is enough storage space for extra future users. Finally, densification can also be pursued by densification of the existing tissue (e.g. the use of 'leftover' spaces, time-sharing).

A second strategy for multiple land use is concerned with mixing functions and activities. This can be done either by enabling juxtaposition without the functions or activities being connected to each other or by a proper interweaving of functions and activities in such a way that separate functions and activities benefit from proximity to one another. At least four 'interweaving concepts' can be distinguished (Poesen-Vandeputte and Bachus 2003):

- exchange of streams between interwoven functions (e.g. creation of jobs for neighbouring residents);
- overlap in which interwoven functions benefit from the same characteristics of the project site, without being directly dependent on each other (e.g. public space used for different activities);
- common third activity in which a concentration of activities attracts other activities (e.g. business services or restaurants);
- separation in which the impact of one activity on another activity is taken away (e.g. noise insulation).

A third and last strategy for multiple land use is the transformation of land use. This ranges from the re-use of buildings and land without changing their structure or form in the reconversion to restoration of old buildings, landscapes or heritage.

Quantitative indicators of the degree of interweaving of activities and functions such as those based on the ratio of housing to non-housing functions, or of number of residents to number of jobs, help to characterise the degree of mixing of strategic project areas, but do not say much about how activities and functions are mixed and interwoven and how much they benefit from proximity to each other. Indicators of the level and quality of local service provision can help to put indicators of the degree of interweaving and mixing into perspective. Since urban areas that fulfil a central function will most likely have a higher density and mix in services, it seems more appropriate to compare the service level of the project area with the average service level in the city (rather than the regional average).

REACHABILITY, ACCESSIBILITY AND PERMEABILITY

The reachability profile of a location is the set of characteristics that determines its reachability, including most notably the distance to population concentrations and other central places, the distance to public transport networks and the sensitivity to congestion. There is an inverse relationship between the reachability profile of a location and the amount of time, money and effort a person needs to transport him or herself or goods in a convenient and qualitative way (Provincie Noord-Brabant 2003; B&A Groep 2000). Accessibility is concerned with the optimisation of land use from the perspective of the social inclusion and participation of all social groups in society. The permeability profile or porosity is concerned with the relationship between green and built-up space, open and closed-off spaces, and public and private spaces and the degree to which these different types of spaces are linked to each other and accessible.

Careful and multiple land use in strategic projects thus has to be supported by reachability, accessibility and permeability (Albrechts *et al.* 2010). To improve reachability and accessibility, strategic projects are preferably located on the principal spatial structure of an efficient, multi-modal transport network. Compact building and multiple land use concentrates a critical mass of users within walking or cycling distance of public transport nodes, while the proximity of diverse functions and activities increases the share of 'soft' transport modes for internal transport. Sustainable strategic projects should strive for maximum permeability by avoiding gated communities and other forms of privatisation of public space and instead make closed-off spaces permeable by building local parks and sharing space among different types of users. At the same time, the private character of dwellings and gardens should be guaranteed.

It is difficult to develop indicators and quantitative norms for many aspects that determine the reachability, accessibility and permeability profile, such as the location of the strategic project in the wider area, the accessibility of local services for different social and cultural groups and the urbanistic and architectural forms that shape permeability and reachability (Albrechts *et al.* 2010). However, some quantitative measures have been developed for the number and proximity of basic services, public open and green space and spaces for children to play, which are crucial for the reachability–accessibility–permeability profile of an area. Exemplary attempts at operationalisation here are to be found in the Flemish City Monitor for liveable and sustainable cities, the concretisation of the Dutch spatial planning vision in a number of detailed notes (e.g. for mobility) and the reachability and accessibility norms developed by the Greater London Authority. The Flemish City Monitor strives for a good balance between reachability and critical mass for neighbourhood provisions and uses a geographical information system

(GIS) application to monitor the proximity and reachability of basic provisions (in terms of the number of people who have a particular provision at a specified distance)[1] (Block *et al.* 2008). The City Monitor works using a walking distance of 400 m for daily needs, while the distances for care provisions vary. For public transport (buses and trams), the City Monitor opts for frequently served stops at less than 500 m from dwellings, following the Flemish decree for basic mobility. In the 'Nota Mobiliteit', in which the Dutch government specifies the mobility aspects of its general spatial planning vision, the distances to public transport are diversified according to the scale of different public transport networks[2] (Ministerie van Verkeer en Waterstaat and Ministerie van Volkshuisvesting, Ruimtelijke Ordening en Milieubeheer 2004). The indicators are also different for dwellings on the one hand and companies and provisions on the other, and take into account the frequency and convenience (number of changes) of the different modes of public transport.

The Greater London Authority has developed an integrated policy framework for project developments that takes reachability and accessibility as one of its guiding principles. The development of green areas and playgrounds is planned, designed and managed as part of a broader network of open space. The Greater London Authority's playground policy does not prescribe exactly how much playground space boroughs must provide, but formulates a matrix of minimum norms (that boroughs have to aim for) and distances according to age groups (100, 400 and 800 m for children of less than five years, five to eleven years and more than twelve years respectively), the number of children and youngsters and the availability of opportunities to play in the wider area (Greater London Authority 2008: 40–67). This matrix functions as a context-sensitive instrument to provide the necessary space for playgrounds in concrete strategic projects.[3] Apart from the aforementioned minimum norm that is imposed on strategic projects, when including playgrounds in new strategic projects, the demographic profile, socio-economic and poverty indicators, spatial characteristics (density and mix), etc. of the area and the opportunities for renewing the existing tissue are also analysed and taken into account.

EPILOGUE

In this chapter we describe how sustainable development became a central concern for spatial planning and design. We argue that sustainable development is a constraint, rather than a goal of spatial planning and design. Sustainability, hence, is a necessary dimension of spatial quality. We then develop a specifically spatial perspective on sustainable development, calling attention to the active role that man-made space can play in sustainable development. This planning and design focus on space as a resource for sustainable development is then operationalised for strategic spatial projects by distinguishing and defining three components of sustainable land use, namely careful land use, multiple land use and reachability–accessibility–permeability, and proposing strategies to implement and tools to assess them.

More research is needed to further operationalise the spatial dimensions of sustainable development for strategic projects. Improving indicators, norms and guidelines to monitor and promote sustainable spatial development will certainly need to be part of this future research. This kind of research would not only strengthen the scientific basis of the design and planning disciplines, but also help to operationalise discussions on sustainable spatial development. However, from a spatial planning and design perspective, it is crucial to understand that these indicators, norms and guidelines for sustainability will not produce spatial quality in themselves. The latter requires creativity in order to translate indicators, norms and guidelines for sustainable development in qualitative spatial concepts, plans and designs. The concepts of and strategies for multiple and careful land use and reachability, accessibility and permeability described in this chapter offer solid building blocks for spatial quality in strategic spatial projects.

NOTES

1 For example, public transport within 500 m, a primary school within 400 m, neighbourhood shops for daily food staples within 400 m (or a supermarket within 800 m), a minimum of 2000 m^2 of neighbourhood green space within 400 m, public play and meeting places within 400 m, youth places within 800 m, a local service centre within 1,500 m, etc.

2 For example, a railway station for intercity trains within 3 km of dwellings and 1.5 km for provisions and corporations, metro stations or fast trams within 750 m for dwellings and 600 m for corporations and provisions, etc.

3 For the basic principles concerning the provision of playgrounds in new strategic projects, see Table 4.7 in Greater London Authority (2008: 60).

REFERENCES

Albrechts, L., Van den Broeck, J. and Segers, R. (2010) *Strategische Ruimtelijke Projecten. Maatschappelijk en Ruimtelijk vernieuwend*, Brussels: Politeia.

B&A Groep (2000) *Synthese bereikbaarheid. Hoofdlijnen*, Rijswijk/Delft: B&A Groep.

Berghauser Pont, M. and Haupt, P. (2005) *Spacemate. The Spatial Logic of Urban Density*, Delft: Delft University Press.

Block, Th., Van Assche, J., Vandewiele, D., De Rynck, F. and Reynaert, H. (2008). *City Monitor for Liveable and Sustainable Flemish Cities*, Brussels: Ministry of the Flemish Community.

Comité Permanent Loyer et Revenu Familial (1973) *Recommandations de Vienne, L'Environnement Direct du Logement*, Luxembourg: IFPH.

European Conference on Sustainable Cities and Towns (1994) *Charter of European Cities and Towns Towards Sustainability*, Aalborg: European Conference on Sustainable Cities and Towns.

European Sustainable Cities and Towns Campaign (2004) *Aalborg +10 – Inspiring Futures*, Aalborg: European Sustainable Cities and Towns Campaign.

Great London Authority (2006) *London Plan Density Matrix Review Housing*, London: Greater London Authority.

Greater London Authority (2008) *Supplementary Planning Guidance. Providing for Children and Young People's Play and Informal Recreation*, London: Greater London Authority.

Hillier, B. (1999) 'Centrality as a process: accounting for attraction inequalities in deformed grids', *Urban Design International*, 4 (3/4): 107–127.

Loeckx, A. and Shannon, K. (2004) 'Qualifying urban space', in A. Loeckx, K. Shannon, R. Tuts and H. Verschure (eds) *Urban Trialogues. Visions_Projects_Co-productions*, Nairobi: UN-Habitat.

Maes, T. (2009) *Developing a Strategy for the Operationalisation of Sustainable Land Use*. SP2SP Working Papers. Ghent: Centrum voor Duurzame Ontwikkeling, Universiteit Gent.

Marcuse, P. (1998). 'Sustainability is not enough', *Environment and Urbanization*, 10 (2): 103–111.

Meadows, D. H., Meadows, D. L., Randers, J. and Behrens, W., III (1974) *The Limits to Growth*, New York: Universe Books.

Ministerie van Verkeer en Waterstaat and Ministerie van Volkshuisvesting, Ruimtelijke Ordening en Milieubeheer (2004) *Nota Mobiliteit. Naar een betrouwbare en voorspelbare bereikbaarheid*, The Hague: Ministeries van V&W en VROM.

Poesen-Vandeputte, M. and Bachus, K. (2003) *Ruimtelijke verweving en hinder*, Leuven: HIVA–K.U.Leuven.

Provincie Noord-Brabant (Werkgroep Bereikbaarheid) (2003) *Korte afstanden, Grootste kansen*. s'Hertogenbosch: Provincie Noord-Brabant.

Stegen, G. (2004) ' "L" Alignement et la forme urbaine'. Paper presented at colloquium Les Formes du Patrimoine Architecturale, March 2004, Strasbourg.

Tjallingii, S. P. (1995). *Ecopolis. Strategies for Ecological Sound Development*, Leiden: Backhuys Publishers.

Tummers L. (ed.) (2007) *OVER(AL)TIJD: De achtergronden: Stedenbouw en veranderende tijdbestedingspatronen*, Delft: Delft University Press.

UN-Habitat (2009) *Planning Sustainable Cities: Global Report on Human Settlements 2009*, London: Earthscan.

United Nations Conference on Environment and Development (1992) *Agenda 21*, New York: United Nations.

United Nations World Commission on Environment and Development (1987) *Our Common Future*, Oxford: Oxford University Press.

Wackernagel, M. and Rees, W. (1996) *Our Ecological Footprint: Reducing Human Impact on the Earth*, Gabriola Island: New Society Publishers.

Wakely, P., You, N. and Meijer, S. (2001) *Implementing the Habitat Agenda: In Search of Urban Sustainability*, London: UN-Habitat and Development Planning Unit, University College London.

Wheeler, T. and Beatley, S. M. (eds) (2004) *The Sustainable Urban Development Reader*, London: Routledge.

CHAPTER 10

UNDERSTANDING LAND-USE CONFLICTS IN STRATEGIC URBAN PROJECTS

LESSONS FROM GENT SINT-PIETERS

TOM COPPENS

INTRODUCTION: UNDERSTANDING LAND-USE CONFLICTS IN STRATEGIC PROJECTS

Community protest and conflicts over strategic projects with local inhabitants or users are often important barriers to project implementation. There are abundant examples of strategic projects that were delayed or even stranded in the face of intensive community opposition and fierce juridical battles. Coping with community opposition poses serious challenges for strategic planners and city officials. They tend to see conflicts as disturbances consuming a lot of 'negative' time and money and as a distraction from more productive endeavours. Conflicts challenge the technical expertise of planners and city officials and are often a source of organisational and psychological stress.

Planning theory has addressed conflicts from a prescriptive point of view by developing approaches for planners to work with conflicts. There is a rich and abundant literature on participative or collaborative planning methods used in public disputes, such as Innes' collaborative planning (Innes 1995, 1996; Innes and Booher 1999) or Susskind and Field's mutual gains approach (Susskind and Field 1996; Susskind et al. 1999, 2000; Susskind and Cruikshank 1987) or Carpenter and Kennedy's advice on public disputes (Carpenter and Kennedy 2001). Many of these collaborative approaches in land-use planning and urban disputes, such as mediation or alternative dispute regulation, have been developed in order to provide more constructive solutions to land-use dispute than can be achieved by litigation. However, there has been less attention paid to the analysis of conflicts. The explanatory literature on conflicts within planning is rather fragmented, and conflicts have been addressed from different theoretical perspectives. A popular explanation of conflicts in spatial planning processes draws on the concept of spatial externalities, an approach sometimes referred to as the 'not in my backyard' (NIMBY) literature. This literature explains community conflicts as conflicts over the uneven distribution of the externalities of land-use changes. But, as Wolsink (1994) argues, the NIMBY literature is based upon a rather static conception of conflicts. It identifies some of the potential underlying reasons for land-use conflict but it fails to explain the empirical variety of community responses and conflict dynamics. There are, for instance, cases of land-use changes with only marginal externalities that result in fierce conflicts, but also land-use changes with considerable externalities that are not contested at all.

In this chapter I will argue that this empirical variety in conflicts and conflict dynamics can be better understood by elaborating an interactionist perspective on conflicts. In such a view, conflict is conceptualised as a social interaction pattern between adversaries. There have been many theories in the social sciences that have sought 'objective' sources of conflict, such as theories on relative deprivation (Gurr 1970) or theories on uneven development, scarcity or class struggle (Marx and Engels 1998). Although an interactionist approach does not necessarily ignore 'objective' sources of conflict in society, it postulates that the actual emergence, escalation and settlement of conflict is best explained by an analysis of the particular perception and conflict behaviour of parties in their interaction with adversaries (Kriesberg 2003; Pruitt and Kim 2004). Inspiration is sought in the field of the social psychology of conflict research, which seeks to formulate theories on the causes of conflict and conflict behaviour, conflict escalation, conflict management and conflict outcomes for a wide range of conflicts (organisational conflict, interpersonal conflict, social conflict, war and armed conflicts, etc.). Because of its emphasis on agency, an interactionist approach is of particular interest to planners and city officials, who want to understand not only how and why their own conduct and approach in interaction with other parties in land-use conflicts in strategic projects could trigger and escalate conflicts, but also how it could result in more constructive conflict outcomes. More specifically, this chapter will address three research questions in mobilising a theoretical framework of conflict research:

1   Why and how do community conflicts about strategic projects emerge?
2   Why do these conflicts escalate and why are they persistent?
3   How do these conflicts come to an end?

These three research questions will be addressed through a case study of community conflict around a major strategic project for the redevelopment of the railway station area in the Belgian city of Ghent.

I start by elaborating an interactionist perspective on conflict. Next, I propose a four-stage approach to conflict and present a framework that explains the transformation from one conflict stage to another by analysing changes in the parties, issues and relationships. This framework is then specified for the different stages and assessed on the basis of a case study analysis of the strategic project concerning the redevelopment of the railway station area in the Belgian city of Ghent.

ANALYSING CONFLICTS IN STRATEGIC PROJECTS: A CONCEPTUAL FRAMEWORK

DEFINING CONFLICTS

Before starting to analyse land-use conflicts in strategic urban projects it is necessary to give a more general definition of conflict. Within an interactionist perspective of conflict, analytical attention is on the perceptions and behaviour of the actors in the conflict, and the interaction patterns between antagonists. Kriesberg (2003) defines social conflict as the process that arises when two or more individuals or groups of individuals recognise that they have incompatible goals. When a conflict party is a group, there are some similarities with the processes of individual conflict, but there are also other distinctive processes at work. If the conflict parties are composite actors, their existence is not self-evident and it needs to be explained how individual grievances turn into collective issues and lead to collective action.

According to Thomas (1992), this interaction process starts when the conflicting parties perceive that their goals are incompatible with the goals of other parties. The word 'perception' suggests that the way the parties themselves assess a situation is crucial. Circumstances that some external observers might regard as putting people in a competitive or exploitative relationship do not in themselves constitute a conflict. The incompatibility has to be recognised by the actors themselves, before they can or will engage in a conflict relationship. It is not enough therefore to identify 'objective' and 'underlying' reasons for incompatibilities, because these often do not evolve into overt conflict (Kriesberg 2003; Klandermans 1997; Pruitt 1983; Pondy 1992). The word 'goals' in the definition is used in a broad sense. Goals can be tangible assets such as money or land, or intangible assets such as power, prestige or knowledge. Thomas (1992) distinguishes between perceptions, interests and values. A conflict over perceptions is then referred to as a judgement conflict or controversy, a conflict over interests as a distributional conflict and a conflict over values as a moral conflict.

Land-use conflicts are a special class of social conflicts. Following the above definition of social conflict, land-use conflicts are the social interaction patterns that arise when a group of people holds the perception that a planned land-use change is incompatible with their interests, values or needs. I am particularly interested here in conflicts in which the opposing parties are collective actors such as neighbourhood committees or action committees, because these are the most common in strategic projects. The term 'planned land-use change' refers to an intended land-use transformation by a public authority in which the zoning plans or the development rights of a site are changed. Most strategic projects belong to this class of land-use changes. My analysis will hence not refer to private initiatives in land-use change, which can be realised within the frame of existing development rights, and in which the intervention of a public authority is restricted to delivering permits.

A FOUR-STAGE MODEL OF LAND-USE CONFLICTS

Conflict scholars identified regularities in the patterns of conflict interaction early on. Authors in different fields of study, such as organisational sociology, psychology and peace studies, have argued that conflict interaction patterns develop through different stages (Pondy 1992) or episodes (Kriesberg 2003). In this approach towards land-use conflicts, I will make use of a four-stage model, which offers a descriptive device for studying social conflicts and provides a fertile ground for theory building on the emergence, escalation and termination of land-use conflicts.

The four-stage model of conflict implies that each conflict can be conceptualised as a serial succession of stages in which each stage of conflict has a particular interaction pattern with its own distinct internal logic and development. This model of conflict defines the different stages of interaction as latent conflict, emergent conflict, conflict escalation and conflict de-escalation. Latent conflict refers to the antecedent or underlying preconditions of conflict. It is the stage in which an incompatibility between interests or goals is created, which may later form a source of conflict between two or more parties. Emergent conflict is the stage in which at least one party in the conflict develops an awareness of its incompatible interests, needs or values. Escalation refers to the process in which the conflict strategies and tactics of the different parties are developed and in which their incompatible goals are pursued. Finally, in the de-escalation stage the intensity of a conflict decreases. A de-escalated conflict can result in a sustainable solution for all parties involved or a new cycle of escalation and de-escalation.

The stage model sees each stage as a necessary but not sufficient condition for a conflict to evolve into the subsequent stage. Thus, it is only under certain conditions that a latent conflict is transformed into an emergent conflict, and only some emergent conflicts become escalating conflicts, and so on. In this way, conflict dynamics are approached as a funnel; from the whole set of latent conflicts, only a subset of conflicts emerge and escalate. In this chapter, I aim to propose and test a set of hypotheses regarding (1) the specific dynamics of conflict in the different stages and (2) the conditions under which a conflict is likely to transform from one stage into the next one.

PARTIES, ISSUES AND RELATIONS AS FACTORS OF CONFLICT TRANSFORMATION

I advance the general hypothesis that transformation moments in conflicts are the result of the changing interplay between parties, issues and their relations. The parties are the actors who perceive themselves as in disagreement and who are ready to involve themselves in a conflict. The issues are the substantial points of disagreement around which the conflict revolves and the goals of the parties differ. The relations between the parties in a conflict can be characterised in terms of unequal power.

My hypothesis here is that transitions between the stages are caused by changes in at least one of the elements of the model (Figure 10.1). Changes in the parties, relations or issues will induce changes in all of the other elements and will result in an overall conflict transformation. Changes can be the result of choices made by the parties themselves, but they can also be related to the external context of the conflict. For instance, when substantial issues emerge due to external

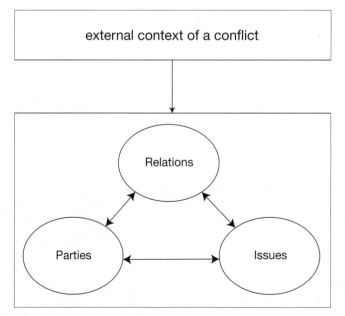

Figure 10.1 Conceptual scheme of land-use conflicts.

events, new parties will form or existing parties will transform. This may have an impact on the forms of interdependency between the actors in the conflict and/or change the issues around which the conflict revolves.

Having laid out a four-stage model of conflicts and proposed a general framework to analyse the dynamics within and the transitions between the different stages, I can move on to the actual analysis of conflict dynamics and develop and test hypotheses for each stage and each transition between stages. I will do so on the basis of a case study of a large-scale strategic urban project on railway development in the Belgian city of Ghent.

CASE STUDY ANALYSIS: GENT SINT-PIETERS

The land-use conflict over a large-scale strategic project around the main railway station in Ghent was analysed over a ten-year period between 1999 and 2009 during which the conflict went through all four stages. The project began in 1999 when the financing partners – Ghent city council, the Belgian national railway company NMBS, the Flemish public bus company De LIJN and the Flemish regional government – decided to renew the main railway station in Ghent and redevelop adjacent strips of land (Figure 10.2).

Figure 10.2 Development scheme Gent Sint-Pieters. Source: Euro-immostar, adapted by author.

The strategic project consisted of four main parts. First, it aimed to renew the existing railway station and the adjacent tram and bus station in order to increase passenger capacity. Second, it aimed to build a new underground car park with 2,800 spaces next to the railway station for commuters and for local users of the office park. Third, it aimed to develop 200,000 m^2 of offices, shopping facilities and dwellings adjacent to the railway station. Some of the buildings are high-rise buildings of up to 90 m. Fourth, a new road would be built to connect the new car park and the railway station directly to the outer ring road of Ghent. Between 2002 and 2005, the project plans were studied and elaborated by the four partners, who by 2005 had reached a consensus on the financial and technical aspects of the project. Construction of the first phase of the project started at the end of 2006.

Although some inhabitants protested against the project from the start, organised protest only emerged in 2005. The inhabitants of the area established an action committee, 'Buitensporig',[1] and organised several actions to alter or block the project in the period between 2005 and 2006. In 2006, the project was taken to court by several organisations and individuals; in 2007, the project partners started a dialogue with inhabitants of the area. By the end of 2007, when it became clear that most of the lawsuits had been decided in favour of the project, the protest subsided.

The data for the following case study analysis were collected through different sources. I analysed newspaper articles, media coverage, planning and policy documents, the action committee minutes and the content of its website in order to reconstruct the conflict dynamics and its different stages and to identify the main parties to the conflict and their goals. Subsequently, door-to-door structured interviews ($n = 117$) were held among the inhabitants living within a 100-m radius of the strategic project. Finally, I interviewed eleven key actors in depth (city officials, external observers such as academics, neighbourhood activists, representatives of environmental organisations, project partners, etc).

LATENT CONFLICT: EXTERNALITIES AS PRECONDITIONS FOR SPATIAL CONFLICT

As noted earlier, latent conflict refers to the antecedent conditions or underlying causes of land-use conflicts (underlying causes refer to potential issues in a land-use conflict). There seems to be a consensus in the literature that the underlying causes of land-use conflicts can be explained by the distribution of the externalities of land-use changes (Cox and Johnston 1982; Cox et al. 2007; Lake 1993; Wolsink 1994; Dear 1992; Takahashi and Dear 1997). In mainstream economics externalities are defined as actions that affect the utility of other market actors in a way that is not reflected in market pricing (Just *et al.* 2004). Spatial externalities, which are a common occurrence in strategic projects, are the effects of land-use transformations on 'neighbouring' actors not directly involved in the transformations and hence not factored into the associated 'costs'. In addition, these externalities often relate to the use value of particular places: accessibility to other functions, connectivity to all sorts of networks, including social networks, the provision of clean air, the beauty of a natural landscape or a scenic view, silence and so on. These indirect utilities are spatially confined, unique and attached to a specific location (hence spatial externalities).

When a strategic project is developed for a particular place, this can have a far-reaching impact on the use value, both positive and negative, that different groups draw from it. Negative externalities of strategic projects such as noise, air pollution, decreasing accessibility or safety affect the local public good or local spatial quality. The devaluation of the use value of a place is a powerful motive for a conflict of interests between those involved in the strategic project and those who are not involved but who are subject to its impact. The distribution of the externalities of strategic projects varies across the relevant space. In the project Gent Sint-Pieters, for example, the positive externalities are mainly located on the supra-local level in terms of increased accessibility of the railway station, whereas the negative externalities are strongly locally concentrated in terms of increased traffic and associated noise and air pollution. Such targets of protest have been dubbed 'locally unwanted land use' (Popper 1987), while the hostile reaction of opponents to such land uses is sometimes described by the popular acronym NIMBY. Of course, by identifying spatial externalities that may (or may not) give rise to conflicts, we need to take into account that they are, to a certain extent, socially constructed. Given that I have defined particular distributions of 'spatial externalities' as the main precondition for conflicts and that the impact of the spatial externalities of a strategic project tends to decline with distance, I expect that potential opponents will be situated within a certain range of the strategic project zone and that opposition will mostly take the form of local community protest.

LATENT CONFLICT IN GHENT

The first design proposal for the strategic project concerning the railway station area in Ghent was made in 1999. The negative externalities of the proposed strategic project formed the basis for a latent conflict between the project partners and part of the local community. These negative externalities surfaced in several studies carried out as part of the development of the strategic project. The (obligatory) 2005 environmental impact assessment analysed its expected impact on local traffic, air quality, the water and soil system, noise, the landscape and human beings for different time periods of the project. An important distinction was made between the impact during the construction phase (2008–2015) and the impact after completion (after 2015).

One of the crucial findings in the report related to the distribution of the traffic load after implementation of the strategic project. Construction of a new road between the railway station and Ghent's outer ring road would lead to a significant increase in traffic in other parts of the neighbourhood (while reducing it in others where streets were being used as connecting roads to the railway station). The redistribution of traffic load would also impact on noise, 'particulate matter' and air pollution and traffic safety. For instance, in some streets with a heavier traffic load, noise levels would increase by 1–3 dBA, while in others with a lighter load noise levels would decrease by 6 dBA. The report concluded that the overall air quality would increase because of a reduction in particulate matter (nitrogen dioxide and PM10), with the exception of two streets.

A second negative externality concerns the effect of the high-rise buildings along the Fabiolalaan, the road adjacent to the project site. In 2004, the Amsterdam Administration for Spatial Planning examined the effects of high-rise buildings on a number of aspects such as sun exposure and radiation, wind climate, feelings of security and visual impact (Gemeente Amsterdam 2004). The study observed only a minor impact on existing houses as regards visual aspects and sun radiation exposure, a conclusion confirmed by the environmental impact assessment, but also noted a potential conflict between the size of the existing houses and the size of the new developments. The project impact zone, as identified in these studies, was fairly restricted. According to the environmental impact assessment, the impact would be felt no further than a range of 500 m from the actual strategic project site, affecting about 13,000 inhabitants.

To conclude, the objective conditions for the emergence of a conflict were present in the strategic project for the redevelopment of the Ghent railway area. I will now focus on the factors which caused this latent conflict situation to be transformed into a real conflict that eventually threatened the implementation of the strategic project itself.

EMERGENT CONFLICT: THE LOGIC OF COLLECTIVE ACTION IN CONFLICTS

The crucial factor in the transformation of a latent conflict situation into a real conflict is the emergence of collective social entities or parties around one or more negative externalities of the strategic project. The stage of conflict emergence hence starts with the transformation of uncoordinated groups of local people affected by the negative externalities into an organised, collective entity. Part and parcel of the development of such a collective conflict party is the framing and selection of conflict issues and the formation of relations with other parties in the strategic project.

The precondition for the development of a conflict party is the presence of individual awareness of incompatible goals or values among potential future members of conflict parties (Kriesberg 2003; Pruitt and Kim 2004). In order to start opposing strategic projects, it is necessary (1) to be minimally informed about the nature of the changes brought about by the strategic project, but also (2) to form an opinion of the potential future harm of the externalities of the pro- ject. In the environmental risk perception literature, there is substantial research on the variation in people's perceptions of future harm (or risk) and in how experts calculate risk on the basis of scientific methods (Kahneman and Tversky 1979; Kunreuther and Patrick 1991; Petts 1992; Rogers 1998; Wester-Herber 2004).

But since protest implies collective forms of action, individual awareness is not a sufficient condition for socially organised protest to emerge. Here, the theory of conflict group mobilisation gives us more insight into how group protest emerges out of individual grievances (Coleman 1957; Tilly and Tilly 1981; Dahrendorf 1959). The theory starts with what Dahrendorf calls a quasi-group with latent interests, that is, a set of people who have interests (or grievances) in common but are not yet aware of each other. More specifically, they are subject to similar nega- tive externalities. The process of group mobilisation usually starts with an external triggering event that alarms or arouses people in the quasi-group. This triggering event functions as a catalyst for communication about their shared grievances among the members of the quasi-group. Group mobilisation is dependent on the capacity to communicate and to recruit (Dahrendorf 1959; Kriesberg 2003; Pruitt and Kim 2004) and on the organisational capacity of the members of the group.

The capacity to communicate and recruit among members of the conflict party is affected by the numbers in the quasi-group, their proximity and density, their social and technical skills, the presence of a common language and the social and non-social links between them (Krieberg 2003). The number and density of people with grievances in strategic project conflicts are proportional to the density and the reach of the project impact zone. Research also demonstrates that pre-existing networks linking individuals and small groups are crucial in the development of conflict parties (Pruitt and Kim 2004). These pre-existing groups and links facilitate communication and the creation of new collective identities.

The second factor affecting conflict group mobilisation is the organisational capacity of the members of the quasi-group. Crucially important is the availability of community leaders who are able to formulate protest group goals, to iden- tify adversaries, to create group identity and to organise group actions. Since strategic projects and the assessment of their environmental and social impacts can be very technical, it is probable that the community leaders will have some substantial or procedural expertise in spatial planning, based on previous experience, or professional activities, or expertise developed through participation in voluntary associations such as environmental organisations.

Issues of disagreement are selected and criticisms formulated as part of the development of a conflict party. Klandermans (1997) and Lewicki and colleagues (2002) argue that the generation of collective action frames is crucial for the emergence of conflict. Such a collective action frame includes a set of common ideas on the shared grievances of the group, the goals it seeks to achieve and the identification of its opponents. In strategic projects, the ease with which group goals and a common identity are developed is very much related to the local distribution of negative externalities. When these externalities are distributed in such a way that inhabitants in the impact zone are likely to pursue different goals, it is very difficult to achieve a collective protest identity for the whole zone. When different groups living in the zone pursue opposite goals, the legitimacy of these groups is more easily questioned. Community leaders therefore play an important role in developing a consensus about group goals. If there are opposing goals within the impact zone, the population will have to find protest arguments that transcend the arguments of the different parts. A collective action frame is hence always a socially negotiated frame, in which internal tensions between different individuals and subgroups remain present.

In the course of the development of conflict groups, relations with opponents are also established. These relations are strongly influenced by the power resources of both parties. Some authors, such as Coleman (1957), Kriesberg (2003) and Kriesi and colleagues (1993), stress that protest is unlikely to emerge when a perception exists among members of the quasi-group that ability to change unsatisfactory conditions is very low. Thus, the theory of protest emergence states that members of a protest group must come to believe they can improve their position of power vis-à-vis their adversaries, either by boosting their own resources or by undermining those of their adversaries.

CONFLICT EMERGENCE IN GHENT

The conflict in Gent Sint-Pieters emerged rather slowly. Although the first plans for the strategic project were drawn up by the city and its allies in 1999, it took until 2005 for collective protest to emerge. One reason for this was the lack of information on the project among the inhabitants. In the period between 1999 and 2005, the only information received by the public came from one public hearing in 2004 concerning the aims and ambitions of the project. The limited availability of information was a deliberate strategy by the project partners. In particular, the semi-public partners of the project, most notably the regional bus company, were very reluctant to communicate actively about the strategic project before the project partners had agreed the basis of the plan and the financial means to implement it (Stad Gent 2003). The city council also made a deliberate choice not to communicate about the project in its early phases. The result was that the project plans were hardly known in the neighbourhood until 2004–2005, so there was no awareness of incompatible goals even on an individual basis.

Nevertheless, on the basis of scanty project information spread by the local press, some quasi-conflict groups in the neighbourhood had already formed, but independently and without knowledge of each other. In the Fabiolalaan, some inhabitants had organised a petition as early as 2001 against the high-rise buildings proposed in the plan (Nieuwsblad 2001). Other inhabitants in the northern part of the area were already involved in an ongoing conflict over car traffic and parking in their neighbourhood, and they perceived the new plans as creating an unacceptable additional traffic load on their streets. In the southern part of the project zone, some inhabitants were active members of a local environmental organisation (Milieugroep Sint Pieters Aaigem), which acquired information on an individual basis. This organisation had already opposed other related spatial planning interventions, including organising some small protest actions (Nieuwsblad 2003), and was now concerned about the loss of natural habitats and the increased noise levels caused by the new road linking the railway station car park with the outer ring road.

The triggering event that brought the quasi-groups together occurred in the spring of 2005. In reaction to the lack of information, several local environmental organisations jointly organised a public debate on the strategic project. The purpose of this hearing was to raise general awareness of the project and to stimulate public opposition. At the end of the meeting, about fifty inhabitants volunteered to participate in protest actions, and, there was no shortage of organisational capacity among them. The core of the action committee comprised an expert in environmental law, the chairperson of the local environmental group and two functionaries from the Flemish government. Furthermore, the action committee received help on occasion from local inhabitants in crucial positions and/or with pertinent capabilities: planning experts, architects, local politicians and activists from environmental organisations. Some committee members were well aware of procedural, juridical and substantive aspects of planning and also possessed the capacity to organise protest.

In the following months, these volunteers organised several meetings, which eventually resulted in the formation of a stable conflict party. The purpose of these meetings was to develop a shared identity involving a shared set of grievances and a collective strategy to oppose the plans. Since the goals of the different quasi-groups were complementary, it was relatively easy to develop such a consensus. The different issues brought forward by these quasi-groups (high-rise buildings, the new road through the natural reserve, additional traffic) were aggregated into group goals. In its first newsletter, the action committee Buitensporig developed a mission statement and presented itself to the community as follows:

> The aim of the action committee Buitensporig is to change the project Gent Sint-Pieters, in dialogue with the project partners, in order to increase the liveability of the neighbourhood. The action committee is an open, non-political group of engaged citizens, which critically analyses the project Gent Sint-Pieters, formulates alternatives, involves other inhabitants and takes appropriate action.
>
> (Buitensporig 2005)

In this mission statement, several elements are present that come together to make a coherent action frame. The members of the protesting party are identified ('open, non-political group of engaged citizens'), grievances are named ('liveability of the neighbourhood'), the adversary partner is named ('project partners'), and the goals are stated ('critically analyse and formulate alternatives'). In conjunction with this mission statement, Buitensporig developed an extensive critique of the strategic project, together with a counter-proposal. The counter-proposal argued for a substantial reduction in the amount of new development along the Fabiolalaan and a reduction in the number of parking spaces and proposed a development scheme without a new road connection. They argued instead for further development of public transport to bring commuters to the railway station.

The transformation of a set of loosely organised individuals and quasi-groups into a full-blown conflict party inevitably changes the relations with other conflict parties. As individuals or quasi-groups, the chances of impacting on the decision-making process of a large-scale strategic project are limited. Individual actions, such as sending emails or letters to the city council, or starting petitions, had little effect on the decision-making process. But through the mobilisation of resources, the action committee Buitensporig was able to pool the necessary knowledge and networks to increase its power. The opportunity for protest was shaped by the internal transformation and resource pooling of the conflict party, which also created concrete opportunities to deploy protest strategies. In 2006, the project partners started the necessary legal procedure to approve the zoning plan for the project. The juridical experts on the action committee saw opportunities for juridical tactics to increase their bargaining power. In addition, the upcoming municipal elections offered opportunities for political tactics.

The case demonstrates that the emergence of conflict started with the transformation from loose groupings of individuals and quasi-groups into a conflict party. The development of a conflict party enabled the selection and negotiation of party issues and altered relationships with adversaries.

ESCALATING CONFLICT: HOW CONFLICT BREEDS FURTHER CONFLICT

With the emergence of conflict, and the formation of protest parties, the different parties then engage in an overt conflict relationship with their adversaries. The process of overt conflict starts with the development of a conflict strategy and tactics by all the conflict parties; conflict behaviour is dependent on the strategic intentions of the conflicting parties. Most models of conflict (Thomas 1992; Blake and Mouton 1964) have distinguished five basic strategic intentions in a conflict, based upon two underlying dimensions developed in the dual concern model (Pruitt 1983; Pruitt and Kim 2004). The strategic orientation of a conflict party depends on the nature of its relationship with other conflict parties: the degree of cooperativeness (intention to satisfy the concerns of others), as well as the degree of assertiveness (intention to satisfy its own concerns). The five basic intentions that follow from combinations of these two dimensions are competitive, collaborative, compromising, avoiding and accommodating.

Furthermore, the strategic orientation of a conflict determines the repertoire of tactics that parties develop during the conflict. For instance, a competitive intention will develop conflict tactics that undermine the power of the other party. A collaborative intention will develop conflict tactics oriented towards joint problem-solving. Tactics used in a conflict situation range from coercion to reward and persuasion. When one or more parties choose a competing intention and competitive tactics, it is highly likely that conflict escalation will occur (Pruitt and Kim 2004). Deutsch and Coleman (2000) define escalation as the increasing use of heavier methods of influence, especially coercive or punishing tactics, by each party in opposition to those of the other party. In this process new issues arise and existing issues become polarised, new parties are added to the conflict, and the conflict strategies and tactics harden.

The tactics used by action committees are explained by resource mobilisation theory (McCarthy and Zald 1977), which argues that the success of a social movement in attaining its goals is related to its success in recruiting active members or supporters who can deliver resources in terms of support, time and money. These resources in turn can be used to gain power over decision-making. Proponents such as the public authority are institutionally authorised to take legitimate decisions on strategic projects. Opponents, however, have no direct power in the main to influence decision-making and have to develop tactics to increase their bargaining power. Through the use of these conflict tactics, however, important transformations occur in issues as well as in the parties and the relationships between them. The use of opposition tactics is likely to lead to new issues of conflict. For instance, through resource mobilisation, the opposing party will attract additional powerful parties sympathetic to its own goals, and, in the formation of such new coalitions, new issues will be raised or stressed. The result is that new issues are added and that specific issues become more general. In the search for litigation strategies, new issues, such as procedural ones, will emerge. Although these issues are initially juridical means to achieving a goal, they can quickly evolve into new conflict goals.

During escalation of the conflict, parties will develop psychological and group changes (Pruitt and Kim 2004). The psychological changes include selective perception and attributional distortion. Selective perception is the tendency to gather, interpret and evaluate information according to previously held beliefs. Attributional distortion, on the other hand, is the tendency towards biased ideas about the behavioural motives of another conflict party. Information that confirms initial ideas concerning the other party's behaviour will be seen as dispositional, whereas information that is contrary to observed behaviour will be seen as situational. The individual tendency towards self-reinforcement and selective perception is also present at group level, but through different mechanisms. For instance, previously held group beliefs can be reinforced by group thinking, while further radicalisation of opinions will be reinforced by militant leadership.

In the escalation stage, processes of further polarisation occur between the conflict parties, and direct communication becomes more difficult or even impossible. Through processes of selective perception or attributional distortion, the view of the other party will change, resulting in stereotyping of the other party.

Conflict escalation in Ghent

After several meetings among the inhabitants in the summer of 2005, the action committee Buitensporig developed its conflict strategies. As stated in its mission statement, the initial aim of Buitensporig was to start a dialogue with the city and its partners, so the committee initially took a collaborative orientation towards the conflict. The project partners, on the other hand, initially took an avoiding orientation towards the protest. Requests for dialogue from the action committees were either ignored or rejected. There are several reasons that explain this reaction from the project partners. For city officials and politicians the project was considered to be of supra-local importance; local protest was therefore perceived as less legitimate than supra-local interests. In the perception of the project partners it was legitimate to accept local negative externalities for much larger presumed benefits on the supra-local level. In addition, the project was also considered as an implementation of the long-term spatial development vision of the city and the Flemish region. The decision to develop a strategic project in this area had already been discussed in the Ghent structure plan; hence the city council regarded the discussion on this issue as closed. Furthermore, the city, the regional bus company and the national railway company had been negotiating for two years on a compromise for the realisation of the strategic project. The compromise involved the specifics of the design, the financial distribution of the costs and the roles and positions of the different partners in the decision-making process. The partners had already signed a contract for the elaboration of the project before the protest emerged. If new demands from the inhabitants were to be added, this could re-open the discussion and lead to a new round of negotiations, with further delays as a result. Therefore, all the partners agreed that there could be no further discussion on the basic components of the plan – the parking provisions, the new road and the high-rise development.

The avoiding orientation of the project partners caused the protest committees to shift from a collaborative towards a more competing intention. The action committee developed mobilisation tactics, oriented to gain more support for its goal. This mobilisation tactic was directed towards different target audiences. Local mobilisation was oriented towards attracting support and resources from among those affected in the neighbourhood. One crucial goal was to increase social awareness of the project's negative impact (to stimulate further conflict emergence) and to convince the local inhabitants of the opportunities for protest. Supra-local mobilisation was oriented towards attracting the support of sympathetic and influential bystanders outside the area. This was done by directly contacting influential elites such as politicians, architects and planners, but also through media coverage in regional newspapers. Political tactics aimed at influencing the decision-making process complemented mobilisation tactics. In 2006 new municipal elections were coming up. When the conflict emerged, the city council of Ghent was dominated by a coalition of socialists and liberals. The major, who was the key person in the realisation of the project, was a member of the Socialist Party. Although both parties – socialist and liberal – intended to continue with the coalition after the election, polls before the elections showed that they were uncertain to achieve a majority. Thus, the chances were high that a third party would be needed to form a majority coalition after the elections, and the best candidate was the Green Party. So the action committee focused on collaboration with the Green Party. The Green Party strongly opposed some parts of the project, and refused to enter into a coalition unless these were revised. The project thus became the stake of the elections. This strategy failed, however, as the socialists and the liberals achieved enough votes to form a coalition without the Green Party.

Apart from mobilisation and political tactics, litigation tactics were crucial in gaining decision or bargaining power for the action committee. These tactics are oriented to increasing bargaining power through juridical lawsuits. In many[3] cases, these lawsuits slow down, or even threaten, project implementation. In Ghent, litigation tactics were used very early in the protest. The driving force behind these tactics was an expert in environmental legislation, who skilfully used his knowledge of the latest juridical innovations. Already in 2005, very soon after the emergence of the action committee, the first juridical steps were taken to block the building permit for the strategic project. In 2007, a juridical bombardment was launched by different organisations and for different juridical institutions. The local Green Party, some environmental organisations and some local inhabitants sued the project partners with substantive and procedural arguments in different law courts.

The tactics employed by the action committee triggered counter-reactions from the public authorities, for instance by increasing the communication activities of the city. There was a steep increase in the number of communication activities (newsletters and public hearings) from 2006 onwards as a reaction to the local mobilisation strategies of the action committee, which started at the end of 2005 (Figure 10.3). Underlying this communication campaign was the idea that the

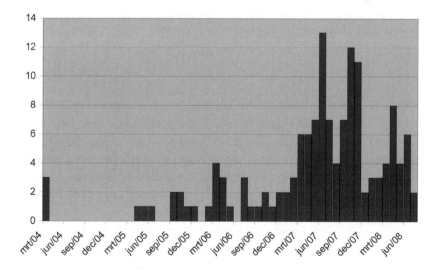

Figure 10.3 Number of communication activities by the city of Ghent over time, including hearings, newsletters and debates.

information distributed by the action committee is biased towards the negative impact of the project. The city and its partners hoped that by providing 'objective' information, the perceptions would change towards a more positive appreciation of the project.

During the escalation new conflict issues developed. For instance, the use of litigation tactics led to a deterioration in personal relationships between the leaders of the action committee and the city representatives and the theme of air pollution and fine dust particles came to dominate the protest argumentation. Although the impact on air pollution had been on the agenda of the action committee from the start, it had been only a secondary issue. This is clearly visible, for instance, in the shift of the arguments used in protests. Early protest actions, such as demonstrations, stressed grievances over high-rise buildings, whereas in later protest actions particulate matter became more important.

Because of the litigation strategies, in particular, the relationships between the city and its partners and the action committee deteriorated quickly and stereotyping emerged. In the national newspaper *De Standaard* (2007) an important project partner commented on the Ghent protest as follows: 'Many people suffer from the Nimby (not in my backyard) syndrome. We lose a lot of time because people try to block the project purely out of their own selfish interests'.

The alderman also commented on the role of the action committee in the project:

> With the project of Ghent Sint Pieters we create 1000 jobs. I want these projects to be feasible and liveable. I agree that the towers cannot throw their shadow on the houses the whole day, but they also resist the new road connection. It is very egoistic of them to refuse particulate matter in their backyard.
>
> (*De Morgen* 2006)

From these quotes it is clear that the project partners blamed the local action committee for parochial selfish behaviour. The action committee, from its side, contrasted a similar strategic project in the Belgian city of Leuven with that in Ghent, calling them the 'beauty and the beast', in which the 'beast' referred to the strategic project in Ghent. The result of this battle for public opinion was that both conflict parties hardened their positions and strengthened their oppositional identity, and direct communication became impossible.

The case shows that during escalation, the parties, the issues and the relationships change and that these changes bring the conflict into a negative spiral in which the conflict strategies and tactics increasingly harden.

CONFLICT DE-ESCALATION

All conflicts eventually come to an end. De-escalation is the stage of a conflict in which an escalation process stops and the number of parties and issues diminishes. According to Kriesberg (2003) de-escalation can be the result of (1) internal changes within one or more parties, (2) a change in the relationship between the parties or (3) a change in the conflict's external context. The outcome of a conflict may be withdrawal from the conflict by one or more parties (because of internal disagreement, exhaustion of the possibilities for attaining its goals, etc.) or the victory of one party over another. But de-escalation can also be the result of equal power balances between the conflict parties. Zartman's (1989) conflict ripeness theory states that conflicts are likely to de-escalate when the parties find themselves in a mutually hurtful stalemate and realise that every new conflict tactic will be answered by an equally hurtful counter-action by the other party. Pruitt and Kim (2004) define a perceived stalemate as a situation in which one of the parties perceives that it cannot make further progress in the conflict at an acceptable cost and that further efforts to win through escalation are unworkable and/or unwise. When two parties enter into a perceived hurtful stalemate, it is very likely that opportunities for voluntary conflict settlements will emerge.

DE-ESCALATION IN GHENT

In Ghent, at the end of 2005, the project partners started to realise that juridical threats could impose a real risk for project implementation. The action committee had already taken juridical steps to fight the issuing of building permits for the project, but together with local and supra-local environmental organisations it also prepared several lawsuits for several courts. Some of these lawsuits were based upon new legislation, for which no jurisdiction had yet been developed and for which the outcome was unpredictable. The perceived risk of juridical procedures opened the door to dialogue.

The city and the other project partners realised that they could no longer ignore the action committee, and decided to offer a compromise by allowing the inhabitants to participate on an 'advisory committee' (with no binding decision-making power). The aim of this committee was to inform the inhabitants about the strategic project and to allow discussion on the design. The city stated clearly that the basic choices – the car park, the high-rise development – were not open for discussion. Furthermore, the city invited not only the action committee, but also several other organisations which acted as representatives for the local inhabitants and users of the area. A neutral expert in public administration chaired the committee. Representatives of the action committee participated in this advisory committee, but felt that the conditions stipulated by the city provided an insufficient guarantee of open discussion and continued with their litigation and mobilisation strategies. The early meetings of the advisory committee were very limited because of the ongoing litigation processes, but in 2008 it became clear that none of the verdicts found in favour of the action committee. The hope of achieving any fundamental changes in the strategic project largely vanished and the action committee considerably decreased its protest activities. However, minor changes to the design of the 200,000 m² development were achieved in 2009, through the aid of an expert panel controlling the project's spatial quality. These small changes in favour of the inhabitants were, however, too limited to satisfy the action committee.

To summarise, all three conditions in Kriesberg's de-escalation theory played a role in the de-escalation of the conflict around the strategic project in Ghent. Changes in the relationship between the parties occurred because of equalising power balances. In seeking an acceptable compromise, the pattern of interaction shifted from mutual stigmatisation, through indirect communication in the media, to direct communication, however limited. However, the action committee's power base soon disappeared after the different lawsuits delivered verdicts in favour of the project partners, and the committee lost a significant part of its organisational and mobilising capacity.

CONCLUSION

In this chapter I have developed a four-stage model for the analysis of conflict dynamics in strategic projects. This model conceptualises conflicts as a serial pattern of social interaction between adversaries. Applying this analytical model to conflicts in strategic projects, I explored the conflict dynamics within each stage and the conditions under which such conflicts emerge, escalate and de-escalate. To do so, I argued that conflict dynamics could be understood by analysing the shifting interaction between issues, parties and relationships. This model is deliberately general to enable it to be applied to a broad empirical variety of local community protest against strategic projects.

I now turn back to my initial research questions. On the question of how and why community protest emerges, I showed that the emergence of community conflict is not just dependent on the characteristics of the land-use changes and its externalities brought about by strategic projects as explained in NIMBY theory. Equally important are the social characteristics (leadership, organisational capacity and capacity to communicate) of the actors involved in the area in which the strategic project is located. Thus, the issues are a result not only of 'objective' underlying reasons, but also of how they are socially negotiated and constructed. On the question of why conflicts can persist, we found that escalation could be driven by the avoiding tactic or non-responsiveness of the project partners. This position 'forced' the opposing party to increase its resources and power base. However, the use of these tactics caused the issues to enlarge and the relationships to polarise. Finally, de-escalation became possible through a renewed and structured interaction between some of the conflict parties in the advisory committee. However, the case in Ghent also shows that the result was only partially constructive. The action committee could achieve minor changes to its advantage, but the main reason for the de-escalation of the conflict was the diminishing power base of the action committee. However, the fact that many members of the action committee are still frustrated with both the strategic project and the decision-making process might lay the basis for a new cycle of protest.

An interactionist perspective on community protest puts emphasis on conflict interaction patterns between adversaries, and shows that this interaction plays an important role in the way potential conflicts become real conflicts, and how they escalate and de-escalate. It also tells us that the existence of underlying contradictory interests in a particular strategic project is not that problematic as such, but that the way in which public authorities respond to this determines the extent to which these conflicts develop in more constructive or destructive ways.

NOTE

1   Buitensporig means both 'excessive', but also 'off the tracks'. It refers mainly to the issue of high-rise buildings.

REFERENCES

Blake, R. R. and Mouton, J. S. (1964) *The Managerial Grid Key Orientations for Achieving Production through People*, Houston: Gulf Publishing.

Buitensporig (2005) Pamphlet Buurtcomité Buitensporig.

Carpenter, S. and Kennedy, W. J. D. (2001) *Managing Public Disputes: A Practical Guide for Government, Business, and Citizens' Groups*, New York: John Wiley & Sons.

Coleman, J. S. (1957) *Community Conflict*, New York: Free Press.

Cox, K. R. and Johnston, R. J. (1982) *Conflict, Politics and the Urban Scene*, London: Longman.

Cox, K. R., Low, M. and Robinson, J. (2007) *The SAGE Handbook of Political Geography*, Los Angeles: Sage.

Dahrendorf, R. (1959) *Class and Class Conflict in Industrial Society*, London: Routledge and Kegan Paul.

Dear. M. (1992) 'Understanding and overcoming the NIMBY syndrome', *Journal of the American Planning Association*, 58: 288–302.

De Morgen (2006) Interview with Daniel Termont, 7 September.

De Standaard (2007) 'Mondige burgers worden lastpakken', 19 May.

Deutsch, M. and Coleman, P. T. (2000) *Handbook of Conflict Resolution: Theory and Practice*, San Francisco: Jossey-Bass.

Gemeente Amsterdam (2004) Hoogbouweffecten rapportage, project Fabiolalaan Gent, Amsterdam (unpublished report).

Gurr, T. R. (1970) *Why Men Rebel*, Princeton, NJ: Princeton University Press.

Innes, J. E. (1995) 'Planning-theory emerging paradigm – communicative action and interactive practice', *Journal of Planning Education and Research*, 14: 183–189.

Innes, J. E. (1996) 'Planning through consensus building', *Journal of the American Planning Association*, 62: 460.

Innes, J. E. and Booher, D. E. (1999) 'Consensus building and complex adaptive systems: a framework for evaluating collaborative planning', *Journal of the American Planning Association*, 65: 412.

Just, R. E., Hueth, D. L. and Schmitz, A. (2004) *The Welfare Economics of Public Policy: A Practical Approach to Project and Policy Evaluation*, Cheltenham: Edward Elgar.

Kahneman, D. and Tversky, A. (1979) 'Prospect theory: An analysis of decision under risk', *Econometrica*, XLVII: 263–291.

Klandermans, B. (1997) 'Mobilization and participation: social-psychological expansisons of resource mobilization theory', *American Sociological Review*, 49: 583–600.

Kriesberg, L. (2003) *Constructive Conflicts from Escalation to Resolution*, 2nd edn, Lanham, MD: Rowman & Littlefield.

Kriesi, H., Saris, W. E. and Wille, A. (1993) 'Mobilization potential for environmental protest', *European Sociological Review*, 9: 155–172.

Kunreuther, H. and Patrick, R. (1991) 'Managing the risks of hazardous waste', *Environment*, 33: 12.

Lake, R. (1993) 'Rethinking Nimby', *Journal of the American Planning Association*, 59: 87–93.

Lewicki, R. J., Gray, B. and Elliott, M. (2002) *Making Sense of Intractable Environmental Conflicts: Frames and Cases*, Washington, DC: Island Press.

McCarthy, J. D. and Zald, M. N. (1977) 'Resource mobilization and social-movements – partial theory', *American Journal of Sociology*, 82: 1212–1241.

Marx, K. and Engels, F. (1998) *The Communist Manifesto: A Modern Edition*, London: Verso.

Nieuwsblad (2001) 'Geen torens aan Sint-Pieters', 2 July.

Nieuwsblad (2003) 'Weg met weg door schoonmeersen', 28 April.

Petts, J. (1992) 'Incineration risk perceptions and public concern: experience in the UK improving risk communication', *Waste Management and Research*, 10: 169–182.

Pondy, L. R. (1992) 'Overview of organizational conflict – concepts and models', *Journal of Organizational Behavior*, 13: 255.

Popper (1987) 'The environmentalist and the LULU', *Environment*, 27: 7–40.

Pruitt, D. G. (1983) 'Strategic choice in negotiation', *American Behavioral Scientist*, 27: 194.

Pruitt, D. G. and Kim, S. H. (2004) *Social Conflict: Escalation, Stalemate, and Settlement*, 3rd edn, London: McGraw-Hill.

Rogers, O. G. (1998) 'Siting potentially hazardous facilities: What factors impact perceived and acceptable risk?', *Landscape and Urban Planning*, 39: 265–281.

Stad Gent (2003) Minutes of the steering committee VII, 20 May 2003.

Susskind, L. and Cruikshank, J. L. (1987) *Breaking the Impasse: Consensual Approaches to Resolving Public Disputes*, New York: Basic Books.

Susskind, L. and Field, P. (1996) *Dealing with an Angry Public: The Mutual Gains Approach to Resolving Disputes*, New York: Free Press.

Susskind, L., McKearnan, S. and Thomas-Larmer, J. (1999) *The Consensus Building Handbook: A Comprehensive Guide to Reaching Agreement*, Thousand Oaks, CA: Sage.

Susskind, L., Van der Wansem, M. and Ciccarelli, A. (2000) *Mediating Land Use Disputes*, Cambridge, MA: Lincoln Institute of Land Policy.

Takahashi, L. M. and Dear, M. J. (1997) 'The changing dynamics of community opposition to human service facilities', *Journal of the American Planning Association*, 63: 79–93.

Thomas, K. W. (1992) 'Conflict and negotiation processes in organizations', in M. D. Dunnette and L. M.Hough (eds) *Handbook of Industrial and Organizational Psychology*, Palo Alto, CA: Consulting Psychologists Press. pp. 651–717.

Tilly, L. A. and Tilly, C. (1981) *Class Conflict and Collective Action*, London: Sage.

Wester-Herber, M. (2004) 'Underlying concerns in land-use conflicts: The role of place-identity in risk perception', *Environmental Science & Policy*, 7: 109–116.

Wolsink, M. (1994) 'Entanglement of interest and motives: assumptions behind the nimby theory on facility siting', *Urban Studies*, 31: 851–867.

Zartman, I. W. (1989) *Ripe for Resolution. Conflict and Intervention in Africa*, Oxford: Oxford University Press.

COMMENTARY ON PART III

STRATEGIC PROJECTS

FROM SUSTAINABILITY TO RESILIENCE?

JEAN HILLIER

INTRODUCTION

The overall introduction to this volume proposes a definition of strategic spatial planning as 'a method for collectively reimagining the possible futures of particular places and translating these into concrete priorities and action programs' (p. 1). In Chapter 9 Oosterlynck and colleagues define strategic spatial projects as 'those that, in terms of content as well as process, contribute to the liveability (in a broad sense) of particular places for all citizens by providing for their real current needs without shifting the negative impact onto either other places or social groups, or into the future' (p. 178). It is interesting that neither definition actually mentions the word 'sustainability', although the latter does invoke a concept of liveability in which individuals and groups deal with their own negative impacts, rather than offloading them onto others in time or space.

Nevertheless, sustainability looms large in the consciousnesses of both groups of authors and provides the focus for the two chapters in this part of the volume. The first (by Stijn Oosterlynck, Trui Maes and Han Verschure) offers a selection of detailed techniques and examples of how strategic spatial planners might operationalise sustainability, while the second (by Tom Coppens) highlights an example of some of the conflicts that practitioners may have to cope with if they wish to implement sustainable major projects.

In this commentary, I discuss four issues that I find of importance in thinking about sustainability:

- the role of non-humans in spatial sustainability;
- space as active;
- moral aspects of planning sustainably; and
- moving forward from sustainability to resilience.

I then propose a potential role for strategic spatial planning in developing resilient projects and cities, rather than merely sustainable ones, and conclude that practising strategic spatial planning through strategic projects may well offer practitioners an adaptable way of planning resilient cities.

THE ROLE OF NON-HUMANS IN SPATIAL SUSTAINABILITY

Doreen Massey (2005a: 354) raises the 'thorny issue of how the voice of (the practice of) the non-human can be given weight'. Although the 'environment', as such, is generally accorded greater weight than social aspects of spatial sustainability (rhetorically at least), even those groups which claim to have the inherent interests of the non-human at heart use discourses that involve anthropocentric concepts, categories and representations, as the two chapters illustrate. No wonder that Erik Swyngedouw (2010: 299) writes, 'Nature does not exist!'.

As Swyngedouw (2010: 300–301) explains, all too often, we regard Nature as something given, a 'solid foundational (or ontological) basis from which we act' in attempts to 're-balance' 'it' as an entity. Nature is often the 'Other' to us humans: some kind of symbolic idyll – when all goes well – of species living in relative harmony. Nature is thereby invoked as 'the external terrain that offers the promise, if attended to properly [i.e. sustainably] for finding or producing a truly happy and harmonious life' (Swyngedouw 2010: 301).

In urban as well as rural areas, in spaces of major projects as well as green spaces, the spatialised performances of flora and fauna (such as moss on buildings, birds nesting in eaves), plant cells and soil microbes, rainwater, chemicals and sunlight are related, connected and aligned in heterogeneous ways and directions: 'turbulent' and 'attentive to the multiplicity of possible paths "in-between" where things pick up speed and take on consistencies and directions of their own' (Whatmore 2002: 124). Non-humans are active: they perform. Whether acid in rain dissolving limestone façades of monumental buildings detracting from aesthetic 'quality' and spatial sustainability, or lotus flowers and koi in water features enhancing spatial worlds, urban living spaces involve far more than human beings.

Authors such as Ingold (2000), Hinchliffe and colleagues (2005) and Haraway (2008) are increasingly recognising the limitations of a view that regards humans acting *on our* worlds rather than relationally *within inclusive* worlds.[1] We need to recognise the active impact of non-humans on our lives, whether spiritual or psychological (e.g. sublime buildings and landscapes), physical (e.g. insect- and parasite-borne diseases, such as malaria), economic (e.g. the commodification of 'beauty' for tourists) and/or social (e.g. dog walking, duck feeding). To be 'response-able' practitioners, as Haraway (2008) might suggest, we have to learn, unlearn and relearn our relationships with space (Beisel 2010) and with other-than-human species and other forms of non-humans. Perhaps every local authority should have an 'animal advocate' as in Zurich?

SPACE AS ACTIVE

Space has not traditionally been appreciated by spatial planners as a sphere of active interaction. Yet, back in 1993, Doreen Massey revealed space to be not a static reality, but active and generative. Architects Bernard Cache, Greg Lynn and Peter Eisenman, for example, have come to regard space as produced and performing through movement, folding, connection and extension. Lynn (1999: 10) conceives space as an event of force and motion rather than a neutral vacuum, while Eisenman's (2005) 'fluid shell' for the City of Culture in Galicia, Spain, performs symbolically – the design references the scallop shell (venera) worn by pilgrims to Santiago de Compostela, and the rivulet streets of the medieval town – physically, socially, aesthetically and economically, attracting tourists – bringing them together and guiding them through the cultural centre – as a facilitator of multiple, indeterminate flows.

The City of Culture clearly demonstrates that every space has a geohistory that should be engaged on its own terms: each is 'territorialised in the landscape by means of human and non-human "agents" guided by a set of institutions, tendencies, trajectories' (Bonta and Protevi 2004: 174). In urban areas, human agency tends to dominate, as we overcode space for economic or other purposes. Yet humans will never completely overcode non-human multiplicities. Non-human agents may operate according to different temporalities from humans and have voice in different manners, but act and speak they will (Hillier 2007).[2]

Space, then, could usefully be regarded as a complex and dynamic, performative multiplicity, rather than as a singular object or resource to be 'used' or 'managed'.

MORAL ASPECTS OF PLANNING SUSTAINABLY

Practitioners are slowly recognising the inherently moral nature of strategic spatial planning (Campbell 2006; Campbell and Marshall 2006; Gunder and Hillier 2007; Healey 2009). As Oosterlynck and colleagues write in their chapter in this part, 'careful land use implies an active, well-reasoned, responsible and critical use of land and environmental resources' (p. 181).

Engagement with the notion of responsibility in planning (and geography) stems largely from the environmental ethics of Hans Jonas, who proposed a future-oriented responsibility towards preserving for humankind, 'the undamaged entirety of his [sic] world' (1984: 9). More recently, McNamee and Gergen (1999) have called for a relational responsibility in order to recognise and legitimate the often conflicting understandings of people from different life worlds. Iris Marion Young (2006) proposes a 'social connection model' of responsibility which suggests that an actor's moral obligation extends to all other actants (human and non-human) whom the actor assumes in performing his or her activities. Donna Haraway (2008) takes this further with her notion of response-ability, which calls for a cultivation of sensitivity towards the other and especially to any suffering that our actions might cause (inadvertently or otherwise). For example, a local authority refusing a planning application for ship recycling facilities in the UK, which may result in those ships being broken up by hand on Asian beaches (see Hillier 2009), spraying public open space with insecticide so that families can picnic without being bitten by mosquitoes or midges (see Beisel 2010), or legislating dog-free beaches all involve response-ability.

But how far should spatial planners' responsibility extend? Should spatial planners and procurement agents of local governance be morally responsible for consequences that they cannot prevent (such as Asian ship dismantlers dying from emphysema because of working with asbestos in unprotected conditions, or depleting rainforest ecosystems and further threatening orang-utan survival by agents procuring Indonesian hardwood for decking in a piazza, for instance)? As Massey (2005b: 9) argues, space is 'the product of interrelations; as constituted through interactions, from the immensity of the global to the infinitely tiny'.

A transport interchange and public squares in the Ghent railway station area strategic megaproject sit within economic, environmental and social networks that span the globe. Some will be in tension, as Coppens' case study demonstrates. Despite being a transport interchange geared to increasing public transport use associated with high-density live–work–shop lifestyles in a theoretically sustainable transit-oriented development[3] (environmental sustainability) and despite their predominantly public sector status,[4] the financing partners would require a return on their 400 million euro investment.[5] Hence, 700 home units and 80,000 m^2 of commercial space were proposed in buildings up to 90 m high. Such economic viability (or economic sustainability) conflicted with local residents' amenity perceptions (social sustainability). Unfortunately, the project managers, eager to see the project under way, adopted a decide–announce–defend (dad) approach rather than a participatory, collaborative strategy that could have averted much of the conflict.

Similarly, Oosterlynck and colleagues' search for an 'optimal density' for 'liveable' projects may risk the reification of quantification. Quantitative indicators may be convenient tools for evaluating aspects of 'sustainability', but there is always the danger that practice becomes indicator driven, with practitioners ticking boxes on checklists rather than thinking for themselves. As Oosterlynck and colleagues recognise, 'general norms, whether in the form of threshold or target norms, are insufficient to operationalise sustainable land use in strategic spatial projects'. There is a need for creativity in terms of flexibility and adaptability of attitudes, plans, systems and cities if strategic spatial planning is to be physically, environmentally, socially and economically useful in the future.

Moving forward: from sustainability to resilience

Flexible and adaptable strategic spatial planning requires flexible and adaptable thinking! As Oosterlynck, Albrechts and Van den Broeck write in their introduction to this volume, a long-term strategic perspective should not specify a fixed end state, but operate as a flexible framework for spatial development.

In this section, I suggest that sustainability has become such an empty signifier – meaning everything and nothing – that it has outlived its usefulness. Moreover, Gunder and Hillier (2009: 136) argue that 'the narrative of sustainable development is often deployed simply to further the interests of an entrepreneurially-supportive state and its institutions', as the Gent Sint-Pieters case study illustrates. This is a pro-market interpretation of sustainable development that dilutes the concept of sustainability to that of 'business as usual' with 'at best, an objective to partially reduce urban consumer energy consumption and waste outputs, while still maximising the potential for economic growth' (Gunder and Hillier 2009: 136).

The term 'sustainability' has become an almost unchallengeable doxa, structured in fantasies of environmental stability, social harmony and economic growth. But, as is increasingly being argued (e.g. Cascio 2009), sustainability is 'insufficient for uncertain times'. Sustainability is inherently static. It assumes that if we can find the 'right' combination of behaviour and technology, then the environment will stabilise in a 'steady state' – until the next disruptive shock. Sustainability is brittle, therefore. Unanticipated changes can cause its collapse.

I argue that strategic spatial planners should resist and overcome the barriers raised by the master signifier of sustainability and consider the concept of resilience instead. Whereas sustainability represents the idea of survival by patching up cities and the world as best we can, the aim of resilience is to thrive or flourish (Cascio 2009). Resilience is, thus, more than sustainability. Recognising that change is inevitable and focusing on adaptability rather than resistance or 'patching up', resilient strategies would evolve: plans and projects would represent temporary fixities in flows of turbulence.[6]

We can identify three different aspects of resilience:

1 persistence or resistance – in which a system (of humans and/or non-humans) possesses or develops the capacity to absorb disturbance, maintaining its identity and function.
2 adaptability – the capacity of a system to adapt its structure, function, identity, etc. in accordance with dynamic contingencies.
3 transformability – the capacity of a system to steer away from undesirable trajectories by transforming its structure and so on.

Resilience by resistance tends to be characteristic of closed systems (e.g. a sea wall built to resist ocean waves, a dam wall etc.), whereas resilience by adaptation and transformation are found in open systems. Most sustainability policies and plans tend to assume closed systems, with measurable and predictable risks or threats to be thwarted or 'resisted'. However, there are few, if any, closed systems in the reality of spatial planning. One of the main problems with attempts to achieve sustainability, I would suggest, is that they seek resistance, but do not recognise its requirement for a closed system. They therefore fail to account for the complexity of the open systems in which they struggle to make an impact. Even so, resistance may be possible in circumstances of small perturbations – such as occasional storm waves battering against a sea wall, small cracks in a dam wall, or one or two shops closing in a shopping arcade or mall – but they nevertheless build up and if the structure is too rigid and fails to adapt it will break. The same principle may be applied to humans resisting change, whether practitioners resisting new ways of working or local residents resisting new land-use developments.

For this reason, I disagree with Coppens, who views community protest as a barrier to project implementation. In an adaptive or transformative resilient system – rather than in a resistant system – change offers the potential for creativity and innovation. A resilience approach would shift attention towards adapting to and working with change, rather than attempting to control it. I argue, therefore, that spatial planning needs to move beyond dad behaviours (as in Ghent), with their powerful expert knowledges and subjectivations of actants, and even beyond the indicator-led control mechanisms of Oosterlynck and colleagues. The four-track approach of Louis Albrechts and Jef Van den Broeck, mentioned in the overall introduction to this volume, offers a potential foundation for thinking about and planning flexibility and resilience.

Inspired by Albrechts and Van den Broeck's tracks and by the potential of post-structuralist theory in an uncertain, indeterminate world, I have developed a multi-planar approach to strategic spatial planning as strategic navigation[7] in which longer-term broad trajectories (or visions) – such as liveability – act as frames of reference that provide justification and navigational context for short- or medium-term substantive actions, such as major projects. As particular projects are developed by a local authority or received as planning applications from developers, attention can be paid to how these projects fit into the longer-term vision for the city. I propose that this might be practised through a pragmatic methodology of strategic navigation.

Navigating strategically would require practitioners sensing and discerning connections and patterns in what is taking place and trying to understand the underlying dynamics and interdependencies between elements, in order to appreciate the diverse possibilities of what is happening and what might happen, and to respond by designing actions that align with the intentions and values of the longer-term strategic trajectory (Hames 2007: 114), but which are contextually appropriate, not copy-pastes of other, previous or 'best' practices (Hillier 2010).

I suggest a methodology of tracing and mapping inspired by Gilles Deleuze and Michel Foucault. Tracing entails looking back in a systematic manner to disentangle or unfold the conditions of possibility of 'how something came to be'. It investigates 'the ontological conditions of the relationships of macrolevel structures and microlevel movements and flows' (Eriksson 2005: 603); for instance, in Ghent, the relations between public and private infrastructure capital, national agencies of governance and interest groups actualised in materialities and discursivities such as texts, meetings, demonstrations, lawsuits, etc. It is an analysis 'of how forces of different types come to inhabit the same field' (Due 2007: 145). It would examine power relations, knowledges and subjectivations (from Foucault), the roles that components played and the processes of stabilising, destabilising and restabilising systems or assemblages of land uses, regulations and plans (from Deleuze and Guattari).

Strategy production may have merely followed a best practice exemplar or a procedural rule book (Healey 2009: 453), or it might have resulted from financial or other pressures. Tracing offers a series of stories of what happened, unpacking the relations between elements and highlighting the power games in play.

Deleuze and Guattari (1987) suggest that tracings should be put on maps. To map involves the discovery of landmarks as something to head towards: 'a furtive glance sideways into an undecidable future' (Bosteels 2001: 895). Mapping begins to develop an 'opportunity structure' (Healey 2009) for spatial strategy-making through envisaging relations between forces, what potential trajectories the force relations may take and whether the conditions of possibility could exist for such trajectories to eventuate. It is a 'what might happen if . . .?' approach, which asks completely different questions to those based on projections of quantified 'evidence'.

Questions might include: Which actants may have potentially what kinds of relations with which others, and which may be excluded? Who and what might form powerful alliances? What knowledges might become important? What conflicts might emerge? (Hillier 2010). It is a prospective exercise of strategic experimental anticipation or speculation. In Ghent, for instance, it would have been relatively easy, I suggest, to anticipate local resistance to high-rise towers and increased traffic and the conflicts that played out.

Strategic navigation monitors and analyses the structures, links, relationships and information flows between humans and non-humans that 'really matter' to different people, in different geographies, over time (Hames 2007: 256). Monitoring is required to ensure that shorter-term projects do not 'veer off' the broader trajectory of the longer-term strategic vision, 'seduced' either by inertia or by the 'latest flavour of the month' (Hames 2007: 250) – another iconic building or commercial centre. Monitoring should also ensure that longer-term visions remain relevant and are adapted or transformed as appropriate. Strategic practice would thus proceed more or less by flexibility, experimentation and creative adaptation rather than by adhering rigidly to some predetermined, but rapidly irrelevant, master plan or sustainability plan.

Urban resilience as a whole depends not only on institutional structures or processes, but also on social dynamics, the non-human environment and ecosystem, and the metabolic flows of production, supply and consumption. Persistence or resistance to change, in attempts to achieve sustainability, implies limitation of opportunity. Sustainability may be part of resilience, but is not sufficient alone to produce resilience. Adaptability and transformability, however, through foresight, flexibility, collaboration, diversity and so on, increase opportunities for cities to flourish in the face of unexpected events, 'turbulence' or disturbances.

THE ROLE OF STRATEGIC SPATIAL PLANNING AND STRATEGIC PROJECTS IN RESILIENCE

Performing resilience and strategically planning resilient cities will require transformation of bureaucratic approaches, land-use regulation, urban maintenance and the delivery and management of public services (Chapter 1 of this volume, p. 1). I advocate (Hillier 2007; 2010) a multi-planar, strategic navigation approach in which longer-term strategic planning would involve an inclusive, democratic open and creative imagination of the past–present–future in which there is foresighting of potential future trajectories and ongoing collaborative, critical discussions about the potential consequences for different human and non-human actants. Strategic projects would facilitate small movements along these dynamic trajectories, reinforcing the 'action orientation of planning, paying careful attention to how it relates to the long-term visions for the wider area, the co-production of specific actions with a variety of actors and the promotion of social innovation' (Chapter 1 of this volume, p. 8).

Strategic spatial planning practice would be concerned with navigating 'journeys rather than destinations' (Hillier 2010) and with establishing conditions for development of alternatives, facilitating adaptability and transformability as appropriate. Through tracing and mapping, practitioners could develop relational understandings of the conditions of possibility for events to actualise in a 'what might happen if . . .?' approach of foresight, anticipation and inclusive creative collaboration between actants, including non-humans, local communities, multinational enterprises and agencies of governance.

If we commence strategic spatial planning with goal setting towards some desired end state of sustainability, rather than learning about how our situations came to be (tracing) and how we might potentially address them (mapping), we inevitably risk implementing predetermined, often universal, 'solutions' that themselves tend to define and pre-shape the very issues and problems that they seek to address (see Gunder and Hillier 2009). We must be careful not to allow the solution to define the problem (e.g. what 'best practice' ordains). Solutions are actual – real, stable identities – whereas problems are virtual – inexhaustible 'open fields' (May 2005, in Gunder and Hillier 2009). Solutions might lie in the implementation of Oosterlynck and colleagues' list of operational techniques, but in doing so we risk constraining potentialities through the imposition of overdetermined structures. I hope that practitioners will learn to live with uncertainty; to plan resiliently – flexibly and adaptively – through pragmatic use of strategic projects geared to strategic spatial trajectories. As Rajchman (1998: 33) suggests, 'the aim of the game is not to rediscover the eternal or the universal but to find the conditions under which something new may be created'.

NOTES

1 See the papers in the special issue of *Environment and Planning D,* 'When species meet', by Hinchliffe, Beisel, Davies and Loftus, and Haraway (all 2010).
2 For instance, bulldozing coastal sand dunes flat in order to provide million-euro views for beachfront mansions is inevitably a temporary measure as prevailing winds will gradually blow sand back across the beach, into gardens and swimming pools.
3 On transit-oriented developments, see Cervero (1998), Cervero *et al* (2004), Center for Liveable Communities (1998) and Reconnecting America (2007).
4 Gent Sint-Pieters is being developed as a public–private partnership.
5 Including a large European Regional Development Fund (ERDF) grant.
6 I regard turbulence and its indeterminacy as exciting, creative and opportunistic. Whilst turbulence may be complex, it also involves structure, organisation and coherence (see Hillier, 2007).
7 After Richard Hames (2007) as suggested to me by Cathy Wilkinson.

REFERENCES

Beisel, U. (2010) 'Jumping hurdles with mosquitoes?', *Environment and Planning D, Society and Space*, 28 (1): 46–49.

Bonta, M and Protevi, J. (2004) *Deleuze and Geophilosophy: A Guide and Glossary*, Edinburgh: Edinburgh University Press.

Bosteels, B. (2001) 'From text to territory: Félix Guattari's cartographies of the unconscious', in G. Genosko (ed.) *Deleuze and Guattari: Critical Assessments of Leading Philosophers*, Vol. II, New York: Routledge.

Campbell, H. (2006) 'Just planning: The art of situated ethical judgement', *Journal of Planning Education and Research*, 26 (2): 92–106.

Campbell, H. and Marshall, R. (2006) 'Towards justice in planning: a reappraisal', *European Planning Studies*, 14 (2): 239–252.

Cascio, J. (2009) 'The next big thing: resilience', *Foreign Policy*, 15 April 2009. Online. Available at http://www.foreignpolicy.com/articles/2009/04/15/the_next_big_thing_resilience (accessed 9 March 2010).

Center for Liveable Communities (CLC) (1998) 'Building liveable communities: a policymaker's guide to transit-oriented development'. Online. Available at http://www.lgc.org/publications/center/clcpubs.html (accessed 9 March 2010).

Cervero, R. (1998) *The Transit Metropolis*, Washington, DC: Island Press.

Cervero, R. *et al.* (2004) 'Transit-oriented development in the United States', TCRP Report 102, Transit Cooperative Research Program, Transportation Research Board. Online. Available at http://gulliver.trb.org/publications/tcrp/tcrp_rpt_102.pdf (accessed 9 March 2010).

Davies, G. and Loftus, A. (2010) 'On the politics of lapdogs, Jim's dog and crittercams', *Environment and Planning D, Society and Space*, 28 (1): 50–52.

Deleuze G. and Guattari F. (1987) [1980] *A Thousand Plateaus: Capitalism and Schizophrenia* (trans. B. Massumi), London: Athlone Press.

Due, R. (2007) Deleuze, Cambridge: Polity Press.

Eisenman, P. (2005) *Codex: The City of Culture of Galicia* (ed. C. Davidson), New York: Monacelli Press.

Eriksson, K. (2005) 'Foucault, Deleuze, and the ontology of networks', *The European Legacy*, 10 (6): 595–610.

Gunder, M. and Hillier, J. (2007) 'Problematising responsibility in planning theory and practice: on seeing the middle of the string', *Progress in Planning*, 68 (2): 57–96.

Gunder, M. and Hillier, J. (2009) *Planning in Ten Words or Less*, Farnham: Ashgate.

Hames R. (2007) *The Five Literacies of Global Leadership,* San Francisco: Jossey-Bass.

Haraway, D. (2008) *Where Species Meet*, Minnesota: University of Minnesota Press.

Haraway, D. (2010) 'Where species meet: staying with the trouble', *Environment and Planning D, Society and Space*, 28 (1): 53–55.

Healey, P. (2009) 'In search of the "strategy" in spatial strategy making', *Planning Theory and Practice*, 10 (4): 439–457.

Hillier, J. (2007) *Stretching Beyond the Horizon: A Multiplanar Theory of Spatial Planning and Governance*, Aldershot: Ashgate.

Hillier, J. (2009) 'Assemblages of justice: the "ghost ships" of Graythorp', *IJURR*, 33 (3): 640–661.

Hillier, J. (2010) 'Strategic navigation across multiple planes: towards a Deleuzean-inspired methodology for strategic spatial planning'. Paper presented at K.U.Leuven, February.

Hinchliffe, S. (2010) 'Where species meet', *Environment and Planning D, Society and Space*, 28 (1): 34–35.

Hinchliffe, S., Kearnes M., Degen M. and Whatmore, S. (2005) 'Urban wild things: A cosmo-political experiment', *Environment and Planning D, Society and Space*, 23: 643–658.

Ingold, T. (2000) *The Perception of the Environment: Essays on Livelihood, Dwelling and Skill*, London: Routledge.

Jonas, H. (1984) *The Imperative of Responsibility*, Chicago: University of Chicago Press.

Lynn, G. (1999) *Animate Form*, New York: Princeton Architectural Press.

McNamee, S. and Gergen, K. (eds) (1999) *Relational Responsibility*, Thousand Oaks, CA: Sage.

Massey, D. (1993) 'Power-geometry and a progressive sense of place', in J. Bird, B. Curtin, T. Putnam, G. Robertson and L. Tickner (eds) *Mapping New Futures*, London: Routledge.

Massey, D. (2005a) 'Negotiating nonhuman/human place', *Antipode*, 37 (2): 353–357.

Massey, D. (2005b) *For Space*, London: Sage.

May, T. (2005) *Gilles Deleuze*, Cambridge: Cambridge University Press.

Rajchman, J. (1998) *Constructions*, Cambridge, MA: MIT Press.

Reconnecting America (2007) 'TOD 101: Why transit-oriented development and why now?'. Online. Available at http://www.reconnectingamerica.org/public/download/tod-101full (accessed 9 March 2010).

Swyngedouw, E. (2010) 'Trouble with nature: "Ecology as the new opium for the masses"', in J. Hillier and P. Healey (eds) *The Ashgate Research Companion to Planning Theory: Conceptual Challenges for Spatial Planning*, Farnham: Ashgate.

Whatmore, S. (2002) *Hybrid Geographies*, London: Sage.

Young, I. M. (2006) 'Responsibility and global justice: a social connection model', *Social Philosophy and Policy Foundation*, 23: 102–130.

PART IV

CONCLUSION

CHAPTER 11

EPILOGUE

TOWARDS A FUTURE RESEARCH AGENDA

STIJN OOSTERLYNCK, JEF VAN DEN BROECK AND
LOUIS ALBRECHTS

The chapters in this edited volume all testify to the capacity of strategic projects to bring about effective change by intervening concretely in space and society. They show how strategic long-term visions for socio-spatial transformation result from the confrontation of different social and spatial challenges, potentials, needs, ambitions, claims, interests and bodies of knowledge (scientific, practical and local). The main challenges addressed in this book are how strategies and concrete actions can be linked, how relevant actors (including non-conventional actors and disadvantaged groups) can be involved and empowered and how the most adequate planning instruments, whether existing or yet to be created, can be mobilized. These challenges, throughout this book referred to as action orientation and socio-spatial innovation, have been explored through a set of different thematic dimensions, namely socio-spatial innovation, design and spatial quality and sustainability. The chapters on socio-spatial innovation have shown that strategic spatial projects, if taking into account a broad set of local and other needs and ambitions, do not only lead to spatial transformations but also have a positive impact on need satisfaction and social relations in particular areas. They transform existing governance arrangements and trigger the emergence of new ones by involving and empowering different actors, including non-conventional and disadvantaged groups, in visioning, in decision-making processes and in implementation processes. In this way they facilitate collective learning among all involved actors. This requires, as shown in the case studies on Angus Locoshops in Montréal and the First Quarter in Antwerp, the mobilization of tools other than traditional spatial planning instruments and requires close attention to the institutional frames in which planning instruments (understood narrowly as technical tools) are embedded.

The chapters on design and spatial quality stress the important role of spatial design in linking planning and implementation and involving different actors in strategic projects. Design – in a broad sense – with its creative, integrative and imaginative capacities is a crucial complement to the more analytical, technical land-use methods and instruments often still used in planning and strategic projects. Through a design process actors can jointly develop a shared language of spatial quality. As several case studies in Part II show, this proves especially useful for the sense dimension of spatial quality, which is less transparent and more difficult to transform into hard requirements. The place-based focus of design and the way it starts from the particular spatial context of a strategic project make it particularly well positioned to integrate the spatial claims of different stakeholders within a clear and challenging vision and, by thus generating social and political support for it, enhance the action operation of strategic projects. The chapters on sustainability deal with the question of how strategic projects can promote sustainable development. Although sustainable development is broadly accepted in the field of spatial planning and design, its operationalization remains something of a challenge. An argument is made for a specifically spatial reading of sustainable development, acknowledging the different ways in which space can play an active role in making development more sustainable through the use of strategies for careful and multiple land use and sustained attention to accessibility, reachability and permeability. Since strategic projects aim for socio-spatial transformation, conflicts over land-use changes frequently emerge and slow down or even undermine their implementation. Case study work on the redevelopment of the railway station area in Ghent shows that leading actors in strategic projects need to take conflicts seriously rather than bury or ignore them, at least if they want to avoid an escalation of the conflict, which may even lead to the project not being realized. The attitude towards conflict hence has an important impact on the project's social sustainability.

The conclusions from the research presented in this edited volume and briefly summarized above suggest a number of interesting avenues for future research. The focus of the strategic planning approach on *socio-spatial* transformation advocated in this book requires further research on the possibilities and modalities of a rapprochement between strategic spatial planning approaches, including design-based methods, and social innovation in strategic projects. The chapters in Part II of this book have explored and analysed how the involvement of a multiplicity of (non-conventional) actors in the planning and designing of places strengthens the action orientation of strategic planning processes. From a social innovation perspective, however, more attention should be paid to the socio-spatial relations between the actors involved and how these are (or are not) transformed in planning and design processes. Vanempten's reference to Amin's 'politics of propinquity', which points to the potential of spatial juxtaposition as a field of engagement between different social actors, provides, however, an interesting step towards a social innovation reading of strategic spatial planning and design processes. The chapters on social innovation in Part I of this book on the other hand analysed the socio-spatial innovation dimension of strategic planning processes, but did not fully address the role of spatial planning and design and insufficiently explored the relative autonomy of space. However, by pointing out how the temporary physical, as well as social, indeterminacy of the Angus Loco-shops brownfield site facilitated the emergence of civil society plans for the site, Van Dyck offers an interesting starting point to couple strategic spatial planning and social innovation processes in strategic projects, starting from the particular characteristics of space as raw material to generate the social as well as the spatial substance of the project. Pieter Van den Broeck's conceptual framework for assessing the socio-territorial innovation capacity of planning instruments in strategic projects offers a further bridge between social innovation and spatial planning and design, as it could be used to assess the extent to which planning and design-based planning instruments can promote social innovation. More research is needed, then, on how planning and design can not only involve different actors, their diverse understandings of spatial quality and multiple spatial claims, but also do so in ways that empower non-conventional actors and disadvantaged groups in creating and implementing alternative futures for the places in which they live. The strategic-relational institutionalist approach developed by Pieter Van den Broeck seems to offer a promising perspective for further exploration of the different kinds of institutional frames in which planning methods and instruments can be embedded and for finding out whether, and under what conditions, these can be guided by socio-spatial innovative rationalities.

Another promising avenue for future research is in the field of the operationalization of sustainable development within strategic spatial projects. The chapter in this book on sustainable land use offered only a partial, though spatially sensitive, operationalization of sustainable development. The authors highlighted, however, that indicators, norms and guidelines in themselves will not produce the spatial quality and sustainability aimed for by planners and designers and suggested an important role for the creativity of planning and design in translating these into qualitative and operational spatial concepts, plans and actions. The context sensitivity of planning and more specifically research into design and its capacity to work with and integrate different types of knowledge seems particularly promising here, but also requires more insights into the institutional dimensions of planning instruments. When defined in general terms, everyone seems to agree that sustainable development is important. However, when it is operationalized and translated into more concrete strategies and norms, conflicts quickly ensue, pointing to social and governance dimensions of sustainability. Future research could explore whether or not research by design is a suitable planning instrument to investigate and negotiate different understandings of sustainability.

INDEX